HARMFUL INVASIVE SPECIES: LEGAL RESPONSES

HARMFUL INVASIVE SPECIES: LEGAL RESPONSES

Marc L. Miller
Robert N. Fabian
Editors

ENVIRONMENTAL LAW INSTITUTE
Washington, D.C.

The designation of geographical entities in this book, and the presentation of the material, do not imply the expression of any opinion whatsoever on the part of IUCN concerning the legal status of any country, territory, or area, or of its authorities, or concerning the delimitation of its frontiers or boundaries.

The views expressed in this publication do not necessarily reflect those of IUCN.

Cover Photo: The J. Paul Getty Museum, Malibu, California. Attributed to Eagle Painter [Painter] (Greek (Caeretan), active 530 B.C. - 500 B.C.), Caeretan Hydria, about 525 B.C., Terracotta, H: 44.6 cm; Diameter [rim]: 22.9 cm; Diameter [body]: 33 cm.

Harmful Invasive Species: Legal Responses

Table of Contents

Acknowledgments

Multi-authored books pose special challenges to authors and editors especially if the volumes as a whole are to be of greatest benefit to the widest range of readers. Such volumes work well when authors and editors keep in mind the larger goals of the volume.

The chapters in this volume began life as several of the short essays presented at a small conference at the Environmental Law Centre of the World Conservation Union (IUCN), in December 1999. The current volume is not, however, the result of this meeting, but the product of three years of revision and editing and the addition of authors (including lead authors) on several chapters. All of the authors responded thoughtfully to the suggestions and requests of editors, and did so in a timely fashion. All of the authors showed grace and understanding throughout the editorial process. And although most of the authors in this volume have met only once, and several have not met their coauthors in person, each acted in a collegial fashion.

The product of this group effort is a volume full of original and important material. Most of the country-focused chapters offer either the first significant writing on the issue of invasive species law and policy or the first significant writing available in English. The cross-cutting chapters (on the relationship between invasive species and the International Plant Protection Convention, world trade, and genetically modified organisms) provide thoughtful and concise treatments of difficult issues. That so much of a multi-authored volume presents dramatically new material testifies not only to the hard work of the authors, but serves also as evidence of the need for far more law and policy work on the topic of invasive species.

The Environmental Law Institute (ELI) has provided superb editorial and intellectual support for this project. In particular, the ELI editor for this volume, Michael O'Grady, already knowledgeable about invasive species issues from work on an earlier ELI volume (Meg Filbey, Christina Kennedy, Jessica Wilkinson, and Jennifer Balch, *Halting the Invasion: State Tools for Invasive Species Management* (August 2002)), added clarity throughout the manuscript with his careful comments and suggestions. Good counsel and support for this project also came from ELI Vice President and *Environmental Law Reporter* Editor-in-Chief John Turner.

We thank IUCN for its concern with invasive species policy and its sponsorship of the original gathering that sparked this volume. In particular, we appreciate the support of Senior Legal Officer Tomme Rosanne Young in helping the contributions in this volume find their way into print.

Among the many people concerned with invasive species science and policy who have been especially helpful to us are Greg Aplet, Bill Buzbee, Carla D'Antonio, Don Kennedy, Julie Mayfield, Peter McAvoy, Keith Pitts, John Randall, Sarah Reichard, Buzz Thompson, and Peter Vitousek. Hal Mooney,

Laurie Neville, and Jeff McNeely deserve special thanks for their assistance with the volume.

The number of biologists concerned with invasive species has been growing over the past decade, followed by a lesser number of lawyers, journalists, and policymakers. One key challenge is to get more policymakers, scientists, journalists, and the general public to recognize invasive species as a major environmental threat—perhaps the most significant global environmental threat other than land change.

This volume reveals that the threat from invasive species is not generally addressed by coherent law and policy. We hope this volume provides a substantial push toward recognizing this serious problem, and toward finding policies that begin to deal with it.

Marc L. Miller
Robert N. Fabian

Atlanta, Georgia
September 2003

INTRODUCTION

BIOLOGICAL AND CULTURAL CAMOUFLAGE: THE CHALLENGES OF SEEING THE HARMFUL INVASIVE SPECIES PROBLEM AND DOING SOMETHING ABOUT IT

by Marc L. Miller[1] and Lance H. Gunderson[2]

N on-indigenous species, and more particularly harmful non-indigenous or "invasive" species, have been widely noted in recent years as a critical environmental problem at many ecological and political scales. At the global level, invasive species have been recognized as a primary driver in the loss of biodiversity and among the top five drivers of global change.[3] Several major international legal instruments and organizations have emphasized the importance of invasive species issues, including the Convention on Biological Diversity (CBD),[4] the International Plant Protection Convention (IPPC),[5] and the World Trade Organization (WTO).

Recognition of the seriousness of the problem of harmful non-indigenous species has led to pleas from biologists, lawyers, nongovernmental organizations (NGOs), farmers, other businesses, and citizens for a more complete and coherent response by all levels of government and by private actors to this threat.[6] Despite the increasing public and indeed global recognition of the problem of harmful non-indigenous species, actual changes to national laws have been quite limited. Indeed, only one country—New Zealand—has even tried to implement a comprehensive policy with regard to non-indigenous species.

In most countries, preexisting laws address the governance of natural and agricultural areas, water, forests, and wildlife, among other topics. Occasionally, countries have targeted laws addressing specific aspects of the harmful non-indigenous species problem, such as quarantine and inspection laws, or laws listing particular excluded species, typically those of particular harm to agriculture and other commercial interests. Many countries with political subdivisions leave most environmental and lands policies to those lower level government bodies (states, counties, lander, etc.).

This volume describes the law and policy regarding harmful non-indigenous species in six countries—New Zealand, Germany, South Africa, Argentina, Poland, and the United States. The volume also addresses three international and cross-cutting dimensions of harmful non-indigenous species policy: quarantine systems, trade issues, and the special and highly controversial concerns raised by genetically modified organisms. Early drafts of these chapters were presented as papers at a small conference at the World Conservation Union (IUCN) Environmental Law Center in Bonn, Germany, in December 1999. The papers have been thoroughly updated and rewritten to provide a complete, current description of the laws in each country and on these cross-cutting topics.

Together, these papers reveal a legal and policy landscape that is dramatically different from the proposals presented in policy instruments, government reports, and scholarly articles. The papers in this volume suggest that generalized calls for improved legal and institutional frameworks for harmful non-indigenous species, while they may be sound in spirit and principle, seem to have ignored the practical, historical, economic, and psychological barriers to effective law and policy in this area.

The six countries surveyed in this volume suggest a number of common issues regarding law and policy regarding harmful non-indigenous species.

First, these countries reveal varying degrees of recognition at the level of law and policy that harmful non-indigenous species are an environmental problem. Indeed, in many of the countries, there are still debates and confusion over some of the basic terminology necessary to define and discuss the problem of invasive species. For example, in Germany, one term describes both native species and long-established non-native species.

While it is clear that non-native species can be beneficial, and indeed are often the cornerstone of modern agriculture, blurring lines between important conceptual distinctions confuses both law and policy. It is often important for sound policy to distinguish between native organisms in their natural, evolved range, organisms native to a country (or other political unit) but outside their natural range, organisms not native to the country but beneficial, non-native organisms that are harmful, and non-native organisms whose impact is unknown. Indeed, the definitional challenges include discussions of the nature of "harm" (economic, ecological, aesthetic), and the need for more precise geographic and biological distinctions, including genetic variation within and among populations and measures of harm across different scales. The concept of what is "native" becomes even more blurred in the context of substantial human transformation of the natural environment. As land and ecosystems undergo long-term, multiple, and pervasive changes, it has become more and more difficult to maintain any notion of what remains natural or wild.

Second, it appears that most countries have not conducted a comprehensive assessment of the status of non-indigenous species, and have instead focused legal and policy efforts at particular non-indigenous species. Indeed, it is not clear that any country has done a comprehensive assessment, though the degree of systematic study of invasive species issues varies greatly. In other words, most countries appear to be reactive rather than proactive with regard to harmful non-indigenous species, even at the level of basic knowledge.

Third, most of the countries surveyed continue to rely on fragmented and incomplete legal authorities. The available laws and policies were typically enacted for purposes other than dealing with harmful non-indigenous species, or developed for only a small subset of non-indigenous species, such as those that threatened specific commercial crops. This theme of "gaps" and excessive (but at the same time incomplete) law and policy is evident in the discussions of Argentina, Germany, Poland, South Africa, and the United States.

The partial exception to this point is New Zealand, which has enacted two general framework statutes to deal with invasive species—the Biosecurity Act of 1993 and the Hazardous Substances and New Organisms Act of 1996. But the chapter on New Zealand explains that the problem of invasive species continues to be critical, and the legal framework has revealed major weaknesses including an absence of measures to judge the impact and success of the system. Moreover, to the extent New Zealand has taken the lead in invasive species policy, the reason may be in part because, as an isolated and long-inhabited island system, the damage from invasive species has been so great.

Fourth, despite several prominent international instruments and increasing global attention to the importance of harmful non-indigenous species as an environmental problem, most of the countries surveyed do not seem to be pursuing dramatic changes in their laws and policies.

The chapters in this volume are thoughtful, nuanced, and highly readable. Each chapter tells its own story, whether about a specific country's policies or one of the cross-cutting themes. Rather than summarize those chapters, each of which justifies careful study, this introduction sets the stage for those detailed descriptions of the relevant laws and policies in each surveyed country, and of the cross-cutting issues, by addressing three points.

We begin by asking why it has taken so long for harmful non-indigenous species to be recognized as a problem of particular concern. We then summarize the leading international instruments with respect to harmful non-indigenous species, since these instruments serve as the background for some of the nation-level discussions. Two of these instruments—the quarantine system under the IPPC[7] and the sanitary and phytosanitary standards (SPS)[8] under the WTO—are discussed in the following chapters, and so the primary focus of this part is on the relevant aspects of the CBD.[9] Finally, given the rather limited state of legal attention in most countries with regard to invasive species, we consider three priorities for countries working to create a sound legal and policy framework for dealing with harmful non-indigenous species.

THE SPECIAL DIFFICULTIES OF THE INVASIVE SPECIES PROBLEM: SEEING AND BELIEVING

The chapters in this volume suggest that in most places, invasive species have been recognized as a problem for some time. Yet these chapters reveal a profound lack of complete or coherent law and policy with regard to invasive species. Why?

Invasive species may be a more difficult problem for individuals and governments to perceive than many other types of environmental problems, such as air or water pollution, extinction of species, or changes in land use. Some of the reasons for the difficulties in perception reflect the limits of everyday human observation of the natural environment. Based solely on experience, it is not hard to make rough judgments about whether an area has been transformed into an urban setting or retains some (perhaps illusory) natural qualities.[10] People can tell the difference between a city and a forest. But without background training or knowledge, it is much more difficult to know whether an organism is indigenous or non-indigenous, and indeed organisms celebrated as part of local culture are often introduced. Even experts have difficulties assessing the biological health of ecosystems.

The problems for wise policy that stem from limitations on human ability to perceive biological pollution are magnified by the absence of settled measures of the biological status of areas or regions. For example, there is no standard measure or language that would help prioritize areas most in need of protection from invasive species, or most harmed by invasive species. At a functional level, few countries appear to have conducted any general biological assessments that would allow policymakers and scientists to map and measure the impact of invasive species. Without an inventory, it is hard to know what is missing, and yet might be restored, or what is present, but should not be.

The ecology of invasions adds its own complexities to everyday and even expert perception. There is often a substantial delay between the act that creates the risk of a new introduction and the visible or substantial presence of that non-indigenous species. There is sometimes further delay between the identification of a new non-indigenous species and judgment about ecological or economic harms. By the time an invasive species is identified, it may be beyond the capacity of even the best modern-day Sherlock Holmes to trace the source or timing of the original introduction, and whether that introduction was intentional or unintentional.

The chapters in this volume show a high level of awareness of particular harmful invasive species. They show a less strong but noticeable awareness of the sources of introduction of harmful invasive species, including laws and policies related to specific pathways (such as ballast water). What is much less common—indeed, what only New Zealand seems to have achieved, to some extent—is the perception of a general problem with the new introduction, spread, and presence of harmful invasive species, and a recognition, in law, of some of the basic categories that should be part of any comprehensive invasive species law and policy.

The difficulty of perceiving and responding to invasive species goes beyond limits on everyday and expert human perception. Many non-indigenous plant and animal species serve as the cornerstones of modern agriculture and commerce. Some of those non-indigenous species appear to post little threat to the natural environment, and to be restricted to the highly altered environment of modern agriculture. Other introduced species that provide huge benefits also impose substantial direct costs from predation and land change. Drawing a line between welcome (strongly beneficial) and unwelcome (harmful or invasive) non-indigenous species is often difficult, a difficulty magnified when the harms and benefits from a species inure to different groups of people.

Indeed, sound laws and policies with respect to invasive species must address the central role in commerce that many non-indigenous species play. Agriculture, horticulture, forestry, and other substantial commercial activities engage in extensive commerce in non-indigenous species. Everyday movement by people and commerce in nonliving objects may pose threats of accidental introduction of invasive species. No amount of law and policymaking with respect to natural areas will be successful if it ignores the interrelationship among natural and developed areas, and between those areas and human and commercial activity. These biological, psychological, and economic points have political implications: no law or policy that imposes substantial costs on commerce and development is likely to be adopted or to succeed unless the benefits are clear, and unless the mechanisms are specified for implementation, enforcement, and measurement of success or failure.

Establishing sound law and policy with regard to invasive species would be hard enough if the puzzles were merely biological, psychological, economic, and political. However, the ultimate questions about the law and policy with regard to non-indigenous species, and invasive species, reflect deep value preferences, values that reflect more general philosophical tenets that may border on religious beliefs. These value questions include which non-indigenous species should be introduced or allowed to remain, which indigenous species should be protected, and which activities should be regulated, and at what cost, if they pose a risk of introducing unwanted invasive species.

This morass of human and social dimensions swirling around the issue of invasive species makes the lack of coherent and comprehensive laws easier to understand, even in the face of long-standing recognition that some non-indigenous species could be very harmful. From an analytic standpoint, this mix of perspectives on the problem of invasive species poses special challenges as well: where, given these complexities, should an evaluation of invasive species law and policy begin?

The chapters in this volume respond to this puzzle by using the laws and policies currently in place in the selected countries as an analytic focal point. These laws are typically easier to identify than the more or less complete information on the full scope of the actual problem they address. These laws are also more accessible than a full analysis of how the laws are in fact implemented, and what impact the laws have. What a law-focused study allows is some reflection of the problems that have been recognized, and the efforts to deal with them. Perhaps a full set of laws should include some explicit mechanisms for stating, assessing, and then periodically reassessing the underlying problem, the goals of the laws, and whether the policies in place achieve their aims.

THE EMERGING INTERNATIONAL CONSENSUS ON THE IMPORTANCE OF HARMFUL NON-INDIGENOUS SPECIES AS AN ENVIRONMENTAL CONCERN

While the principal focus of this volume is on country-specific laws and policies, countries develop their environmental laws in the context of local concerns on the one hand, and in the context of international laws, instruments, and demands on the other. There are a variety of international laws and instruments, multilateral and bilateral, that relate (or might relate) to country-specific law and policy with regard to invasive species.[11] However, three basic and widely applicable international legal frameworks dominate any discussion of international policy with respect to invasive species: (1) the quarantine laws under the IPPC; (2) the related SPS promulgated as part of the WTO; and (3) the CBD.

The country studies in this volume make few references to any international agreements or standards other than the CBD. These three key international frameworks (IPPC, SPS, and CBD) are discussed in the following paragraphs.

The IPPC aims to prevent the introduction of plant pests. Under the IPPC, countries have established plant quarantine systems, now typically referred to as "phytosanitary" systems. The traditional focus of such systems has been on pests that threaten agricultural and other commercial lands and products, but the trend has been to expand phytosanitary systems to reflect concerns for plant pests that threaten the natural environment as well. John Hedley, in his chapter in this volume on the IPPC and invasive species, describes the history and scope of the IPPC, and explains the importance of phytosanitary systems to limiting the introduction and spread of harmful non-indigenous species.

The SPS Agreement, promulgated in 1994 as part of the trade talks that also instituted the WTO, provides a more general international law framework for the development of national phytosanitary standards and international mechanisms for enforcing those standards. The WTO has given three organizations the responsibility to develop international phytosanitary standards. One of those organizations is the IPPC, which has the responsibility to develop international standards with regard to plant health (with issues of food safety and animal health left to other international bodies). The SPS Agreement also limits the authority of Member countries to draft standards so as to avoid national laws that unnecessarily or unjustifiably interfere with trade. One of the major issues, addressed in the chapter by Jacob Werksman and Nattley Williams, is whether the SPS Agreement reaches too far and in fact limits countries from implementation of sound measures to protect against harmful non-indigenous species.

The CBD "is the only globally applicable, legally binding instrument to address generally alien species introduction, control and eradication across all biological taxa and ecosystems."[12] The 179 Parties to the CBD include, of the countries studied in this volume, New Zealand, South Africa, Argentina, Poland, and Germany.[13] The United States is not a Party to the CBD. Article 8(h) of the CBD provides: "Each Contracting Party shall, as far as possible and as appropriate . . . . Prevent the introduction of, control or eradicate those alien species which threaten ecosystems, habitats or species."[14] Article 8(h) appears as part of a list of "in-situ conservation" measures. In-situ conservation is defined by the CBD as "the conservation of ecosystems and natural habitats and the maintenance and recovery of viable populations of species in their natural surroundings and, in the case of domesticated or cultivated species, in the surroundings where they have developed their distinctive properties."[15]

Article 8(h), by itself, provides a weak foundation on which to build consistent, coherent, or strong invasive species policies in Member states. Surely it is good that the CBD explicitly recognizes that alien species can cause harm, and Article 8(h) usefully encompasses concern both for new introductions, and for control and eradication of invasive species—the general steps for any comprehensive invasive species policy. But the language of Article 8(h) appears too narrow for comprehensive invasive species policies to the extent it limits concerns to natural systems. Many of the issues with regard to harmful non-indigenous species involve developed areas and commercial and other human activities.

Moreover, the recognized harms from invasive species are limited even by this short text to threats to "ecosystems, habitats, or species." These types of harms are both too broad, since invasive species can threaten smaller and different ecological units and processes, and too narrow, since invasive species may also threaten human health, economic, and aesthetic values. Finally, the general limitation in Article 8 that demands action on each aspect of that Article only "as far as possible and appropriate" provides governments with substantial wiggle room.

The CBD is a large and complex document. Other provisions may strengthen the brief and somewhat cryptic language of Article 8(h).[16] In addition, the CBD is not only a document—it is also a process. The general provisions of the basic document are illuminated and nurtured by two administrative structures set up under the convention: the Conference of the Parties (COP) and the Subsidiary Body on Scientific, Technical, and Technological Advice (SBSTTA).

In 1998, the COP requested that the SBSTTA "develop guiding principles for the prevention, introduction and mitigation of impacts of alien species."[17] In February 1999, the Executive Secretary of SBSTTA produced a document describing the development of guiding principles, to be presented at its Fourth Meeting in Montreal in June 1999.[18] The February 1999 document addresses some of the shortcomings of Article 8(h). The document emphasizes the role of alien species in threatening biological diversity in many contexts. The document notes that "alien species are known to affect biological diversity whether within or outside protected areas and to influence ecosystems, natural habits and surrounding populations."[19] Indeed, the document recognizes harms from alien species entirely outside the context of "protected areas" by linking such harms to CBD provisions in Article 6 addressing "general measures for conservation and sustainable use."[20]

At the same time, the February 1999 document restricts alien species policies by focusing on "geographically and evolutionarily isolated ecosystems."[21] The February 1999 SBSTTA document is largely a restatement of other documents and research, albeit with strong (and inelegant) summaries, such as the statement that "the ecological threats posed by [alien] species are potentially and often actually enormous, they tend to evolve in an unpredictable way, and are virtually irreversible; the economic implications that derive from those threats are equally serious."[22]

In terms of new policy recommendations, the February 1999 document has only modest suggestions, mostly focusing on further process with little new substantive direction. One step combining some substance and more process is a recommendation that "parties urgently submit available case studies on alien species to the Executive Secretary."[23] It is odd to see a request for case studies without an explanation of the gap in knowledge they are meant to fill. Put another way, there is wide consensus on the existence of knowledge gaps regarding many aspects of the science and policy regarding invasive species, but it is not obvious how case studies might respond to any of those gaps.

In February 2000, the SBSTTA presented a document with 10 recommendations and 15 guiding principles for consideration by COP at its Fifth Meeting in Nairobi in May 2000.[24] A version of this document, with modifications in light of discussions at the COP meeting, was adopted and then published in June 2000 as part of the official report of that meeting.[25] The June 2000 document urges, endorses, invites, and requests CBD Parties to do various things, mostly procedural. For example, COP "[u]rges Parties, Governments and relevant organizations to submit case-studies."[26] As with the February 1999 SBSTTA document, the functional role of such case studies is not explained, though COP added to the earlier document a request that the case studies "particularly focus on thematic assessments."[27] Most of the recommendations in the June 2000 document are of sufficient generality that it is hard to imagine the recommendations having much impact (or at least any way to test or measure any impact).

The February 2000 SBSTTA document included a specific and practical recommendation that was not subsequently included in the June 2000 document, that the Executive Secretary "develop a paper . . . setting out options for future work of the Convention on Biological Diversity, which would provide practical support to Parties, Governments and organizations."[28] Some of the difficult issues obscured by abstract discussions of the "importance" of the invasive species problem and the various harms invasive species cause might be revealed by documents that wrestle with "practical support," and the elimination of this SBSTTA recommendation by COP is therefore unfortunate.

A potentially significant new contribution to invasive species policy included in the June 2000 document is a list of 15 "Interim Guiding Principles for the Prevention, Introduction, and Mitigation of Impacts of Alien Species," along with a corresponding recommendation urging parties, governments and relevant organizations "to apply the interim guiding principles."[29] Those principles are worth quoting and reading, despite their length, as they provide the most direct, compact, and active set of principles currently available for invasive species policy.

A. *General*

Guiding Principle 1: Precautionary Approach

Given the unpredictability of the impacts on biological diversity of alien species, efforts to identify and prevent unintentional introductions as well as decisions concerning intentional introductions should be based on the precautionary approach. Lack of scientific certainty about the environmental, social and economic risk posed by a potentially invasive alien species or by a potential pathway should not be used as a reason for not taking preventative action against the introduction of potentially invasive alien species. Likewise, lack of certainty about the long-term implication of an invasion should not be used as a reason for postponing eradication, containment or control measures.

INTRODUCTION

Guiding Principle 2: Three-Stage Hierarchical Approach

Prevention is generally far more cost effective and environmentally desirable than measures taken following introduction of an alien invasive species. Priority should be given to prevention of entry of alien invasive species (both between and within States). If entry has already taken place, actions should be undertaken to prevent the establishment and spread of alien species. The preferred response would be eradication at the earliest possible stage (principle 13). In the event that eradication is not feasible or is not cost-effective, containment (principle 14) and long-term control measures (principle 15) should be considered. Any examination of benefits and costs (both environmental and economic) should be done on a long-term basis.

Guiding Principle 3: Ecosystem Approach

All measures to deal with alien invasive species should be based on the ecosystem approach, in line with the relevant provisions of the Convention and the decisions of the Conference of the Parties.

Guiding Principle 4: State Responsibility

States should recognize the risk that they may pose to other States as a potential source of alien invasive species, and should take appropriate actions to minimize that risk. In accordance with Article 3 of the Convention on Biological Diversity, and principle 2 of the 1992 Rio Declaration on Environment and Development, States have the responsibility to ensure that activities within their jurisdiction or control do not cause damage to the environment of other States or of areas beyond the limits of national jurisdiction. In the context of alien invasive species, activities that could be a risk for another State include:

(a) The intentional or unintentional transfer of an alien invasive species to another State (even if it is harmless in the State of origin); and

(b) The intentional or unintentional introduction of an alien species into their own State if there is a risk of that species subsequently spreading (with or without a human vector) into another State and becoming invasive.

Guiding Principle 5: Research and Monitoring

In order to develop an adequate knowledge base to address the problem, States should undertake appropriate research on and monitoring of alien invasive species. This should document the history of invasions (origin, pathways and time-period), characteristics of the alien invasive species, ecology of the invasion, and the associated ecological and economic impacts and how they change over time. Monitoring is the key to early detection of new alien species. It requires targeted and general surveys, which can benefit from the involvement of local communities.

Guiding Principle 6: Education and Public Awareness

States should facilitate education and public awareness of the risks associated with the introduction of alien species. When mitigation measures are required, education and public-awareness-oriented programs should be set in motion so as to inform local communities and appropriate sector groups on how to support such measures.

B. *Prevention*

Guiding Principle 7: Border Control and Quarantine Measures

1. States should implement border control and quarantine measures to ensure that:

(a) Intentional introductions are subject to appropriate authorization (principle 10);
(b) Unintentional or unauthorized introductions of alien species are minimized.

2. These measures should be based on an assessment of the risks posed by alien species and their potential pathways of entry. Existing appropriate governmental agencies or authorities should be strengthened and broadened as necessary, and staff should be properly trained to implement these measures. Early detection systems and regional coordination may be useful.

Guiding Principle 8: Exchange of Information

States should support the development of database(s), such as that currently under development by the Global Invasive Species Program, for compilation and dissemination of information on alien species that threaten ecosystems, habitats or species, to be used in the context of any prevention, introduction and mitigation activities. This information should include incident lists, information on taxonomy and ecology of invasive species and on control methods, whenever available. The wide dissemination of this information, as well as national, regional and international guidelines, procedures and recommendations such as those being compiled by the Global Invasive Species Program should also be facilitated through, inter alia, the clearing-house mechanism.

Guiding Principle 9: Cooperation, Including Capacity-Building

Depending on the situation, a State's response might be purely internal (within the country), or may require a cooperative effort between two or more countries, such as:

(a) Where a State of origin is aware that a species being exported has the potential to be invasive in the receiving State, the exporting State should provide information, as available, on the potential invasiveness of the species to the importing State. Particular attention should be paid where exporting Parties have similar environments;
(b) Agreements between countries, on a bilateral or multilateral basis, should be developed and used to regulate trade in certain alien species, with a focus on particularly damaging invasive species;
(c) States should support capacity-building programs for States that lack the expertise and resources, including financial, to assess the risks of introducing alien species. Such capacity-building may involve technology transfer and the development of training programs.

C. *Introduction of Species*

Guiding Principle 10: Intentional Introduction

No intentional introduction should take place without proper authorization from the relevant national authority or agency. A risk assessment, including environmental impact assessment, should be carried out as part of the evaluation process before coming to a decision on whether or not to authorize a proposed introduction. States should authorize the introduction of only those alien species that, based on this prior assessment, are unlikely to cause unacceptable harm to ecosystems, habitats or species, both within that State and in neighbouring States. The burden of proof that a proposed introduction is unlikely to cause such harm should be with the proposer of the introduction. Further, the anticipated benefits of such an introduction should strongly outweigh any actual and potential adverse effects and related costs. Authorization of an introduction may, where appropriate, be accompanied by conditions, e.g., preparation of a mitigation plan, monitoring procedures, or containment requirements. The precautionary approach should be applied throughout all the above-mentioned measures.

Guiding Principle 11: Unintentional Introductions

1. All States should have in place provisions to address unintentional introductions (or intentional introductions that have established and become invasive). These include statutory and regulatory measures, institutions and agencies with appropriate responsibilities and with the operational resources required for rapid and effective action.
2. Common pathways leading to unintentional introductions need to be identified and appropriate provisions to minimize such introductions should be in place. Sectoral activities, such as fisheries, agriculture, forestry, horticulture, shipping (including the discharge of ballast waters), ground and air transportation, construction projects, landscaping, ornamental aquaculture, tourism and game-farming, are often pathways for unintentional introductions. Legislation requiring environmental impact assessment of such activities should also require an assessment of the risks associated with unintentional introductions of alien invasive species.

D. *Mitigation of Impacts*

Guiding Principle 12: Mitigation of Impacts

Once the establishment of an alien invasive species has been detected, States should take steps such as eradication, containment and control, to mitigate the adverse effects. Techniques used for eradication, containment or control should be cost-effective, safe to the environment, humans and agriculture, as well as socially, culturally and ethically acceptable. Mitigation measures should take place in the earliest possible stage of invasion, on the basis of the precautionary approach. Hence, early detection of new introductions of potentially invasive or invasive species is important, and needs to be combined with the capacity to take rapid follow-up action.

Guiding Principle 13: Eradication

Where it is feasible and cost-effective, eradication should be given priority over other measures to deal with established alien invasive species. The best opportunity for eradicating alien invasive species is in the early stages of invasion, when populations are small and localized; hence, early detection systems focused on high-risk entry points can be critically useful. Community support, built through comprehensive consultation, should be an integral part of eradication projects.

Guiding Principle 14: Containment

When eradication is not appropriate, limitation of spread (containment) is an appropriate strategy only where the range of the invasive species is limited and containment within defined boundaries is possible. Regular monitoring outside the control boundaries is essential, with quick action to eradicate any new outbreaks.

Guiding Principle 15: Control

Control measures should focus on reducing the damage caused rather than on merely reducing the numbers of the alien invasive species. Effective control will often rely on a range of integrated techniques. Most control measures will need to be regularly applied, resulting in a recurrent operating budget and the need for a long-term commitment to achieve and maintain results. In some instances, biological control may give long-term suppression of an alien invasive species without recurrent costs, but should always be implemented in line with existing national regulations, international codes and principle 10 above.[30]

These are an excellent set of working principles. While they share the fault of excessive generality common to "guidance" documents, including the other documents produced as part of the CBD processes, and while many puzzles remain about each of the principles, they are sufficiently short and well structured that they might actually be of use to a country trying to develop its invasive species policies.

Among the most important of these principles is Guiding Principle 10, relating to intentional introductions of new alien species (not just those known to be invasive). One basic and very useful policy distinction is between alien species brought into a country, region, or area intentionally—with the knowledge or purpose of an individual or corporate entity—and those alien species brought into the country unintentionally or accidentally—through the lack of knowledge or negligence of an individual or corporate entity. Reckless behavior, where an individual or the representatives of a corporate entity know that there is a substantial risk of introducing alien species, but act anyway, is an important category of behavior that can be analogized to either intentional or unintentional behavior, depending on the degree of the risk, the level of awareness of that risk, and the purpose of the classification, such as preventive policy, regulation, civil liability, or criminal liability.

Among the easiest aspects to understand of the problem of harmful invasive species is the intentional introduction of alien species that then cause harm. Many harmful species have been intentionally introduced leading, eventually, to the question of why a person would bring in a harmful organism (a biological time bomb), and why a government would allow such acts to occur. The answer, in retrospect, is often that intentional introductions were not intended by the introducer to cause harm (even if the introduction itself was intentional)—indeed, as with the case of biological controls, or a new horticultural or pet species, the new species may have been intended to provide benefits. From the government side, the answer is often that no (or minimal) process existed to limit, identify, or screen new intentional introductions.

INTRODUCTION

Guiding Principle 10 directs that a risk assessment process be created for every "intentional introduction," that each risk assessment include an EIA, that introductions be allowed only for "alien species . . . unlikely to cause unacceptable harm" and where anticipated benefits "strongly outweigh any actual and potential adverse effects and related costs," that a person proposing an introduction bears the burden of proof, and that any authorization may be accompanied by specific conditions related to any identified risks.

Guiding Principle 10 establishes, in simple language, the basic framework for a screening system. From the perspective of those concerned about the rate and manner of new intentional introductions, it will be necessary to specify what qualifies as an "intentional introduction" triggering this screening mechanism. Does it apply only to species never before introduced, or any species alien to the proposed place of introduction? Is the concept of "place" defined in terms of political or ecological boundaries? What kinds of risks will be considered? Will there be a mechanism for oversight and follow-up? What kinds of penalties will attach to introductions that are allowed but eventually cause harm?

From the perspective of relevant industries concerned about burdensome and costly regulations and processes, Guiding Principle 10 may appear to be a simple assertion of the need for a so-called White List where only approved alien species may be introduced, and where industry must carry an impossible burden—proof that an alien species will in no circumstance cause harm—for each introduction.

The chapters in this volume suggest that few countries have developed a comprehensive or strong screening system, with New Zealand providing the example of the most substantial system. Australia—an important country with respect to policies regarding invasive species—has shown that a strong screening system can be practical and assess proposed introductions efficiently.[31] Characteristics of alien species can be identified that make them more or less likely to prove invasive and harmful. Levels of screening can be instituted so that many species (including those where there have been prior introductions and records established) can be reviewed very quickly (in a matter of hours or days), while only a modest proportion of proposed introductions require more searching (and time-consuming and costly) review.

Another important principle is Guiding Principle 11, related to unintentional introductions. In this principle, COP recognizes, though perhaps not as clearly as they might, that for unintentional introductions, waiting to identify and assess alien species once they are in place is unworkable, and that the mechanisms of transmission or "pathways" must be identified and regulated. The identification of pathways for unintentional introductions highlights some of the limits of classic risk assessment or cost-benefit analysis, or at least emphasizes that risk and cost principles must be applied not only to individual acts, but to social and commercial activities as well.

One of the most controversial and confusing of the Interim Guiding Principles is Principle 1, which encourages countries to use a "precautionary approach" in invasive species law and policy. Like most complex ideas, the notion of a precautionary approach is not self-defining. The idea has been particularly controversial because it is susceptible to several very different readings, some highly problematic.

If the precautionary principle highlights invasive species policy as an area where there may be greater levels of uncertainty than in other areas, given the complexity of invasion biology, the time delays, and the other barriers to perception, this is a useful principle, but should not be highly controversial. However, the precautionary principle has not been limited to the context of invasive species policy. For example, the CBD Preamble provides that lack of scientific certainty "shall not be used as a reason to postpone measures to avoid or minimize a threat of significant reduction or loss of biodiversity."[32] Similarly, the Rio Declaration, Principle 15 states "lack of full scientific certainty shall not be used as a reason for postponing cost effective measures to prevent environmental degradation."[33]

To the extent that the precautionary principle merely highlights that important decisions must sometimes (and perhaps always) be made on incomplete information, and based on assessments of probabilities and risk, surely it is correct, but says little that is worthy of the controversy this concept has generated. The precautionary principle makes sense to the extent it rejects the requirement of an unrealistic and rigid perfectionism (scientific certainty) as a basis for policy or action. A sound reading of the precautionary principle should also reject an equally dangerous and sloppy requirement of action in the face of scientific *uncertainty*—what might be called "actionism" (an assumption that actions are positive, and that any action is better than non-action, or that necessarily the benefits of action outweigh the costs of non-action).

The controversy arises from the ambiguity inherent in these various statements and the extent to which they are seen to include a normative preference for action or action in the face of uncertainty. Both action and non-action have costs and benefits. To the extent that the precautionary principle is intended to encourage governmental action without adequate reflection or justification, it should be rejected. Similarly, to the extent the precautionary principle is intended to encourage inaction (or a rejection of proposed action) in the absence of full or complete justification or proof of the safety of that action, it should also be rejected. In other words, the "precautionary approach" is a useful principle to the extent it highlights the high levels of risk (and associated harm) and lack of knowledge in the area of invasive species policy and decisionmaking.

In some situations, uncertainty and lack of knowledge may be a basis for action; in other contexts, they may be a basis for inaction. Any use of the "precautionary principle" should include a more detailed statement of the underlying premises. If the ambiguities in this controversial phrase cannot be settled or clarified through more detailed statement, then perhaps the term should be removed from policy dialogue. By making the precautionary principle Interim Guiding Principle 1, COP has obscured the other useful and clearer principles that follow.

The tension between action and planning or study has been part of resource management discussions for decades. One assumption of the action approach is that some action is better than none. Yet an increasing number of examples from large-scale resource systems indicate that there is a great likelihood that intended actions will often be wrong, and lead to unintended consequences.[34] On the other hand, the precautionary principle responds in part to a perhaps overly cautious approach to dealing with natural resource issues that assumes a requisite understanding of these complex systems is needed prior to any intervention.

One possible answer to the dilemma between action based upon imperfect knowledge and no action arising from a conservative interpretation of the precautionary principle is an approach called adaptive environmental assessment and management. Since it's inception in the late 1970s at the International Institute for Applied Systems Analysis (IIASA), adaptive management has proved to be an effective technique for assessing and managing complex environmental issues. Successful applications in large-scale regional systems include forests in Canada; water management in the Everglades of Florida and hydropower/endangered species management in the Colombia River Basin, both in the United States; and the Great Lakes of North America.[35]

Adaptive environmental assessment and management is based upon three assumptions. One is that information and understanding will always be partial and imperfect. The second is that even with applications of the best available science, for a number of technical reasons (nonlinear interactions, cross-scale dynamics, and inherent complexity of variables) predictability of interventions will always be limited. The third is that the inherent uncertainty in resource systems should be confronted in a process where learning is linked with action. These assumptions provide the points of departure for assessment and management.

The implementation of an adaptive management approach might prove valuable for dealing with global invasive species problems. An adaptive approach views policies as hypotheses and management actions as tests of those hypotheses. Once actions are implemented and key parts of systems are monitored, then policies can be evaluated and modified through a process of learning and increased understanding.

The single largest problem with the Interim Guiding Principles from the perspective of a country trying to develop policy is that there is still no clear starting point, no first principle or principles that might lead to a complete and coherent set of invasive species policies. It is likely that a starting point for developing those principles could be found in an integrated assessment that has played a central role in the debates about global climate change. The second largest problem with these principles is that they do not include as a basic principle the proper measurement of the general problem of invasive species (as opposed to studies of specific invasive species) and corresponding measurement and feedback on the effectiveness and efficiency of any policy initiatives.

Put another way, the chapters in this volume, describing invasive species policies in selected countries, are hard to line up with the June 2000 set of guiding principles. The last part of this introduction considers where countries should begin in developing wise invasive species policies. In light of the studies in this volume, and the solid general principles suggested by the COP "Interim Guiding Principles," what steps should come first?

THREE POLICY PRIORITIES: BIOSTATUS, PREVENTION, AND HOLISTIC THINKING ABOUT DYNAMIC MANAGEMENT

Lining up the ideas of the Interim Guiding Principles (or a similar set of principles in the IUCN Guide)[36] with the chapters in this volume suggests a considerable gap between idea and reality. Indeed, the gap is sufficiently large that the first question for the countries discussed in this volume, or any country considering its invasive species policies, might be where invasive species legal and policy work should *begin*. This part suggests three steps should come first: an assessment of the status of alien species in the country; a focus on prevention of new introductions; and the integration of a holistic approach, aware of the social, psychological, and commercial aspects of the invasive species problem.

Biostatus Evaluation and Reports: Describing the Problem

The chapters in this volume highlight the degree to which countries do not know the extent of alien species present, how many of those species are harmful, and in what ways, and the time and manner of their introduction. It is hard to understand a problem or design a wise solution unless the problem is carefully described and its relevant dimensions defined. The first priority in designing wise invasive species laws and policies is a comprehensive biological survey that describes the presence and extent of indigenous and non-indigenous species throughout the country, and that articulates and prioritizes the current harm and potential threats from the alien species.

Careful biological assessment—the biostatus of the entire country—and a clear and understandable statement of the nature and scope of the problem are critical to inform legislators and administrators who must authorize, design, and apply new policies. Such information is also critical to generating public and commercial understanding and support for new policies, and for assessing the effectiveness and efficiency of all policy efforts.

Biologists have not yet developed terms that convey the scope of biological invasion or biological integrity, or the degree of threat from invasive species. Nor have they developed a broad theoretical base that is adequate to generate an advancement of understanding of the problem of biological invasion. Only at the ends of the spectrum can biologists convey in a clear way the role of invasive species, noting, for example, that some bays and rivers have become biological cesspools, or that some remote areas retain a high degree of biological integrity. Information about particular invasive species or lists with numbers of species do not provide information that is particularly useful at other scales. Nor do such lists provide a framework that will allow adaptive assessment and feedback of any future policy efforts. Like measurements of air quality or water quality or urban sprawl or wildlands preservation, biologists must develop one or more measures of biological integrity and threat from invasive species and link those key response variables to the processes (both ecologic and social) that influence those measures.

Once information is gathered, and measures developed to convey the scope of the invasive species problem, biologists and others must find ways to report that information to audiences with varying levels of sophistication and who will use the information in different ways. Different reports, including suggestions prioritizing and explaining the costs and benefits of various policies, and describing feedback mechanisms, should then be provided to legislators, policymakers, administrators, journalists, academics, and the general public.

Without the development of basic information and sound measures of the invasive species problem—a clear specification of harm from current policies and the benefits of policy change—invasive species may become only an environmental fad, moved by dramatic stories and occasional political insight, but too easily undermined by those who dislike the costs that any regulations will impasse, and who will be able to specify and quantify those costs with greater precision.

Prevention Is a Priority, but Only a Partial Solution

Invasive species policy documents typically suggest that efforts at prevention take priority over efforts at controlling spread or eradication of harmful invasive species already in place. For example, the IUCN Guide states:

> The duty to take preventive measures is laid down by all international instruments that concern alien species and also forms the cornerstone of most national legal frameworks that address this subject. Prevention is more cost effective and environmentally desirable than remedial measures taken after the introduction of alien invasive species. Once an introduced species becomes invasive, eradication may be impossible and the ecological damage irreversible.[37]

Similarly, COP Interim Guiding Principle 2 offers a three-stage hierarchical approach, and places prevention first (followed by preventing spread and eradication, and lastly long-term control). Principle 2 states: "Prevention is generally far more cost effective and environmentally desirable than measures taken following introduction of an alien invasive species. Priority should be given to prevention of entry of alien invasive species (both between and within States)."[38]

While there appears to be substantial agreement on the priority that should be given to preventing new introductions, the chapters in this volume suggest that preventing introductions has not been given priority in most countries. Countries conflate long-established quarantine systems that focus on known dangers with a system of screening all new intentional introductions and commerce and travel that directly or indirectly threaten new harmful introductions.

The realities of increasing world trade, and increasing trade and travel in many countries, along with the real technological limits on identifying unintentional introductions, should not prevent, and indeed should encourage, a strong statement of principle limiting introduction of alien species. Laws and policies should bar all introduction or movement of alien species, whether already present in the country or not, unless the risk from the species (where known) or the activity (for pathways which enable unintentional introductions) are identified and assessed based on the best available science.

Even with prevention of entry or biotic quarantines, introductions of new invasive species will still occur. In many cases, substantial numbers of invasive species may already be present in a system, but which of those species will become harmful has not been revealed. The bottom line is that even with the most effective "filtering" of species movement among states, movement of species across political boundaries will occur. But without a strong statement of principle and supporting processes and resources for wise decisionmaking to prevent new introductions, any effort to deal with invasive species already present will be doomed to fail.

Holistic Thinking About Dynamic Management

The reasons that have kept the invasive species problem from becoming a primary focus of environmental policies in many countries are likely to limit efforts at new law and policy, even as the importance of the problem becomes more widely recognized. The COP Interim Guiding Principle 6 encourages countries to "facilitate education and public awareness of the risks associated with the introduction of alien species."[39] This is only one piece of a larger challenge, which is to recognize the huge variety of social, cultural, and commercial activities and psychological predilections that have an impact on the introduction and spread of invasive species.

With even initial and partial invasive species law and policy, countries and organizations will need to recognize the behaviors and beliefs that have led to the introduction and movement of harmful invasive species in the past. Policies structured in a technical fashion, focusing only on specific kinds of decisions (e.g., new introductions), responses (e.g., screening systems), or institutions (e.g., border control agencies), are likely to be overwhelmed by social, cultural, psychological, and commercial realities.

The chapters in this volume confirm that invasive species management is a complex and dynamic problem. New species appear in regions, through unknown means. Some species classified as harmful in one area are benign in others. Which species will prove harmful and which will not cannot be predicted. All of this suggests that the nature of the invasive species challenge will change over time and space. What is suggested as appropriate policies and practices now is strikingly different from policies that were suggested or in place 30 years ago, and will likely be very different from those written 30 years hence. Because of the ever-changing nature of the invasive species problem, policies and implementations, assessments, and management actions must be dynamic and structured in ways to increase knowledge and understanding of changing ecosystems.

CONCLUSION

This volume reflects both hope and concern about the present and future of invasive species policies. The hope comes from the universal recognition by the countries described in this volume that non-indigenous species present a distinct and important environmental threat, and that the threat from harmful non-indigenous species deserves a substantial policy response. The concern reflects the lack of a comprehensive response from most of the countries, and substantial limitations on the scope and effectiveness of the invasive species policies even for New Zealand, the country that has, so far, gone farthest in developing such policies.

It has taken most countries many years to recognize harmful non-indigenous species for the significant ecological, economic, and aesthetic threat they pose. Recognition of the problem, however, only starts a country, group, or institution down the path to a sensible solution. For each country and locality, and for NGOs and international bodies concerned with environmental policy, the first task is to recognize the serious problems caused by harmful non-indigenous species. The second task is to appreciate the immense scope and complexity of that problem, and to work on responses with that inherent complexity in mind.

Thoughtful models exist for comprehensive invasive species policies. The chapters in this volume reaffirm the need for such policies, and highlight how far most countries have yet to go in responding to the threat from invasive species.

Introduction Endnotes:

1. The author is a Professor of Law, Emory University School of Law, Atlanta, Georgia. E-mail: mmiller@law.emory.edu. He would like to thank Greg Aplet, Anita Bernstein, Bill Buzbee, Nick Fabian, Peter McAvoy, Richard Orr, Keith Pitts, Sarah Reichard, Robert Schapiro, and Ron Wright, each of whom offered insights on earlier drafts, and Stephanie Allen, Terry Gordon, Jason Herman, and Wendy Phillips for research support. The author wishes to express his appreciation for the insights into invasive species policy and politics provided by the National Invasive Species Council Policy and Regulation Working Group, on which he served as nonfederal co-chair. *See* INTERIM REPORT: POLICY AND REGULATION WORKING GROUP OF THE INVASIVE SPECIES ADVISORY COUNCIL (2000), *available at* http://www.invasivespecies.gov/council/PR%20interim%20final2%20703.doc (last visited June 10, 2003).

2. Associate Professor of Environmental Studies, Emory University, Atlanta, Georgia. Prof. Lance Gunderson attended the University of Florida, receiving a bachelor's degree as well as a master's degrees in botany and a Ph.D. in environmental engineering sciences. He worked for over a decade as a botanist with the U.S. National Park Service in the Big Cypress and the Everglades regions of southern Florida. He then worked for a decade as a research scientist in the Department of Zoology at the University of Florida. He has been chair of the Department of Environmental Studies at Emory University since January 1999. He was the executive director of the Resilience Network, a program of the Beijer International Institute for Ecological Economics, Swedish Royal Academy of Sciences, Stockholm. He currently serves as vice chair of the Resilience Alliance and on the Science Advisory Board of the Grand Canyon Monitoring and Research Center.

3. Peter Vitousek, *Human Domination of Earth Ecosystems*, 278 SCIENCE 5335 (1997).

4. 31 I.L.M. 818 (1992).

5. United Nations (U.N.) Food and Agricultural Organization (FAO), International Plant Protection Convention New Revised Text Art. II (1997) (approved by FAO Conference at its 29th Session in Rome).

6. A summary of such proposals, and a set of ideal proposals for both international and national policymaking appear in CLARE SHINE ET AL., WORLD CONSERVATION UNION (IUCN), A GUIDE TO DESIGNING LEGAL AND INSTITUTIONAL FRAMEWORKS ON ALIEN INVASIVE SPECIES (2000) [hereinafter IUCN GUIDE].

7. *See supra* note 5.

8. *See* WTO, *Agreement on the Application of Sanitary and Phytosanitary Measures*, *in* THE RESULTS OF THE URUGUAY ROUND OF MULTILATERAL TRADE NEGOTIATIONS. THE LEGAL TEXTS (1994). *See generally* Marc L. Miller, *NIS, WTO, SPS, WIR: Does the WTO Substantially Limit the Ability of Countries to Regulate Harmful Non-Indigenous Species?*, 17 EMORY INT'L L. REV. (forthcoming 2003).

9. 31 I.L.M. 818.

10. Ecologists are increasingly attuned to the idea that qualities of wildness can be expressed both in highly natural and highly artificial settings. *See* Gregory Aplet, *On the Nature of Wildness: Exploring What Wilderness Really Protects*, 76 DENV. U. L. REV. 347 (1999).

11. These many instruments are catalogued and discussed in the IUCN GUIDE, *supra* note 6.

12. *Id.* at 14.

13. *See Convention on Biological Diversity, at* http://www.biodiv.org/Index.html (last visited June 11, 2003).

14. 31 I.L.M. 818, art. 8(h) (1992).

15. *Id.* art. 2.

16. *See* IUCN GUIDE, *supra* note 6.

17. *See id.* at 15.

18. SBSTTA, DEVELOPMENT OF GUIDING PRINCIPLES FOR THE PREVENTION OF IMPACTS OF ALIEN SPECIES BY IDENTIFYING PRIORITY AREAS OF WORK ON ISOLATED ECOSYSTEMS AND BY EVALUATING AND GIVING RECOMMENDATIONS FOR THE FURTHER DEVELOPMENT OF THE GLOBAL INVASIVE SPECIES PROGRAM (1999) (UNEP/CBD/SBSTTA/4/8).

19. *Id.* ¶ 9.

20. *Id.* ¶ 10.

21. *Id.* ¶ 2.

22. *Id.* ¶ 54.

23. *Id.* ¶ 75.

24. COP CBD, REPORTS OF THE SUBSIDIARY BODY ON SCIENTIFIC, TECHNICAL, AND TECHNOLOGICAL ADVICE (2000).

25. COP CBD, REPORT OF THE FIFTH MEETING OF THE CONFERENCE OF THE PARTIES TO THE CONVENTION ON BIOLOGICAL DIVERSITY 111-19 (2000) (UNEP/CBD/COP/5/23).

26. *Id.* V/8, recommendation no. 3.

27. *Id.* The document provides no definition or justification of the notion of making the case studies "thematic." Perhaps COP recognizes that case studies in isolation—even studies organized around the authorized one page outline—may not provide any insight into the general problems of invasive species biology, law, or policy.

28. *Id.* V/8, Annex 1, at 113.

29. *Id.* V/8, recommendation no. 1.

30. *Id.* Annex 1, at 114-17.

31. *See* Richard Sharp, *Review of Australia's National Environmental Impact Assessment Processes in the Control of Alien Species in Order to Prevent Biodiversity Loss*, 16 ENVTL. & PLAN. L.J. 92 (1999); Curtis Daehler & Debbie Carino, *Predicting Invasive Plants: Prospects for a General Screening System Based on Current Regional Models*, 2 BIOLOGICAL INVASIONS 93-102 (2000); Roger Pech, *Managing Alien Species: The Australian Experience, in* PROCEEDINGS OF THE NORWAY/U.N. CONFERENCE ON ALIEN SPECIES, TRONDHEIM JULY 1-5, 1996, at 198-203 (Odd Sandlund et al. eds., 1996). *See also* DEPARTMENT OF AGRICULTURE, FISHERIES & FORESTRY, AUSTRALIA, GUIDELINES FOR IMPORT RISK ANALYSIS (2001) (Draft), *available at* http://www. affa.gov.au/content/publications.cfm?Category=Biosecurity%20Australia&ObjectID= 85B98CC3-86DE-48AE-8A76D4A40F33245A (last visited July 7, 2003).

32. 31 I.L.M. 818, pmbl.

33. Rio Declaration on Environment and Development, U.N. Conference on Environment and Development, princ. 15, U.N. Doc. A/CONF.151/5 Rev. 1, 31 I.L.M. 874 (1992). *See generally* Cass R. Sunstein, *Beyond the Precautionary Principle*, 151 U. PA. L. REV. 1003 (2003).

34. For examples, see LANCE H. GUNDERSON ET AL., BARRIERS AND BRIDGES TO THE RENEWAL OF ECOSYSTEMS AND INSTITUTIONS (1995); KAI LEE, COMPASS AND GYROSCOPE (1993).
35. *See id.*
36. IUCN GUIDE, *supra* note 6.
37. *Id.* at 33.
38. *See supra* note 25, Annex 1, princ. 2, at 112.
39. *Id.* Annex 1, princ. 6, at 115.

CHAPTER 1:
INVASIVE SPECIES LEGISLATION AND ADMINISTRATION: NEW ZEALAND

by Mark Christensen[1]

The New Zealand government has identified the continuing decline of indigenous biodiversity as the major environmental issue facing the country. More than 200 years of introductions of invasive species, both intentional and unintentional, have played a significant part in this decline. During the past decade, the government has taken several key steps to combat the threat from invasive species and the decline of indigenous biodiversity.

In particular, the government of New Zealand has enacted two main statutes that address invasive species. the Biosecurity Act of 1993 and the Hazardous Substances and New Organisms Act of 1996 (HSNO Act). The Biosecurity Act aims to prevent the unintentional introduction of invasive species and their spread within the country. It sets standards for all imports that might pose a biosecurity threat, controls the passage of goods across the border by way of inspections and border control, and requires post-entry quarantine. For an invasive species already established in New Zealand, the Biosecurity Act provides for either the eradication or the ongoing management of that species by way of pest management strategies at both a regional and a national level. Pest management strategies establish who is responsible for a species, including fiscal, managerial, and "on the ground" responsibilities. Finally, the Biosecurity Act puts in place mechanisms for the gathering, recording, and disseminating of information about invasive species.

The HSNO Act governs the operations and duties of people and organizations that intentionally bring new organisms (including genetically modified organisms (GMOs)) into New Zealand. The HSNO Act requires people who propose to import, develop, field test, or release a new organism to obtain an approval from a specially constituted body, the Environmental Risk Management Authority (ERMA). ERMA is required by the HSNO Act to consider the risks and benefits of such an introduction before granting approval. The HSNO Act also provides for public participation in applications, and approvals may be granted subject to conditions that aim to reduce potential adverse effects, such as accidental release.

Like the Biosecurity Act, the HSNO Act also has provisions that grant wide powers to agencies in the case of an emergency. The Act places a general duty on people dealing with new organisms to avoid, remedy, or mitigate any actual or potential adverse effects of that organism.

As another important aspect of its commitment to the issue, the government established, in 1997, the cabinet portfolio of the Minister of Biosecurity to co-ordinate policy and activities that impact upon the introduction of potentially invasive species.

While the legislative and administrative framework for the control of invasive species and GMOs in New Zealand is detailed and comprehensive, problems remain. Introduced invasive species pose serious threats both to ecosystem functioning and to the survival of indigenous species in many natural areas, both on public and private land. Pest and weed problems are pervasive and widespread and are increasing in both number and distribution; the costs of pest and weed control are high, and insufficient resources currently limit the effectiveness of controls.

A 2000 report by the independent Parliamentary Commissioner for the Environment has highlighted a number of major weaknesses in the current system, including a lack of clearly defined outcomes against which the success or otherwise of the system can be judged. The report also pointed out that progress has been slow in developing strategic directions for biosecurity, including policy, research, and operational policies, particularly in relation to risks to indigenous biodiversity. The commissioner's report makes a number of recommendations to the Minister of Biosecurity and to various biosecurity agencies on how the biosecurity system might be improved and more effectively implemented from an environmental management perspective.

This has contributed to the release in December 2002, of a draft Biosecurity Strategy by the Biosecurity Council, which makes further recommendations including the nomination of lead agencies for terrestrial and freshwater biosecurity (Ministry of Agriculture and Fisheries) and marine biosecurity (Ministry of Fisheries) and the reconfiguration of the Biosecurity Council as a stakeholder advisory body.

INTRODUCTION

The decline of indigenous biodiversity has been identified as the major environmental issue facing New Zealand.[2] One of the primary reasons for this decline is the impact that introduced mammals and plants have had, particularly since Europeans arrived some 200 years ago.[3] For decades successive governments have tried to deal with those pests and weeds that have threatened the country's agricultural base.[4] More recently, however, the government has also recognized the major impact of invasive species on New Zealand's unique biodiversity.

In an effort to fight more effectively what many see as a losing battle, New Zealand has, within the last decade, introduced a comprehensive and unified approach to minimize the introduction of new invasive species and manage those invasive species that are already present. This chapter examines the current legislative and administrative framework that deals with potential and actual invasive species. After briefly reviewing New Zealand's experience with invasive species, the chapter considers the separate legal and administrative regimes that apply to intentional and unintentional introductions of invasive species. It also addresses the way in which New Zealand deals with the eradication or management of species already present within the country.

Despite this comprehensive and unified approach, problems remain. As a result, New Zealand's legislative and administrative framework for biosecurity is currently subject to significant review. A substantial 2000 report to Parliament by the Parliamentary Commissioner for the Environment,[5] while recognizing the many positive features of the current system, has made a number of recommendations on how New Zealand could significantly improve its biosecurity operations and infrastructure.[6]

NEW ZEALAND'S EXPERIENCE WITH INVASIVE SPECIES

New Zealand's biodiversity is more primitive in character than that of many other countries, having a limited representation of higher plants and animals, e.g., angiosperms and mammals, but a high representation of older plants and animals, e.g., mosses, liverworts, ferns, flatworms, snails, spiders, wingless crickets, solitary bees, leiopelmid frogs, sphenodon reptiles, and ratite birds. Many of these older species are endemic to New Zealand.[7]

Alien species threaten one-third of New Zealand's protected forests (1.8 million hectares) and put pressure on smaller reserves and individual species.[8] The 1997 report on the State of New Zealand's Environment confirmed what conservation managers had known for a long time: an army of predatory and browsing animals and aggressive weeds, introduced by previous generations, now threaten New Zealand's remaining natural habitats; costly animal pest and weed control is a necessary and constant part of ecosystem management.[9]

For example, there are estimated to be approximately 70 million possums occupying a large portion of the country.[10] The number of goats and deer appears to be rising. Rats, stoats, and feral cats continue to devastate endemic bird populations. Native fish are at risk from introduced trout.

The Department of Conservation manages almost one-third of New Zealand's land area (approximately eight million hectares). In 1999, over NZD22 million was spent by the Department of Conservation alone on animal pest control.[11] Spending includes 170 possum control operations over 850,000 hectares, 140 goat control operations over 1.1 million hectares, and 6 tahr control operations over about 7,000 hectares in 5 "mainland islands."[12] By 2002, this had increased to over NZD26 million.[13]

Table 1[14]
Key mammals which have reduced New Zealand's biodiversity

Species		Population	Status
Rabbits		Tens of millions (1995)	Occupy 56% (15 million hectares) of the land area. Pose a high to extreme risk to pasture over 1 million hectares of South Island high country where they are prone to dramatic population explosions
Goats		Farm: 337,000 (1995) Feral: 300,000-1 million	Farm goats peaked at 1.3 million (1988). Feral goats were reduced by helicopter shooting in the 1970-1980s, but increased during the farming downturn. They occupy three million hectares, two-thirds of Department of Conservation land
Tahr		10,000-14,000 (1994)	Peaked at 60,000 (1970s). Were reduced by helicopter shooting to about 6,000 (1983)
Deer		Farm:1.8 million (1995) Feral: 250,000 (1993)	Farm deer still increasing. Wild (mostly Red) deer peaked in 1970-1975, and are now controlled by hunting
Pigs		Farm: 431,000 (1995) Feral: at least 300,000	Farm pigs peaked at 771,000 (1964). About 100,000 feral pigs are killed annually. Problem areas are Northland, Nelson/Marlborough, the Chatham Islands, and Auckland Island
Possums		70 million (1993)	Occupy more than 90% of the country, still spreading, and subject to widespread control operations
Mustelids	Stoats Ferrets Weasels	Possibly millions Possibly millions Probably thousands	Absent from Stewart and Chatham Islands. Stoats are common in forests, including Fiordland beech forests. Ferrets are common in open country where rabbits, their main prey, are abundant. Weasels are uncommon
Rats	Ship rats Norway rats Pacific rats (kiore)	Tens of millions Tens of millions Tens of thousands	Ship rats are common in forests, especially podocarp-hardwoods. Norway rats peaked before stoats arrived and are now limited to towns, farms, water margins, and islands. Pacific rats are now limited to Fiordland and about 50 islands
Cats		Pets: ca. 770,000 (1991-1992) Feral: Possibly millions	Almost one-half the nation's homes have pet cats. Feral cats are widespread. Population trends unknown
Dogs		Pets: ca. 398,000 (1991-1992) Farm: 150,000-300,000 (1992) Feral: Insignificant	Around 29% of homes have pet dogs and at least one-third of the nation's farms have one or more teams of working dogs. Dog population trends are unknown

26

Table 2[15]
The area of Department of Conservation (DOC) land at risk from browsing mammals

Likely impact if no control operations were in place[16]	Total DOC estate (hectares)
Total forest collapse[17]	550,000
Major composition change[18]	1,045,000
Major loss of biodiversity[19]	169,000
Area at risk of major change	1,764,000
Minor loss of biodiversity[20]	1,313,000
Area at risk of major or minor change	**3,077,000**

Invasive introduced plants are also one of the greatest threats to New Zealand's biodiversity. Since 1996, the Department of Conservation has been assessing the nature and scale of the threat posed to indigenous biodiversity from invasive weeds and in 2002 spent almost NZD10 million on direct weed control.[21]

Almost one-half of all vascular plant species growing wild in New Zealand are introduced—about 2,100 species. But at least another 19,000 introduced plant species are present in New Zealand's private gardens and collections, or are being used in agriculture, horticulture, or forestry. Many of these are likely to naturalize in the future. The Department of Conservation's weed database currently lists over 240 naturalized land, wetland, freshwater, and marine plants as actual or potential invasive weeds.[22]

Invasive weeds are one of the main risks to the survival of 61 threatened native vascular plant species, have an impact on another 16 species, and threaten the long-term survival of native animals on many sites. Unless controlled, weed invasions will threaten natural areas covering at least 580,000 hectares in the next 10 to 15 years.

The majority of invasive plants were deliberately brought to New Zealand. More than 70% of invasive weeds were introduced into New Zealand as ornamental plants.[23] A further 12% were introduced for agriculture, horticulture, or forestry.[24] Only 11% were introduced accidentally.[25] For instance, seven of New Zealand's most invasive weeds (contorta pine, old man's beard, wild ginger, pampas, heather, and the aquatic weeds egeria and lagarosiphon) were deliberately brought into New Zealand.[26]

New plant species continue to enter New Zealand deliberately, accidentally, or illegally. The number of known invasive weeds has grown steadily since the 1960s, and this trend shows no signs of slowing. In the Auckland region, more than 615 introduced plant species are known to have naturalized—a figure apparently unmatched by any other city in the world—and 4 new species naturalize there each year.[27] In the marine environment, the number of accidental marine introductions and their impacts are largely unknown.[28]

Despite the significant problems from invasive species, and their potential to have some serious impacts on New Zealand's economy, culture, and health, biosecurity is still not generally recognized as being as strategically important to New Zealand as national security.[29]

LEGISLATION

New Zealand's legal and administrative structure for dealing with invasive species is relatively simple in concept, while aiming to be comprehensive and effective. Two key Acts, implemented during the past decade, form the legislative basis for biosecurity[30] in New Zealand: the Biosecurity Act and the HSNO Act.

The purpose of the Biosecurity Act 1993 is to prevent the unintentional introduction of potentially invasive species, and to enable New Zealand to exclude or to manage effectively invasive species already present in the country. The Act has five major components:

> (1) To set standards for imports[31];
> (2) To control the passage of goods across the border[32];
> (3) To establish post-entry quarantine (an extension of border control)[33];
> (4) To monitor and maintain surveillance of indigenous animal and plant populations[34]; and
> (5) To oversee the eradication and control of invasive species once established or introduced.[35]

The Biosecurity Act is an empowering Act rather than a requiring one. That is, there is no requirement on any particular agency to take action in relation to the presence of a harmful organism.

The HSNO Act is designed to control the intentional introduction of new organisms (including GMOs)[36] into New Zealand. A new organism is defined as a species of any organism that was not lawfully present in New Zealand on July 29, 1998; or a GMO that has not previously been approved for release in New Zealand; or a species of any organism that has not been approved for importation for release or release from containment; or an organism that has been eradicated from New Zealand.[37]

The purpose of the HSNO Act is to protect the environment, and the health and safety of people and communities, by preventing or managing the adverse effects of hazardous substances and new organisms. Approvals from a specially constituted assessment body (called the Environmental Risk Management Authority) are required for the importation,[38] development,[39] field testing,[40] and release[41] of new organisms into New Zealand.

GOVERNMENT RESPONSIBILITY FOR THE MANAGEMENT OF INVASIVE SPECIES

Biosecurity management in New Zealand is administered by a two-tiered governmental structure: the central government and regional councils. A large degree of autonomy is devolved to regional councils, which are administered by publicly elected members.

Regional councils[42] have primary responsibility for the eradication and management of invasive species present in New Zealand. This is primarily carried out by way of pest management strategies under the Biosecurity Act. Council officers also have education and enforcement roles. Regional councils spend over NZD40 million per year on pest management, of which approximately one-half is funded from the central government.[43]

A typical biosecurity program of a regional council has three main components:

> 1. Regional tuberculosis (Tb) control–where the council acts as an agent of the central government's Animal Health Board, controlling pests, e.g., possums and ferrets, that carry bovine Tb in order to reduce bovine Tb in the region;
> 2. Regional animal pest management—to identify and manage significant pests for the region; and
> 3. Regional plant pest management—to identify and manage significant weeds and other plant pests.

In recognition of the significance of invasive species to New Zealand, a new cabinet portfolio was established in 1997: the Minister of Biosecurity. This Minister's responsibilities include coordinating the implementation of the Biosecurity Act, recording reports of and managing the appropriate responses to suspected new organisms, and promulgating national pest management strategies.

Nevertheless, the government department with primary responsibilities for preventing the unintentional introduction of invasive species is the Ministry of Agriculture and Forestry (MAF). To carry out its biosecurity responsibilities, MAF maintains five business groups:

> (1) The MAF Policy group provides policy advice to the Minister of Food, Fibre, Biosecurity, and Border Control;
> (2) The Biosecurity Authority, which was established in July 1999, is responsible for border control, quarantine services, pest and disease surveillance, emergency response capabilities and other disease control programs. It is also responsible for promoting animal welfare policies, providing animal and plant health assurances to New Zealand's trading partners, developing operational and regulatory policy, and overseeing risk management. The Authority's mission is "[t]o protect New Zealand's unique biodiversity and facilitate exports by managing risks to plant and animal health and animal welfare in New Zealand"[44];
> (3) The Food Safety Authority (a semi independent body established in July 2002, with its own Minister of Food Safety) assures that much of New Zealand's exported food is safe and "fit for purpose";
> (4) The MAF Operations group provides a range of core operational businesses, including the quarantine service (the border protection service),[45] the New Zealand animal health and plant pest reference laboratories, and the MAF verification agency, which provides documentation to show that exported products meet other countries' biosecurity requirements; and
> (5) The MAF Forest Management unit manages and administers forestry grants, Crown lease forests on Maori land, indigenous forests, and forest health.

MAF receives around 95% of the government's biosecurity funding. MAF's focus has, until now, been on risks to primary production and trade. Because of the Biosecurity Authority's pivotal role in the coordination of biosecurity activities, it is now being required to demonstrate that greater attention will be given to biosecurity impacts on indigenous biodiversity and marine ecosystems.[46]

The Department of Conservation, the Ministry of Fisheries, and the Ministry of Health also have some biosecurity responsibilities in relation to the unintentional introduction of and the management of invasive species. The Department of Conservation provides policy advice on biosecurity risks to indigenous flora and fauna and biodiversity. The Ministry of Fisheries provides advice on marine biosecurity and the Ministry of Health provides policy advice and specific disease response in relation to biosecurity risks to people's health posed by pests and diseases.

The Minister for the Environment has a key policy and oversight role in relation to the intentional introduction of new organisms and the administration of the HSNO Act. The Minister for the Environment has the power to issue policy directions[47] and to make regulations on a range of technical and procedural matters.[48]

The Environmental Risk Management Authority, established by the HSNO Act, plays a coordinating role in managing the risks and benefits of the intentional importation, development, field-testing, and release of new organisms. Its responsibilities include[49] the assessment of applications for approval, the setting of controls for new organisms that are approved, and the overseeing of compliance and enforcement. The Environmental Risk Management Authority also monitors the HSNO Act's effectiveness in reducing the adverse effects of new organisms on the environment or people. Finally, it enhances public education, engages in continuing investigation and information gathering, and maintains records.

The various activities of these government bodies are coordinated by the Biosecurity Council, which was established as a nonstatutory body in 1997.[50] Its members include the chief executives and chief technical officers of the four government departments with biosecurity responsibilities, the group director of MAF Biosecurity authority, the chief scientific adviser at the Ministry of Science, Research, and Technology, and one representative each from the Ministry for the Environment, the Environmental Risk Management Authority, Te Puni Kokiri (The Ministry of Maori Development), the regional councils, the primary production industry, and environmental organizations.

A Biosecurity Consultation Forum organized by the Council provides an opportunity for other stakeholders, such as the private sector, nongovernmental agencies, and science providers, to contribute their views. The coordination of strategic advice on policy matters by the Biosecurity Council is recognized as a significant strength of the biosecurity system. It fosters good working relationships among the four government departments with biosecurity functions, and the regional councils.[51]

However, a common criticism of the Biosecurity Council is that it lacks a strategic approach to biosecurity: it tends to focus on operational matters affecting individual departments, and does not examine strategic risks or priorities across the whole spectrum of biosecurity interests. In his report, the Parliamentary Commissioner recommended that the Minister for Biosecurity revise the representation on, and responsibilities of the council to encourage participation by Maori, ensure a wider representation of stakeholders and expertise and to provide the Minister with a regular assessment of the effectiveness of the biosecurity system.[52] This criticism has met with some response by the inclusion in the Biosecurity Council of Te Puni Kokiri, and representatives from the primary production industry and environmental organizations. The draft Biosecurity Strategy released by the Biosecurity Council in December 2002,[53] recommends the virtual disestablishment of the council to be replaced with an advisory group made up of stakeholders.

In addition, the report states that it is important that all biosecurity agencies develop formal agreements with the Biosecurity Authority on their respective roles in relation to emergency situations and develop criteria for determining responsibilities for follow-up action.[54] These agreements have now been formalized in the form of memoranda of understanding between all the various agencies. It is also recognized in the report that biosecurity is not an end in itself. It is a means to achieve outcomes such as the protection of primary production systems, indigenous flora and fauna from harmful organisms, etc. Despite its comprehensive nature, New Zealand's biosecurity system does not have a clear set of expected outcomes against which the effectiveness of the system (including the relevant legislation) can be assessed.[55]

An early draft of the Biosecurity Strategy was released in August 1999, which was intended as a first step toward a more comprehensive framework to underpin the biosecurity activities of the agencies represented on the council. The Parliamentary Commissioner in responding to this draft has recommended that the Biosecurity Strategy incorporate the following:

1. A statement that puts biosecurity into perspective, recognizing that biosecurity, like national security, is essential for the protection of the country's key strategic asset—its natural resources.

2. The concept of shared responsibility for managing biosecurity risks, and public participation in monitoring and surveillance.

3. Biosecurity risk management principles that will guide biosecurity decision-making.

4. Criteria for assessing risks to indigenous flora and fauna, biodiversity, ecosystem health, and public health and determining appropriate levels of protection against biosecurity risk.

5. Adoption of the precautionary approach to managing biosecurity risks where information on the impacts on indigenous species is not available, limited or uncertain.

6. A statement that, to be effective, biosecurity should focus on controlling high-risk pathways by which exotic organisms arrive in New Zealand.

7. Frameworks and processes for prioritizing biosecurity research.

8. A statement about the importance of information sharing among

stakeholders to assist biosecurity decision making.

9. Guidance on the public and private sectors' contributions to biosecurity funding, consistent with exacerbator/beneficiary responsibilities.

At the time of this writing the final Biosecurity Strategy was due to be released following the end of public consultation on February 28, 2003. It is likely that the final product will contain priorities similar to those voiced in the December draft as follows:

1. MAF and the Ministry of Fisheries to take leadership roles in implementing this strategy and ensuring a "whole-of-government" approach to biosecurity management;

2. Institute advisory board to help MAF Biosecurity address its expanded role;

3. These lead agencies to identify and meet their responsibilities under the Treaty of Waitangi[56];

4. Lead agencies to formalize a working arrangement with regional government to facilitate pest management and biosecurity policy consultation;

5. Establish surveillance objectives for the full range of biosecurity threats and upgrade programs to get earlier detection of new pests and diseases;

6. Improve decision-making processes so decisions across the system take better account of risks to biodiversity, taonga, human health, and lifestyle;

7. Clarify and reveal where and how value tradeoffs are made in biosecurity decision making;

8. Undertake a continuous improvement plan for management of risk pathways and vectors both prior to and at the border;

9. Engage all New Zealanders in supporting biosecurity programs;

10. Establish science advisory panel to support biosecurity agency decision-making and strategy, including formal research program;

11. Reconstitute Biosecurity Council as a ministerial advisory forum with quarterly stakeholders' meeting; and

12. Undertake step-by-step funding review to improve efficiency, so marginal contribution of new spending becomes transparent.

The draft responds to some, but not all of the Parliamentary Commissioner's recommendations. Of particular interest is the recommendation of a tempered precautionary approach whereby action or inaction is guided by mainstream scientific views because uncertainty will never be eliminated due to the impossibility of proving that something will never happen. It recommends that a precautionary approach needs to recognize that negative decisions also carry risk, such as the World Trade Organization (WTO) sanctions for excluding imported products on the basis of hypothetical risks. It also provides guidance on public/private contributions to biosecurity funding and suggests that cost recovery is ad hoc and inconsistent at present and recommends areas for priority review.

As part of its obligation to implement the Convention of Biological Diversity,[57] the government released a Biodiversity Strategy in early 2000.[58] The Biodiversity Strategy aims to establish a strategic framework for action to conserve, sustainably use, and manage New Zealand's biodiversity. In relation to invasive species, the Biodiversity Strategy sets out a number of specific objectives. It seeks to establish effective methods to assess and manage biodiversity risks from unwanted organisms, as well as to coordinate biosecurity management within and between central and local governments and nongovernmental agencies by clarifying responsibilities. Furthermore, the Biodiversity Strategy aims to maintain and enhance integrated border control measures as the first and most important line of defense for minimizing biodiversity risks to New Zealand's indigenous biodiversity and domesticated and cultivated species. Finally, it plans to manage the introduction of new organisms (including GMOs) in a way that avoids adverse effects on New Zealand's indigenous biodiversity, and to eradicate or contain introduced species that have the potential to become serious threats. For each of these objectives, the Biodiversity Strategy sets out a number of specific actions.

MANAGEMENT OF INTENTIONAL INTRODUCTIONS

The first part of this chapter has provided an overview of New Zealand's legislative and governmental structure. The remainder of the chapter will explore the actual operations of the system in greater detail. I first examine New Zealand's management of the intentional introduction of new organisms. I then consider the more complex management of the unintentional introduction of invasive species.

As explained above, the HSNO Act governs the operations and duties of people and organizations that intentionally bring new organisms (including GMOs) into New Zealand for the first time. Once an organism is present in the country, it is no longer a "new organism" for the purposes of the HSNO Act. Further introductions (both intentional and unintentional) are thus dealt with under the Biosecurity Act.

Information and Application

To bring a new organism into New Zealand, a person or an organization must file an application for approval with ERMA. The application has to include the following specified information[59]:

    (1) the detailed information prescribed;
    (2) identification of the organism;
    (3) information on all occasions where the organism has been considered by the government of any prescribed countries or by any prescribed organization; and any results of such consideration;
    (4) any likely inseparable organisms;
    (5) all possible adverse effects of the organism on the environment;
    (6) the affinities of the organism with other organisms in New

33

Zealand;

    (7) the potential uses for the organism[60]; and

    (8) where the application is for a containment approval, information on the containment system for the organism.[61]

The information required for an application to release a GMO is the same as that for the release of any new organism. But applications either for the development of a GMO in containment or for a field trial must include the identification of the organism, all occasions where the organism has been considered by governmental organizations in other countries and the results of that consideration, the containment system for the organism, and all the possible adverse effects of the organism on the environment.

For approval to develop a GMO in containment, the application requires additional information, including a description of the project and the experimental procedures to be used, the details of the biological materials to be used, and the expression of foreign deoxyribonucleic acid (DNA). The application for a field trial requires additional information as well, including the purposes of the field trial, the genetic modifications of the organism to be tested, and the nature and method of field trial and the experimental procedures to be used.

Assessment of Applications

In considering applications, ERMA must "recognise and provide for" two central principles[62]: the safeguarding of the life-supporting capacity of air, water, soil, and ecosystems; and the maintenance and enhancement of the capacity of people and communities to provide for their own economic, social, and cultural well being and for the reasonably foreseeable needs of future generations.

In addition, ERMA must "take into account" a number of particular matters to achieve the purpose of the Act.[63] First, it must consider the sustainability of all native and valued introduced flora and fauna, the intrinsic value of ecosystems, and public health. It must also heed the relationship of Maori and their culture and traditions with their ancestral land and water sites, waahi tapu (sacred sites), valued flora and fauna, and other taonga (treasures).[64] Furthermore, ERMA must consider the economic and related benefits to be derived from the use of a particular new organism, New Zealand's international obligations; and the principles of the Treaty of Waitangi.[65] Finally, ERMA must take into account the need for caution in managing adverse effects where there is scientific and technical uncertainty about those effects.[66]

To assess applications, ERMA is required to follow a specific methodology,[67] set out in regulations.[68] This prescribed methodology includes the process ERMA follows when considering information provided by applicants, how it evaluates risks, costs and benefits, and how it deals with uncertainty. It requires ERMA, as it considers each application, to examine the following potential impacts:

    (1) the significant displacement of any natural species within its natural habitat;

    (2) the significant deterioration of natural habitats;

(3) the significant adverse effects on human health and safety;

(4) the significant adverse effects on New Zealand's inherent genetic diversity;

(5) the ability of the organism to establish an undesirable self-sustaining population anywhere in New Zealand;

(6) the ease with which the organism could be eradicated if it established an undesirable self-sustaining population; and

(7) the ability of the organism to cause disease, be parasitic, or become a vector for human, animal, or plant disease.[69]

In addition to these methodological requirements, ERMA is also bound by minimum standards set out in the HSNO Act itself. For example, ERMA must decline applications for new organisms[70] that potentially threaten significant displacement of any native species in its natural habitat, significant deterioration of natural habitats, or significant adverse effects on human health and safety. ERMA also must decline applications for organisms that might cause a significant adverse effect on New Zealand's inherent genetic diversity, or that might cause disease, become parasitic, or become a vector for human/animal/plant diseases (unless that is the purpose for the importation or release). Finally, in the case of a rapid assessment, ERMA must determine the ability of the new organism to establish an undesirable self-sustaining population, and the ease with which it could be eradicated if it did [71] There are also certain prohibited organisms, specified in a schedule to the HSNO Act that may not be granted approval by ERMA.[72]

After all of these considerations, ERMA has wide discretion to grant or decline an application. However, it may only grant an approval if it is satisfied that the positive effects of the organism outweigh the adverse effects, or, conversely, decline it if it considers that the adverse effects of the organism outweigh the positive effects.[73] Thus, it is the effects of an organism that are all important in terms of assessing applications.

Controls or conditions may be imposed on approvals to import, develop, or field test a new organism in containment, as opposed to an application to release a new organism.[74] Controls may include measures to prevent accidental release, to exclude unauthorized people from the site, or to prevent the unintended release of the organism by those working with the organism.[75]

Notification and Hearing of Applications

Applications submitted to ERMA for approval are publicly notified in newspapers throughout the country, except in the cases of applications to import new organisms (including GMOs) into containment, applications to develop GMOs in containment where they meet specified "low risk criteria,"[76] and requests to import for release new organisms other than GMOs that meet the rapid assessment criteria set out in the Act.[77]

Anyone can make a written submission on a notified application and request a public hearing of the application. All submitters, as well as the applicant, are entitled to be heard and to present evidence on the application to ERMA. After a hearing, ERMA publicly releases a written decision.[78] There is no right of appeal on the merits from a decision of ERMA. Any submitter may, however, appeal to the High Court on the grounds that ERMA has erred on a point of law.

Consultation with other branches of government is sometimes required even where organisms meet the rapid assessment criteria and in recognition of the special potential of new organisms to damage indigenous biodiversity—consultation is always required with the Department of Conservation, and ERMA must have particular regard to any resulting submissions.[79]

Intentional Introductions Between Regions

Regional Pest Management Strategies issued under the Biosecurity Act control the intentional introduction or movement of invasive or potentially invasive species between regions within the country. A strategy can provide that listed species may not be introduced to or propagated within a particular region, or that specific actions be taken to control or eradicate certain pests.[80] If any person wishes to introduce a listed organism, the strategy may grant an exemption, provided that the council is satisfied of certain criteria.[81]

UNINTENTIONAL INTRODUCTIONS OF POTENTIALLY INVASIVE SPECIES

Managing biosecurity risks at the border is a key aspect of biosecurity for an island nation. The government invests a significant proportion of biosecurity funding into this area. Successes do occur. For example, the white spotted tussock moth was successfully eradicated in 1997. In specific cases, both central and local government agencies have successfully combined resources in attempts to eradicate pests. The rate of detection of biosecurity risks from incoming passengers and luggage at international airports has markedly improved since the introduction of x-ray scanners and detector dogs. Discoveries of biosecurity incursions are not necessarily an indication that the system has failed, but rather evidence of successful vigilance and awareness.[82]

Unintentional introductions of invasive species are minimized by controlling the import of "risk goods."[83] The general rule is that no risk goods may be imported unless an import health standard (IHS) has been issued. For any item or product to be imported into New Zealand for the first time, a disease risk analysis is conducted by MAF, which analyzes factors such as the nature of the product and the likelihood that it may carry "associated organisms," e.g., pests or diseases. Based on the results of this analysis, MAF then develops an IHS that specifies the safeguards or conditions that have to be met before an animal or animal product can enter and be released into New Zealand.[84] Over 350 import health standards for animals and animal products exist.[85]

The requirement of a risk analysis and consultation often means that the development of an IHS takes some time (ranging from four months to two years). Currently, MAF is developing generic risk analyses for broad groups of animals and animal products like dairy and meat products, passerines, ratites, tropical fish, etc., to help speed up the process. Importers may also, in consultation with MAF, commission a risk analysis by independent experts to facilitate the development of an IHS more quickly.

Still, a generic risk analysis and/or IHS must undergo several stages of consultation. This involves internal consultation, including a peer review and intergovernment department consultation, and a full public consultation with direct notification of all people or organizations whose interests might be significantly affected by the matter under consideration. The WTO is also notified in any instance where proposed risk management measures are not substantially the same as international standards, where they exist, and which may have a significant affect on the trade of a WTO Member country.

A 2002 report on biosecurity risks from used cars imported from Japan recommended:

> 1. Biosecurity risk mitigation should focus on pathways, not individual organisms, thereby accommodating both the known and the unknown risks.
> 2. The important biosecurity principle of risk separation between the risk organism and potential establishment sites must be applied.
> 3. Biosecurity strategies should apply risk separation by confining the risks offshore.[86]

Upon arrival in New Zealand, all goods (which include organisms) must go to either a transitional facility or a biosecurity control area. They are then inspected by an inspector, who either gives them a biosecurity clearance or directs them to another transitional facility or containment facility (or in some cases reships or destroys them). The type of transitional facility to which goods are directed will depend on the type of goods in question and on the risk that they may pose. For example, transitional facilities for quarantine are approved for specified kinds of animals to a particular level of security, e.g., the facility may be approved as a high-security transitional facility for the quarantine of avian species. All containment and transitional facilities must be approved and meet standards set out in the Act. Each facility must also have an operator approved to operate that facility.[87]

A transitional facility is approved for a particular purpose, whether the inspection, storage, treatment, quarantine, holding, or destruction of uncleared goods. (Uncleared goods are imported goods that have not been given a biosecurity clearance by an inspector.) Some parts of airports or sea ports are automatically deemed transitional facilities; these are generally those parts of ports where risk goods are off-loaded or held. Unlike other transitional facilities, these places become transitional facilities without having to go through an approval process. The purpose of having these areas is to ensure that there are places at ports where risk goods must go to be inspected. The goods must remain there until they either are given a biosecurity clearance, or are directed to a more appropriate transitional facility, e.g., for quarantine or treatment, or to a containment facility (for holding new organisms).

Containment facilities hold organisms that should not ever become established in New Zealand, even temporarily. Examples of containment facilities include zoos, as well as some research, diagnostic and reference laboratories. In some cases, organisms are released from a containment facility, as when a new biological control agent is released following favorable trials while in containment.

In certain cases, the same facility may be both a transitional facility and a containment facility. For example, a zoo is a containment facility for animals not at large in New Zealand, but it may also have a transitional facility within it to hold animals recently imported until all quarantine requirements have been met. Similarly, many invertebrates imported as potential biological control agents are held in a facility that is both a containment and a transitional facility. The stricter quarantine requirements of the transitional facility are removed when an inspector is satisfied that the invertebrates are not carrying other harmful organisms.

The Biosecurity Act also provides for the declaration of "unwanted organisms." These are defined as organisms that are capable of causing unwanted harm to any natural and physical resources or human health.[88] Classifying an organism as an "unwanted organism" enables the powers of the Biosecurity Act to be deployed in a variety of additional situations, including the importation of risk goods, disease or pest surveillance and management, and response to exotic disease incursions. Deciding in advance that an organism is an unwanted organism gives inspectors and authorized persons the ability to respond rapidly, without first requiring a chief technical officer to make a determination that the organism is an unwanted organism.

MAF is required to maintain a public register of all unwanted organisms, whether determined to be an unwanted organism by an MAF chief technical officer or a chief technical officer appointed in one of the other government departments with operational responsibilities for biosecurity (Department of Conservation, Ministry of Fisheries, or Ministry of Health). (A register is available on MAF's website.)[89] Furthermore, the Biosecurity Council has issued a policy statement on unwanted organisms clarifying the responsibilities of relevant organizations.

One of the categories in MAF's policy on unwanted organisms is termed "notifiable organisms." Notifiable organisms are those organisms for which every person has a duty to notify the chief technical officer if they become aware of the organism in a new place.[90] Notifiable organisms are listed in the Biosecurity (Notifiable Organisms) Order 2000[91] and included in the unwanted organism register on MAF's website.

ERADICATION AND CONTROL OF INVASIVE SPECIES

Pest management strategies (PMS) are the principal mechanism under the Biosecurity Act for the eradication and control of invasive species once established or introduced in New Zealand. The Act provides for both national and regional strategies. Strategies provide direction on control, establish who is responsible for various activities, and designate the funding and compensation arrangements. An amendment to the Biosecurity Act in 2003 clarifies §92 to make it clear that levies to fund PMS can be imposed on people as a result of their status as exacerbators.

For a national PMS, a descriptive proposal document is publicly notified by the Minister. Written submissions are sought from any person or group whose interests may be affected by the proposal. If the Minister finds that there is significant opposition, a Board of Inquiry must be set up to review the proposal. A recommendation is made by the Minister to the Governor General to approve by regulation the PMS when he or she is satisfied with the proposal.[92] Central government has been slow to develop national PMS. At the time of this writing only two had been finalized—one for bovine tuberculosis and one for American Foulbrood, which afflicts honey bees. The next strategy closest to completion was for the varroa mite, which is another parasite of honey bees largely restricted to the northern half of the North Island but with pockets of infection in the lower North Island. These honey bee strategies have been produced at the initiative of bee keepers seeking to prevent the expansion of this pest's distribution.

A regional PMS may be prepared by any person or organization approved by the regional council from the region (or regions) in which it is to apply. Again, the proposal is publicly notified by the regional council and submissions are called for. A public hearing must be held that may be conducted by the regional council or by a hearings commissioner appointed for that particular PMS. The regional council must give public notice of its decision and of the final PMS and advise each submitter of its decision.[93] In contrast to national PMS, regional PMS have been developed for most of New Zealand's regions and impose pest control obligations on landowners.

Any person who made a submission on a proposed regional PMS may refer a particular matter to the Environment Court. A regional PMS must be reviewed within five years. Minor amendments may be made to the regional PMS during this period if rights and obligations of any person are not significantly affected by the change.

PMS are not the only mechanism available to manage invasive species. If there is no PMS in place for a particular species, enforcement officers may be appointed, with direct access to the pest management powers of the Act. But there is less certainty that action will be taken against the harmful organism if this approach is relied on. The advantages of developing a PMS rather than relying on direct access to Biosecurity Act powers are the following:

(1) the management agency can include bodies other than a government department or regional council;

(2) nongovernment employees can be appointed with the powers necessary to undertake the control or eradication actions;

(3) PMS rules can be created that place obligations or duties on identified groups of people;

(4) the compensation requirements, and the basis of payment, can be varied for loss or damage that occurs to private property as a result of using statutory powers to manage the species;

(5) financial contributions can be secured by way of a levy; and

(6) a more secure commitment from funding providers is assured.

One difficulty that has been identified with PMS is that they focus on the control of particular organisms. Experience with PMS suggests that biosecurity can be more effective if the focus is also on the control of pathways, rather than just specific pests.[94]

A regional council may also establish a small-scale management program.[95] The organism must be an unwanted organism as determined by an enforcement officer; it must be capable of causing serious and unintended effects if earlier action is not taken; eradication or control must be possible within three years; the cost of controlling it must be less than NZD100,000; and the control measures should not result in monetary loss to the people unless they contributed to the presence or spread of the organism. A small-scale management program is declared by public notice. The council is required to give land occupiers five days' notice of the work to be carried out unless it believes that the organism may spread beyond that place within that period.

WEAKNESSES OF THE BIOSECURITY ACT

The Parliamentary Commissioner has identified a number of weaknesses in the Biosecurity Act. Unlike the HSNO Act, the Biosecurity Act lacks the following:

1. An over-arching purpose statement and set of principles to guide decision-makers;
2. Reference to the Treaty of Waitangi and associated obligations;
3. A general duty to avoid, remedy, or mitigate adverse effects arising from the introduction of an unwanted organism as a result of the importation of risk goods; and
4. A requirement on any particular agency to take action in relation to the presence of a harmful organism.

The lack of "requiring" provisions and the fact that an organism is not considered to be a "pest" until it is defined as one in a PMS, contrasts with other legislation, in which specific responsibilities for managing the effects of particular activities are assigned to each agency with powers under the Act. The lack of clear responsibilities for responding to potential pests could result in a harmful organism remaining unmanaged.[96]

Each aspect of the Biosecurity Act that involves risk management contains its own set of slightly different criteria for analyzing risks. Some refer to "the economy, human health and the environment"[97] while others refer to "the economy, people and the environment,"[98] "the economy and the environment,"[99] or simply "adverse and unintended effects."[100] In some cases only the costs or potential adverse effects of an activity require consideration,[101] whereas in others a cost/benefit approach is required explicitly (PMS) or implicitly through reference to actions being "in the public interest."[102] The provisions for preparing PMS provide a much greater level of guidance of the types of risks to be considered than the provisions relating to border control activities.[103]

ENFORCEMENT AND EMERGENCIES

While a PMS is the principal mechanism that provides for on-going control, it is not always feasible or practical to develop a PMS. Access to other control mechanisms is sometimes necessary.

The Biosecurity Act gives the government departments with biosecurity responsibilities a wide range of powers to manage or eradicate an unwanted organism.[104] Each department has at least one chief technical officer who is able to determine that an organism is an unwanted organism, and to appoint people who have access to the relevant powers when necessary.

A provisional control program is declared in situations where a harmful organism is suspected but the identity of the organism is unknown or unconfirmed, and sufficient powers are not otherwise available to prevent the spread or development of the organism.[105] Once the identity of the organism becomes known this provision no longer applies, but another control mechanism may be used. A provisional control program enables a Minister to take whatever steps are necessary to control the spread or development of an organism until further information is available. Action can be taken under this provision for up to 60 days, and the program can be extended by one further period of 60 days.[106]

In addition to these more general powers, a "biosecurity emergency" may be declared by the Governor-General on the recommendation of a Minister of the Crown.[107] However, strict criteria govern the declaration of biosecurity emergencies: the organism to be managed or eradicated must have the potential to cause significant economic and/or environmental loss if it becomes established; it must be in the public interest that immediate action is taken against the organism; and sufficient powers must not be otherwise available to manage or eradicate the organism effectively.[108] This last criterion in particular limits the occasions in which a biosecurity emergency may be declared. In the vast majority of situations sufficient general powers will be available to deal with the organism. The principal exceptions are in situations where the movement of people needs to be restricted or equipment commandeered.

Following the declaration of a biosecurity emergency, the Minister is able to take whatever measures are necessary to manage or eradicate the organism, including entering private property.[109] The declaration remains effective for four months unless it is revoked earlier or is extended by parliament.[110]

An amendment to the Biosecurity Act in 2003 has extended the powers of the government to deal with biosecurity threats. An example includes the power to search and inspect places under §109, which has been expanded so that the power can be used to enter a place for the purpose of ensuring compliance with the act. Another is the power under §114a to carry out aerial spraying to eradicate pests. This used to be subject to a mandatory 14-day notice period. The 2003 amendment allows this period to be reduced in cases where the organism concerned could have significant adverse effects and the 14-day notice period would prejudice the chances of eradicating or containing it.

FUNDING OF BIOSECURITY REQUIREMENTS

The costs of carrying out a number of the Biosecurity Act's functions can be recovered under various provisions. The Biosecurity (Costs) Regulations 1993[111] outline the charges to be applied for a number of biosecurity activities, including inspecting and treating various categories of risk goods, issuing import health permits, inspecting transitional facilities, and supervising their operators.

Despite these regulations, there is a recognition that there is still a lack of policy on appropriate public/private sector contributions to biosecurity funding. While biosecurity measures to protect indigenous flora and fauna, biodiversity, and ecosystem and public health are generally in the public interest, and should therefore be publicly funded, private sector contributions for a range of activities need to be reviewed.[112]

The Act also provides a cost-recovery mechanism in the event that a person does not comply with a direction to carry out specified actions or measures. An enforcement agency may authorize the necessary actions to be taken and then recover the costs of those actions from the person to whom the direction was issued.[113]

At present, there is no fund established for the sole purpose of covering costs of an incursion response. Biosecurity agencies either have to draw from their own resources by reprioritizing, or seek cabinet approval for additional funding. The Parliamentary Commissioner has recommended that the government establishes dedicated funding arrangements and criteria to enable rapid and effective responses to biosecurity emergencies.[114] The December 2002, draft of the Biosecurity Strategy recommends a review of funding mechanisms for one-off incursion responses—but does not go further—and recommends the establishment of a dedicated find.[115]

SANCTIONS AND PENALTIES

Both the Biosecurity Act and the HSNO Act set out criminal and civil liability for various failures to comply with the legislation.

Illegal Introductions

The criminal penalties that apply under the Biosecurity Act vary depending on the nature of the offense.[116] The most severe penalty for an individual carries a maximum of five years' imprisonment, a fine of up to NZD100,000, or both.[117] For a corporation, the maximum penalty is a fine of up to NZD200,000.[118] These penalties apply to offenses such as knowingly possessing unauthorized goods, or moving organisms or other goods in breach of a movement control notice.[119]

A person who, on arrival at the border, wrongly declares that they do not possess goods that may pose a biosecurity risk (whether or not they make that declaration knowingly) may be fined up to NZD400.[120] That person may elect to pay an instant fine of NZD200 rather than have the offense heard in court. If the person does not elect to pay an instant fine, they have only 14 days within which to respond.[121]

The existence of the instant fine provision or the payment of such a fine does not prevent prosecution under other offense provisions if a person is believed to have breached those provisions as well. For example, a person who knowingly tries to bring unauthorized goods into New Zealand may be subject to the more stringent penalties discussed above, whether or not the instant fine provisions have been applied to them.

For most offenses, it is not necessary to show any intention to commit the offense, and every person with some degree of responsibility for an action or event constituting an offense may be held responsible. A limited number of defenses are available to offenses of strict liability.

There is a wide range of criminal offenses under the HSNO Act,[122] including when a person develops a new organism in contravention of the HSNO Act, or knowingly imports or releases a new organism in contravention of the HSNO Act.[123] Other criminal offenses include knowingly, recklessly, or negligently importing or developing a new organism without approval, or knowingly, recklessly, or negligently possessing a new organism imported, developed, or released in contravention of the HSNO Act. Penalties range up to a maximum of NZD500,000 (NZD50,000 per day where the offense is a continuing one) or three months imprisonment.[124]

Civil Remedies and Compensation

Civil enforcement is primarily overseen by ERMA, though various other agencies are given day-to-day enforcement powers.[125] There are wide powers of entry and inspection given to a range of agencies and their enforcement officers.

An individual may be required to pay the costs of mitigating or remedying the adverse effects on people or the environment that have been caused by their breach of the HSNO Act, or relating to land where they are an owner or occupier.[126] Furthermore, an enforcement officer may issue a compliance order[127]:

(1) requiring a person to cease, or prohibiting them from commencing, any act which contravenes or is likely to contravene the HSNO Act;

(2) relating to a new organism which is, or is likely to be, dangerous to such an extent that it has, or is likely to have, an adverse effect on the health and safety of people of the environment; or

(3) requiring someone to do something that is necessary to ensure compliance with the HSNO Act, any regulations, controls imposed with any approval, or is necessary to avoid, remedy, or mitigate any actual or likely adverse effects on people or the environment resulting from any breach either caused by or on behalf of that person, or relating to any land that the person owns or occupies.[128]

CONCLUSION

While the legislative and administrative framework for the control of invasive species and GMOs in New Zealand is detailed and comprehensive, a number of significant problems remain. Current pest management efforts on public conservation lands are restricted to priority areas and, in most cases, limited to "holding the line" until new techniques for pest control can be developed. Threats from plant and animal pests and domestic stock to indigenous biodiversity on private land are not yet comprehensively or consistently addressed.

The increase and spread of naturalized, introduced plants that have become (or have the potential to become) invasive weeds represent a latent, but potentially serious, threat to indigenous biodiversity. Gaps in the knowledge about pest species, inadequate pest control methods and technologies, and limited resources limit the effectiveness of pest management. Public and community awareness about the threat of pests and support for pest prevention and control methods, while important, is often lacking.

Having identified these weaknesses and problems, it is now up to the government to address the Parliamentary Commissioner's report and recommendations on desirable improvements to the administrative system and necessary legislative changes. If it does, that will provide an excellent platform from which to effectively address the ongoing environmental threats facing New Zealand from invasive species.

CHAPTER 1: NEW ZEALAND

Chapter 1 Endnotes

1. Mark Christensen is an environmental lawyer and a partner in the New Zealand firm of Anderson Lloyd Caudwell. Mark graduated LLB(Hons)/BA(Hons) in 1984 from the University of Otago. Mark acknowledges the helpful assistance of Michael Cameron in the preparation of this chapter.

2. NEW ZEALAND DEPARTMENT OF CONSERVATION AND THE MINISTRY FOR THE ENVIRONMENT, NEW ZEALAND'S BIODIVERSITY STRATEGY (2000) [hereinafter NEW ZEALAND'S BIODIVERSITY STRATEGY 2000].

3. *See* Table 1 *infra.*

4. *E.g.*, Possums introduced from Australia are primary carriers of bovine tuberculosis; rabbits have impacted large areas of pastoral lands; and gorse introduced from the United Kingdom affects agricultural areas throughout the country.

5. The Commissioner is an independent officer of Parliament who, with the objective of maintaining and improving the quality of the environment, reviews and provides advice on the system of agencies and processes established by the government to manage the allocation, use, and protection of natural and physical resources.

6. OFFICE OF THE PARLIAMENTARY COMMISSIONER FOR THE ENVIRONMENT (PCE), NEW ZEALAND UNDER SIEGE—A REVIEW OF MANAGEMENT OF BIOSECURITY RISKS TO THE ENVIRONMENT (2000) [hereinafter PCE REPORT 2000]; *see Parliamentary Commissioner for the Environment, at* http://www.pce.govt.nz for the *PCE Report 2000* and various background papers.

7. NEW ZEALAND'S BIODIVERSITY STRATEGY 2000, *supra* note 2.

8. *See* Table 2 *infra.*

9. NEW ZEALAND MINISTRY FOR THE ENVIRONMENT, STATE OF NEW ZEALAND'S ENVIRONMENT 9-6 to 9-8 (1997) [hereinafter STATE OF ENVIRONMENT REPORT].

10. *Id.* at 9-7.

11. Hugh Logan, Director-General of Conservation of New Zealand, speech to National Pest Summit (Apr. 7 1997).

12. *Id.*

13. NEW ZEALAND DEPARTMENT OF CONSERVATION ANNUAL REPORT: FOR YEAR ENDING JUNE 30, 2002 (2002).

14. STATE OF ENVIRONMENT REPORT, *supra* note 9.

15. *Id.*

16. In fact, control operations covered 1.3 million hectares in the 1995/1996 year, 70% of the major risk areas. *Id.* at 9-15.

17. Total canopy loss, significant species loss, replacement of forest by shrubland/grassland.

18. Significant canopy and species loss, change in forest structure from complex to simple.

19. Significant species loss and change.

20. Some species loss and change.

21. NEW ZEALAND DEPARTMENT OF CONSERVATION ANNUAL REPORT, *supra* note 13.

22. DEPARTMENT OF CONSERVATION, DEPARTMENT OF CONSERVATION STRATEGIC PLAN FOR MANAGING INVASIVE WEEDS (1998).

23. *Id.*

24. *Id.*

25. *Id.*

26. *Id.*

27. *Id.*

28. W. GREEN, BIODIVERSITY THREATS TO INDIGENOUS BIODIVERSITY—A BACKGROUND REPORT PREPARED FOR THE PARLIAMENTARY COMMISSIONER FOR THE ENVIRONMENT (2000).

29. PCE REPORT 2000, *supra* note 6.

30. "Biosecurity" is not defined in the Biosecurity Act. A draft definition contained in the Draft Biosecurity Strategy defines the term as the "management of risks posed by organisms to the economy, environment and people's health through exclusion, eradication and control." Thus, biosecurity could be described as the management of exotic biological risks that may harm New Zealand's economic, environmental, and social interests. It also includes the management of risks arising from the translocation of species from their natural range within New Zealand. Biosecurity is the means by which these risks are managed rather than being an end in itself. PCE REPORT 2000, *supra* note 6.

31. Biosecurity Act, pt. III.

32. *Id.*

33. *Id.*

34. *Id.* pt. IV.

35. *Id.* pt. V.

36. A GMO is defined as any organism in which any of the genes or other genetic material:

   (a) have been modified by *in vitro* techniques, or
   (b) are inherited or otherwise derived, through any number of replications, from any genes or other genetic material which has been modified by *in vitro* techniques. *Id.* §2.

37. Organism is defined as:

   (a) Does not include human being or a genetic structure derived from a human being;
   (b) Includes a micro-organism;
   (c) Includes a genetic structure, other than a genetic structure derived from a human being, that is capable of replicating itself, whether that structure comprises all or only part of the total genetic structure of an entity;
   (d) Includes an entity (other than a human being) declared to be an organism for the purposes of the Biosecurity Act of 1993; and
   (e) Includes a reproductive cell or developmental stage of an organism.

   Id.

38. "Importation" means:

   (1) For all the purposes of this Act, goods shall, except where otherwise expressly provided, be deemed to be imported into New Zealand if and so soon as in any manner whatever, whether lawfully or unlawfully, they are brought or come within the territorial limits of New Zealand from any country outside those limits.
   (2) Goods whose destination is outside the territorial limits of New Zealand, and ships' stores, shall not be deemed to have been so imported unless, while they are within those limits, they are removed from the ship or

aircraft in which they arrived there, but if so removed they shall for all the purposes of this Act be deemed to have been brought within the territorial limits of New Zealand as aforesaid; . . . .

Hazardous Substances and New Organism Act of 1996, §2(1) [hereinafter HSNO Act 1996].

39. "Develop," in relation to organisms, means genetic modification of any organism; but does not include field testing. HSNO Act 1996 §2(1).

40. "Field test" means, in relation to an organism, the carrying out of trials on the effects of the organism under conditions similar to those of the environment into which the organism is likely to be released, but from which the organism, or any heritable material arising from it, could be retrieved or destroyed at the end of the trials; and includes large-scale fermentation of microorganisms. *Id.*

41. "Release," in relation to new organisms, means to allow the organism to move within New Zealand free of any restrictions other than those imposed in accordance with the Biosecurity Act of 1993 or the Conservation Act of 1987. *Id.*

42. There are 16 regional councils in New Zealand.

43. NEW ZEALAND CONSERVATION AUTHORITY (NZCA), PESTS & WEEDS: A BLUE-PRINT FOR ACTION (1999).

44. New Zealand Ministry of Agriculture and Forestry, *Overview of MAF Biosecurity Roles*, *at* http://www.maf.govt.nz/biosecurity/about/roles.htm (last visited Apr. 1, 2003).

45. The *PCE Report 2000* notes that expenditure by MAF Quarantine on public awareness has declined in recent years from about NZD500,000 to NZD86,000. PCE REPORT 2000, *supra* note 6, at 45. In contrast, the Australian Quarantine Inspection Service budget for quarantine awareness is the equivalent of NZD2.86 million. The report notes that increased funding is needed to maintain an effective public awareness campaign, and that this needs to be supported by increased penalties for noncompliance with biosecurity requirements. At the urging of the New Zealand Green Party, 2002 has seen an increase in public awareness spending with a special government allocation of over NZD2 million for an awareness program including television advertisements featuring "Max the Biosecurity Beagle."

46. PCE REPORT 2000, *supra* note 6.

47. HSNO Act §17.

48. *Id.* §140.

49. *Id.* §11.

50. *See Index of Biocouncil Publications*, *at* http://www.maf.govt.nz/Biocouncil/publications/ (last visited Feb. 24, 2003).

51. PCE REPORT 2000, *supra* note 6.

52. *Id.*

53. GUARDING PACIFIC'S TRIPE STAR: DRAFT BIOSECURITY STRATEGY FOR NEW ZEALAND (2002), *available at* http://www.biostrategy.govt.nz/library/draft-strategy/draft-strategy.pdf (last visited Feb. 24, 2003).

54. PCE REPORT 2000, *supra* note 6.

55. *Id.*

56. Government of New Zealand, *Treaty of Waitangi 1840*, *at* http://www.govt.nz/en/aboutnz/?id=a32f7d70e71e9632aad1016cb343f900 (last visited Apr. 2, 2003).

57. 31 I.L.M. 818 (1992).

58. *See* Government of New Zealand, *Our Chance to Turn the Tide: Biodiversity Information, at* http://www.biodiversity.govt.nz (last visited Apr. 2, 2003).

59. The form required is set out in the Hazardous Substances and New Organisms (New Organisms Forms and Information Requirements) Regulations 1998. SR 1998/218.

60. HSNO Act, §34.

61. *Id.* §40(2).

62. *Id.* §5.

63. *Id.* §6.

64. *Id.*

65. *Id.* §8. The Treaty of Waitangi was signed by the British Crown and various Maori tribes in 1840 and was the basis (at least in part) on which the Crown assumed sovereignty over New Zealand. Since 1840, there has been much debate about the application of the Treaty of Waitangi in domestic law. The Maori people have sought to have the treaty enforced through litigation with some success. However, the treaty has recently become more directly incorporated into the New Zealand legal system largely as a result of specific provisions including in a number of statutes. These include the Treaty of Waitangi Act of 1975, which established the Waitangi Tribunal to consider Maori claims, as well as the State Owned Enterprises Act of 1986, the Environment Act of 1986 and the Conservation Act of 1987, all of which make specific reference to the principles of the Treaty of Waitangi.

66. HSNO Act, §7.

67. *Id.* §9.

68. The Hazardous Substances and New Organisms (Methodology) Order 1998, SR 1998/217, establishes the methodology to be used by ERMA when making decisions under the HSNO Act.

69. *Id.* cl. 10.

70. HSNO Act, §36.

71. *Id.* §37.

72. Second Schedule—"prohibited organisms." The importation or release or development of any organism listed in the Second Schedule is prohibited. *Id.* §50. Examples include snakes of any species, cane toads, predatory snails, witchweed, and the puncture vine.

73. Effect is defined to include any potential or probable effect, any temporary or permanent effect, any past, present, or future effect, any acute or chronic effect, or any cumulative effect that arises over time or in combination with other effects.

74. HSNO Act, §38(2).

75. *Id.* sched. 3.

76. Set out in the Hazardous Substances and New Organisms (Low-Risk Genetic Modification) Regulations 1998. SR 1998/216.

77. A rapid assessment may be made where the organism is not an unwanted organism, and it is highly improbable that after release the organism could do any of the following:

   - form self-sustaining populations anywhere in New Zealand, taking into account the ease of eradication;
   - displace or reduce a valued species;
   - cause deterioration of natural habitats;

- cause disease, by a parasite, vector for human/animal/plant diseases; or
- have any adverse effects on human health and safety or the environment.

HSNO Act, §35.

78. *Id.* §§54 and 60.

79. *Id.* §§53 and 58. An explanation of the Department of Conservation's approach in assessing new organism applications may be found in Michael Cameron, *New Organism Introductions: A Risk Analysis Approach, Used in the Assessment of Whether a Proposed Importation, Development, and/or Release Is in the Interests of Conservation*, in ECOLOGICAL MANAGEMENT (Department of Conservation ed., 2000), *available at* http://www.doc.govt.nz/PUBLICATIONS/004~SCIENCE-AND-RESEARCH/BIODIVERSITY-RECOVERY-UNIT-PUBLICATIONS/ECOLOGICAL-MANAGEMENT/ (last visited Apr. 2, 2003).

80. Biosecurity Act, §80B.

81. *Id.* §80D.

82. PCE REPORT 2000, *supra* note 6.

83. Risk goods are defined as any organism, organic material, or other thing or substance, that (by reason of its nature or origin) it is reasonable to suspect constitutes, harbors, or contains an organism that may—

    (a) cause unwanted harm to natural and physical resources or human health in New Zealand; or
    (b) interfere with the diagnosis, management, or treatment, in New Zealand, of pests or unwanted organisms.

    Biosecurity Act, §2.

84. *Id.* §22.

85. *See* MAF's website, *at* http://www.maf.govt.nz/biosecurity/animals.htm (last visited Apr. 2, 2003).

86. G. HOSKING, BIOSECURITY RISK MITIGATION FOR IMPORTED CARS FROM JAPAN—BEST PRACTICE (2002) (a report prepared for Japan Quarantine Inspections, BioSecurity Services Ltd., Rotorua).

87. Biosecurity Act, §40.

88. *Id.* §2.

89. Ministry of Agriculture and Forestry, *The Unwanted Organisms Register, at* http://www.maf.govt.nz/biosecurity/pests-diseases/registers-lists/unwanted-organisms/index.htm (last visited Feb. 24, 2003).

90. Biosecurity Act, §45.

91. *See supra* note 89.

92. Biosecurity Act, §§56-70.

93. *Id.* §§71-83.

94. PCE REPORT 2000, *supra* note 6.

95. Biosecurity Act, §100.

96. PCE REPORT 2000, *supra* note 6.

97. Biosecurity Act, §7A.

98. *Id.* §22.

99. *Id.* §144.

100. *Id.* §100.

101. *Id.* §§22, 100.

102. *Id.* §§7A, 144.

103. J. SINNER & N. GIBBS, A PROPOSED FRAMEWORK FOR THE MANAGEMENT OF BIOSECURITY RISKS AT THE NEW ZEALAND BORDER (1998) (report prepared for the Biosecurity Council, Wellington).

104. Biosecurity Act, pt. VI.

105. *Id.* §152.

106. *Id.*

107. *Id.*, pt. VII.

108. *Id.*

109. *Id.* §145.

110. *Id.* §146.

111. SR 1993/368.

112. PCE REPORT 2000, *supra* note 6.

113. Biosecurity Act, §128.

114. PCE REPORT 2000, *supra* note 6.

115. GUARDING PACIFIC'S TRIPLE STAR: DRAFT BIOSECURITY STRATEGY FOR NEW ZEALAND (2002), *available at* http://www.biostrategy.govt.nz/library/draft-strategy/draft-strategy.pdf (last visited Feb. 24, 2003).

116. Biosecurity Act, pt. VIII.

117. *Id.*

118. *Id.*

119. The penalties and offenses are outlined in *id.*

120. *Id.*

121. *Id.*

122. HSNO Act, §109.

123. *Id.*

124. *Id.* §114.

125. Minister of Labour for places of work; Director of Land Transport Safety and the Commissioner of Police for motor vehicles, roads, trains, railway lines; Director of Civil Aviation for aircraft and ships; Director of Maritime Safety for ships; Ministry of Health for the protection of public health; Territorial authorities for all other areas.

126. HSNO Act, §114.

127. *Id.* §104.

128. A compliance order may be appealed to a District Court. *Id.* §125.

CHAPTER 2:
INVASIVE SPECIES LAW AND POLICY IN SOUTH AFRICA

by Robyn Stein[1]

South African law governing invasive alien organisms is essentially fragmented. It does not offer a comprehensive or holistic approach to the ongoing negative impacts of alien invasive species on the country's indigenous and precious natural resources. The legislation that has been enacted at both the national and provincial levels of government deals unevenly with invasive species. In consequence, multiplicities of statutes regulating plants, animals, and genetically modified organisms (GMOs) are administered by a number of different government departments, each with its own management objectives and budgetary constraints.

For example, statutory provisions pertaining to alien plants are generally found in national legislation, particularly in the Conservation of Agricultural Resources Act 43 of 1983 (Conservation of Agricultural Resources Act). This Act, which is administered by the national Department of Agriculture, has spawned fairly comprehensive regulations to address the control of "weeds" and "invader plants." However, the Act provides no standard procedures to deal with the intentional introduction of alien invasive plants into the natural or built-up environments. Furthermore, the imposition of penalties when individuals fail to comply with the regulations has, in the past, been unsuccessful. This is a main focus of proposed amendments.

To complicate matters, each of the nine provinces also has nature conservation legislation dealing with the control of invasive plants. However, the definitions are not uniform and the treatment of the problem ranges dramatically. In some provinces, there are statutes that prohibit the importation or trade in certain declared weeds unless the trader/importer holds a permit authorizing him or her to undertake a specific activity with respect to the declared plant. In other provinces, the competent authority is granted powers to take measures, which may include the promulgation of regulations as necessary, to control invasive plants. Since the establishment of the provinces is relatively recent, it is possible that they will, in time, develop a more comprehensive and unified approach.

However, legislation addressing alien plant forms does not stop here. The national government manages water resources through Catchment Management Agencies. The control of alien plants is an important component of the catchment management process, since the impact of these plants on water resources—on a catchment's ability to provide water—is significant. Alien plants thus become an integral part of a Catchment Management Agency's responsibilities. Furthermore, the National Water Act 36 of 1998 (National Water

51

Act) recognizes activities like "stream flow reduction" and plantation forestry as areas subject to control by Catchment Management Agencies.[2]

In addition, the South African government has effectively operated the Working for Water Program over the past few years. This program was launched with the primary purpose of dealing with invasive alien plants and their impact on the nation's scarce water resources. Besides contributing to the control of dangerous invasive alien species in South Africa, the program has been instrumental in promoting public awareness and providing employment opportunities, particularly for previously disadvantaged South Africans.

South Africa's new democratic government has recognized that the existing body of uncoordinated laws addressing alien invasive organisms requires urgent attention. The government has taken steps to introduce a comprehensive law that will aid compliance with South Africa's obligations under the United Nations Convention on Biological Diversity (CBD).[3] Also, a White Paper (an official policy document) on the Conservation and Sustainable Use of South Africa's Biodiversity proposes a number of actions to consolidate and coordinate the laws governing alien organisms (including plants and animals) and GMOs. Although it is not possible to forecast with any precision when the new legislation will be enacted, it should be placed before the legislature for consideration within the next 24 months.

INTRODUCTION

South Africa has one of the highest biodiversity indices in the world.[4] It has the richest flora of all African countries, with more than 20,300 species of plants.[5] Furthermore, South Africa houses two internationally recognized biodiversity hot spots: the Cape Floral Kingdom and the Succulent Karoo (the only arid land hot spot in the world). The Cape Floral Kingdom has the highest recorded species diversity for any similar sized temperate tropical region in the world.

South Africa's marine life is similarly diverse, partly as a result of the extreme contrast between the East and West Coasts. Three water masses—the cold Benguela Current, the warm Agulhas Current, and oceanic water—make the region one of the most oceanographically heterogeneous in the world. More than 10,000 plant and animal species, almost 15% of the coastal species known worldwide, are found in South African waters, with nearly 12% of these occurring nowhere else.

The introduction of invasive alien organisms has had major effects on the terrestrial, freshwater, and marine biodiversity of South Africa, and these organisms are widely regarded as the second-largest threat to biodiversity after direct habitat destruction. Present laws governing the control and/or eradication of invasive alien organisms in South Africa are substantially fragmented and uncoordinated, and there is no comprehensive or holistic approach to deal with the negative impacts of alien invasive species on the country's indigenous and precious natural resources. Plants, animals, and GMOs are unevenly dealt with in legislation enacted at both the national and provincial levels of government. Consequently, multiple statutes are administered by a number of different government departments, each with its own management objectives and budgetary constraints.

This chapter explores the lack of unity and coordination in the laws governing invasive alien organisms in South Africa by examining briefly the governmental structure and then providing an in-depth legislative overview of current laws concerning plants, animals, and GMOs.

Although South Africa has yet to offer a comprehensive approach to the negative impacts of alien invasive species on its biodiversity, it is nevertheless important to acknowledge that the country does have a clear history of recognizing the potential threat of invasive species. This history is demonstrated by the many legal and institutional attempts, however fragmented, to address the threat of invasive plant species, invasive exotic animals, and GMOs.

The chapter concludes by highlighting the problems faced by South Africa in attempting to defeat the negative impacts of alien invasive species and, furthermore, provides some suggestions for overcoming them.

GOVERNMENTAL OVERVIEW

On April 27, 1994, for the first time in the nation's history, South Africa became a constitutional democracy. The Constitution of the Republic of South Africa, which was adopted by Parliament on May 8, 1996, gives the legislature and executive primary responsibility for the creation and adoption of policy and legislation.[6] The role of the judiciary is distinct and independent from the executive and the legislature and becomes relevant only when the state and its organs fail to respect, protect, and fulfil fundamental rights.

Government in South Africa is constituted at three distinct, yet interdependent, spheres: the national, the provincial, and the municipal. These spheres must observe and adhere to the principles enshrined in the Constitution. National and provincial government have concurrent legislative competence over agriculture, animal control, and the environment and nature conservation (excluding national parks, national botanical gardens, and marine resources). Where national government has set norms and standards, and provincial or local government fails to comply with such norms and standards, national government may intervene to ensure compliance. National legislation on the topic of protection of the environment will always trump provincial legislation, and, if it is to be effective, provincial legislation must comply with national legislation on this topic. Furthermore, any national legislation setting norms or standards will trump provincial legislation, provided that such norms and standards are necessary to regulate any matter effectively.

The Department of Environmental Affairs and Tourism and the Department of Water Affairs and Forestry are the most important national authorities responsible for environmental regulatory controls.

LEGISLATIVE OVERVIEW

The Preamble to the Constitution of the Republic of South Africa commits all South Africans and their elected representatives to healing the divisions of the past by establishing a society based on democratic values, social justice, and fundamental human rights. Furthermore, §24 of the Constitution guarantees the right of each person to an environment that is not harmful to health or well-being. This right, which, as part of the Constitution's Bill of Rights, places positive duties on the state, acts as a veritable guide for future government policy and state action in the field of environmental regulation.

With the advent of democracy, South Africa began a number of important environmental law reform initiatives that have resulted in the development of new environmental policies and legislation.

The National Environmental Management Act 107 of 1998 (NEMA) is an overarching environmental protection and management statute, which recognizes that the environment is a functional area of concurrent national and provincial legislative competence and that, in order to promote and fulfill the fundamental environmental rights enshrined in the Constitution, requires the three spheres of government and all organs of state to cooperate, consult, and support one another.

NEMA established both the National Environmental Advisory Forum, which monitors environmental management objectives and priorities—as well as the methods of compliance—and the Committee for Environmental Coordination, which promotes the integration and coordination of environmental functions by the relevant organs of state.

NEMA does not specifically refer to alien invasive organisms, but it does offer mechanisms and institutions through which invasive alien control programs may be implemented and coordinated. One priority of the Act is that development must be socially, environmentally, and economically sustainable. All necessary steps should be taken to avoid the disturbance of ecosystems, the loss of biological diversity, and the pollution and degradation of the environment. Furthermore, NEMA stipulates that sustainable development includes the prevention of negative impacts on the environment by early anticipation of such impacts. Thus, compliance requires that indigenous organisms be protected, but the control of invasive alien species, though it seems clearly to follow from this requirement, is still only implied.

NEMA places responsibilities and obligations on certain people, namely, those who own or control land or premises, or those who have a right to the use of land or premises on which any situation exists that could potentially cause significant pollution or degradation of the environment. All such persons are required to take reasonable measures to prevent such pollution or degradation from occurring.[7] Included in these measures is the need to investigate and evaluate the impact on the environment of all activities.[8] In consequence, as stated above, NEMA creates scope to require reasonable measures to be taken to control invasive organisms that have been shown to cause considerable degradation of the environment.

While NEMA encourages cooperation and coordination between the different spheres and institutions of government, the Environment Conservation Act 73 of 1989 (Environment Conservation Act) in effect reinforces the problems of fragmentation. The Act empowers the Minister of Environmental Affairs and Tourism to identify activities that may have a substantially detrimental effect on the environment.[9]

But several sections of the Act have been delegated to the provincial legislatures, including the authority to designate protected natural environments. The delegation of specific powers to the provinces has resulted in a fragmentation of the statute, with different sections being administered by different spheres of government and, in turn, by different departments, each with its own management objectives.

In 1997, under the auspices of the Act, the Minister of Environmental Affairs and Tourism identified several activities that have a substantial detrimental impact on the environment, including "the intensive husbandry of, or importation of, any plant or animal that has been declared a weed or an invasive alien species; and the release of any organism outside its natural area of distribution that is to be used for biological pest control."[10]

To undertake such activities requires written authorization from the Minister or competent authority, which may be issued only after the consideration of reports concerning the environmental impact of the proposed activity. Protected natural environments the Cape Peninsula, for example—fell under provisions of the Environment Conservation Act's predecessor, namely, the Environment Conservation Act 100 of 1982. The 1982 Act issued directions with which managers of protected natural environments were required to comply.[11] In 1985, a specific directive was issued requiring that *Acacia* and *Hakea*, and any other exotic species that threatened the survival of indigenous plant species, to be eradicated within the Cape Peninsula Protected Natural Environment.

South Africa's ratification of the CBD[12] on November 2, 1995, has had important legal implications for the country's domestic legislation. In terms of the Constitution, South Africa is bound by international agreements[13] and is therefore obliged to ensure that those agreements are implemented in accordance with their stated objectives. Thus, the state is required by the Constitution and the CBD either to develop national strategies, plans or programs, or to adapt existing ones to integrate the conservation and sustainable use of biodiversity into sectoral and cross-sectoral plans, programs, and policies.

South Africa's response is contained within the White Paper on the Conservation and Sustainable Use of South Africa's Biological Diversity,[14] which articulates the country's policy and strategy to achieve the objectives of the CBD.

The White Paper[15] sets out certain policy objectives, one of which aims to prevent the introduction of potentially harmful alien species and to control and eradicate alien species that already threaten ecosystems, habitats, or species.[16] Alien organisms are defined as plants, animals, and microorganisms that do not naturally occur in an area or ecosystem, but are deliberately or accidentally introduced by humans.

The White Paper recognizes that in spite of extensive legislation and various programs that regulate the introduction and spread of alien organisms, past efforts at control have been relatively unsuccessful, particularly because responses have tended to be reactive, with actions taken only after invasive alien species have become a problem. To redress this, the document proposes that the government adopt a proactive, preventative, and precautionary approach to control the introduction and spread of invasive alien organisms and the transfer, handling, use, and release of GMOs.

The White Paper has created a set of guidelines to be followed by government in collaboration with interested and affected parties. It seeks to consolidate and coordinate the law governing alien organisms (including plants and animals) and GMOs. The guidelines aim to streamline existing legislation, develop national policy, and coordinate the efforts of existing institutions.[17]

The Biodiversity Bill, promoting biodiversity in South Africa's indigenous flora and fauna is expected to impact significantly on alien invasive species.

INVASIVE PLANTS

More than 10% of South Africa's plant species are already listed as threatened in the *South Africa Red Data List*,[18] which indicates the conservation status of threatened species and ecosystems. Although only a few cases exist in which there is enough evidence to prove definitively that alien plant invasions have resulted in the extinction of species, an excessive number of species listed in the Red Data List are nevertheless threatened wholly or in part by alien invading plants.

Similarly, the transformation of landscapes by alien trees has been a significant threat to bird species in the Mpumalanga province, many of which are threatened species and are endemic to the area. A rough estimation suggests that invasive alien plants have affected nearly 10 million hectares (8.28% of the total country). The most widespread invading alien plants in South Africa include the Black Wattle, Bug Weed, Lantana, Mesquite, Pine, Port Jackson, Prickly Pear, Rooikrans, and Syringa.

Alien invasive plants are also responsible for reducing stream flow from catchment areas and for reducing groundwater supplies. Most of South Africa's stream flow is generated from upper catchments and these have been found to be the areas most at risk from invasion. It is anticipated that most of these upper catchment areas will become fully invaded if not properly managed. Experiments that examine both the planting of aliens in catchment areas as well as the clearing of them have produced estimates regarding the size and significance of alien water consumption. A 1998 estimate suggests that invading alien plants use 3.3 billion square meters of water in excess of that used by native vegetation every year.[19] Without action these water losses will increase as alien plants invade remaining uninvaded areas.

The problem in South Africa also includes the intentional introduction of non-native plant species. For example, South Africa's timber is produced entirely from plantations of exotic trees (mainly pines, eucalyptus, and wattle), making the timber industry largely responsible for a part of the country's alien invasion. In fact, commercial plantations occupy 38% of the total invaded area. These plantations not only threaten to damage natural ecosystems and alter the hydrological cycle, but they also irrevocably rearrange the character of South Africa's scenery, alter drainage patterns and soils, and destroy the food-growing potential of thousands of hectares of land. Forestry is, however, an important part of the country's economy, contributing ZAR1.8 billion, or 2%, of the gross domestic product and employing a large number of people. Therefore, with the industry already so established, the only solution is to minimize the negative impacts of these plantations to the greatest extent possible. The forest industry is committed to an environmental code of conduct that includes the management of the spread of alien plants on their estates.

The Cape Floral Kingdom is an area particularly exposed to the onslaught of invasive plants. This biodiversity hot spot covers 90,000 square kilometers in the western and eastern Cape provinces. This area, barely 4% of the land surface of southern Africa, is home to 45% of the subcontinent's plant species.[20] The region includes almost 8,600 species of flowering plants and ferns, of which almost 70% are endemic.[21] The kingdom is also the smallest of six such kingdoms into which the world's vegetation is subdivided, and it is the only one that is found entirely within the borders of a single country.

Almost one-third of the kingdom has already been lost to urbanization, agriculture, and forestry and the remaining areas are under severe threat from invading alien plants. Statistics indicate that, of the remaining area, 10.7% is currently under dense stands of alien plants and another 32.9% is lightly invaded. Indications are that southern Africa could lose almost one-quarter of its plant species from these provinces alone due to invading alien plants. Apart from the intrinsic value of the rich biodiversity in this area, the Cape Floral Kingdom needs to be protected on the basis of its tourist industry, its agricultural and horticultural industry, and its role as a site of important research material.

It will become apparent that rather than a holistic or comprehensive approach to the problem, there are instead multiplicities of laws that deal, in differing degrees, with alien invasive plants. These laws are administered by a number of different government departments at both the national and provincial levels. Each of the nine provinces has its own nature conservation legislation that addresses the issue of invasive plants. Definitions are not uniform, and the treatment of the problem ranges dramatically.

Legislation designed to control or to prevent weeds dates back to the 19th century. Historically, the problem has not been a lack of legislation, though some Acts such as the Mountain Catchment Areas Act 63 of 1970 (Mountain Catchment Areas Act) have been difficult to enforce. The problem has often been the failure of authorities to provide sufficient field staff and resources to enforce the legislation.

Traditionally, land owners in South Africa have had absolute rights over their land and its natural resources, including—implicitly—the "right" to neglect and abuse it. The Conservation of Agricultural Resources Act 43 of 1983 and Environment Conservation Act introduced the idea that landowners are obliged to manage their land and natural resources sustainably. Furthermore, this approach, which is consolidated in all recent environmental legislation, argues that failing to take action against invasive weeds is neither sustainable nor efficient. It encourages taking the steps needed to implement existing legislation or any new legislation that replaces it.

Unfortunately, though, much of the South African government's inherited legislation does not adhere to the principle of sustainable development. Confusion arises from the application of both new laws that encourage sustainable development and old ones that are still in force that do not. Furthermore, the administration of legislation is fragmented: the Conservation of Agricultural Resources Act is administered by the Minister of Agriculture and Land Affairs, while the administration of the Mountain Catchment Areas Act has been devolved entirely to provincial nature conservation; the Environment Conservation Act is administered by the Minister of Environmental Affairs and Tourism, though several sections—including the proclamation of protected natural environments—have been delegated to the provincial legislatures.

Statutory provisions pertaining to alien plants are primarily found in the Agricultural Resources Act. The powers to apply the Conservation of Agricultural Resources Act reside in the Minister of Agriculture and Land Affairs, who can appoint an executive officer to exercise the powers and perform duties designated by the Act.[22] The Minister can publish regulations to declare any plant to be a weed or an invader plant, either throughout the republic or in any specific part of the republic.[23] The regulations that the Minister has promulgated under the Act to control "weeds" and "invader plants" have recently been amended. Significantly, however, the Act provides no standard procedures to deal with the intentional introduction of alien invasive plants into the natural environment.

Under the Conservation of Agricultural Resources Act, penalties are imposed when individuals do not comply with the regulations governing the control of certain plants. Landowners found to contravene any section of the Act can be fined, with matters taken further in cases of noncompliance.[24] The selling and/or spreading of weeds (whether "caused or permitted") in agricultural produce or on livestock are prohibited.[25] Only organizations registered under the Plant Improvement Act 53 of 1976, such as the Plant Protection Research Institute, are exceptions.[26] To a certain extent, the Plant Improvement Act interacts with the Conservation of Agricultural Resources Act's prohibitions on weed dispersal. The Plant Improvement Act regulates the nursery industry and any related organizations involved in the breeding and commercial propagation, import, and export of plants and plant material. Any plant (or plant part) must be registered and comply with certain requirements. The Plant Improvement Act does not directly outlaw propagation of weeds, but since weeds are not included in the lists of acceptable species and varieties, their propagation is illegal. There is an initiative underway in South Africa to ensure that nurseries do not sell invasive alien species. The South African Nursery Association, Working for Water, the National Botanical Institute, the Botanical Society, the

Plant Protection Research Institute, and the Council for Scientific and Industrial Research are all involved.

Implementation of the regulations promulgated under the Conservation of Agricultural Resources Act has in the past been unsuccessful, and was one of the main focus areas of amendments. The amendments formulated new categories into which invader plants will be allocated.

Category 1 plants will include weeds that serve no economic purpose and possess characteristics that are harmful to humans, animals, or the environment. These plants must be removed from the land. Category 2 plants include plants that are useful for commercial plant production purposes, but are proven invaders under uncontrolled conditions outside demarcated areas. These plants may be grown only with a permit, and only in a demarcated area. Category 3 plants include plants that are mainly used for ornamental purposes in demarcated areas, but are proven plant invaders under uncontrolled conditions outside demarcated areas. These plants may not be sold or propagated.[27]

The regulations state that if the specified plants occur contrary to the provisions of the regulations, the land user must control those plants effectively by means of certain specified control methods. There are 198 invasive alien plants listed in the regulations. Hopefully, the strengthening of the legislative capacity, the structure of the new regulations and certain empowering provisions will lead to greater compliance, placing an appropriate emphasis on landowners to ensure the combating of invading alien plants.[28]

The Mountain Catchment Management Act empowers provincial authorities to declare any area to be a Mountain Catchment Area. The Minister of Water Affairs and Forestry can, however, prescribe management measures for mountain catchment areas that apply both to the catchment area and to areas falling within five kilometers of the catchment area's boundary. These measures include directions for the conservation, use, management, and control of land, soil, and natural vegetation and the destruction of "intruding" vegetation.[29] Currently, mountain catchment areas have only been proclaimed in the former Cape Province, making the Act applicable only in the eastern and western Cape provinces.

The National Forest Act 84 of 1998 lists specific principles of sustainable forest management that apply to all official decisions affecting forests. Through these mechanisms, the Minister of Water Affairs and Forestry can require that the management of forests include the control of invasive alien plantations. Furthermore, the Minister is empowered to enter into an agreement with the owner and any other interested party to adopt a sustainable forest management plan for the area. Such an agreement could certainly incorporate the removal or control of alien invasive trees. In addition, the National Water Act, administered by the National Department of Water Affairs and Forestry, recognizes activities like "stream flow reduction" as subject to control. At present, plantation forestry is classified as such an activity and is therefore also subject to control in terms of this Act.

The National Water Act replaces the previous water resource regulatory system, which facilitated private ownership of water use rights, with a system in which water is statutorily recognized as a resource common to all South Africans and which is allocated on an administrative licensing basis. Under South Africa's new water regime, "all water, wherever it occurs in the water cycle, is a resource common to all."[30] The right to own water is replaced by the right to its use. Apart from allocating enough water for basic human needs, the National Water Act also recognizes the need to protect and maintain an Ecological Reserve, which refers to the "quantity, quality and reliability of water required to maintain the ecological functions on which humans depend."[31]

Thus, the healthy functioning of catchments and their associated habitats must be conserved to protect their ability to produce water. To meet the challenges of supplying water to all people on an equitable basis and of maintaining the Ecological Reserve, the country's water resources have to be carefully managed. As the custodian of water resources, the government manages water on a catchment basis through Catchment Management Agencies. The control of alien plants forms an important component of the catchment management process since the impact of these plants on water resources, and therefore on a catchment's ability to provide water, is significant. Alien plants consequently become an integral part of a Catchment Management Agency's responsibilities.

In summary, the laws that govern invasive alien plants are essentially fragmented. The Environment Conservation Act and the Mountain Catchment Areas Act devolve the control of weeds down to the nine provinces, whereas the primary legislation relating to weed control, the Conservation of Agricultural Resources Act, has not been devolved to the provinces. Alien invasive plants are, therefore, administered by a number of different national and provincial government departments, each with their own management objectives.

To complicate matters further, provincial nature conservation ordinances predate the creation of the nine current provinces, and no new ordinances have been promulgated yet. However, some of the provinces have promulgated a provincial Nature Conservation Act, some of which repeal the original ordinances and some of which incorporate these ordinances into the provincial framework.

The definitions in these provincial Acts are not uniform, and the treatment of invasive plants ranges considerably. Some of the provincial statutes prohibit trading or importing of certain declared weeds unless the trader/importer is the holder of a permit, which authorizes him or her to undertake a specific activity with respect to the declared plant. In these cases, the procedure for obtaining such a permit is set out in the relevant statute. In other provinces, the competent authority is granted powers to take measures that may be necessary to control invasive plants, which measures may include the promulgation of regulations. Since the establishment of the nine provinces is relatively recent, it is possible that the issue will be more comprehensively dealt with in time.

The provincial ordinances that provide some degree of weed or invasive management are: the Nature Conservation Ordinance 15 of 1974 in Natal; the Nature and Environmental Conservation Ordinance 19 of 1974 in the Cape Province; the Nature Conservation Ordinance 8 of 1969 of the Orange Free

State; and the Nature Conservation Ordinance 12 of 1983 of the Transvaal. Each new province is governed by one of the four ordinances except for Mpumalanga, where Nature Conservation Act 10 of 1998 has repealed the application of Ordinance 12 of 1983.

While these ordinances still designate an "Administrator" as the responsible official, that role has now been transferred to the Minister responsible for environmental conservation, namely, the Minister of Environmental Affairs and Tourism. The ordinances empower an Administrator to proclaim and manage provincial nature reserves in each of the provinces. Apart from containing detailed provisions safeguarding fauna and flora, these ordinances empower each province to declare Provincial Nature Reserves, provide for the establishment of a local authority and allow for the establishment of private reserves by landowners. Where there are proclaimed Mountain Catchment Areas, these areas are also under the authority of the Administrator (Minister) and the appropriate department or board.

The Mpumalanga Nature Conservation Act reassesses the entire legal framework relating to nature conservation in this province. The Schedule to the Act lists 45 plants that are declared to be invasive. Moving beyond the provisions of the Conservation of Agricultural Resources Act, the Mpumulanga Nature Conservation Act provides that no person may possess, sell, purchase, donate or receive as a donation, convey, import into the province, or cultivate a declared invader weed or plant, unless she or he holds a permit which authorizes him or her to do so.[32] Furthermore, the Act provides that the owner or occupier of land upon which invader weeds and plants are found and which threaten the natural biodiversity, must take the necessary steps to eradicate or destroy such plants.[33] Failure to comply with these provisions may result in a fine or imprisonment for a period not exceeding four years, or both.[34] It is interesting to note that the penalties for noncompliance provided in the Conservation of Agricultural Resources Act, with fines from ZAR500 to ZAR5,000, or a period of imprisonment from three months to two years, depending on which provisions of the Act are contravened, are not as stringent as those of this provincial legislation.

EXOTIC ANIMALS

Animals that are not indigenous to South Africa—like the Argentinian ant, the Himalayan thar, the European starling, the house sparrow, and the black rat—are responsible for a reduction in South Africa's biodiversity. Some of the most drastic impacts of invasive animal species have been recorded in South African rivers, where alien fish—and to a lesser extent invertebrate and reptile species—have altered habitats and successfully out-competed native fauna. Up to 60% of the threatened endemic freshwater fish of South Africa may be threatened by introduced fish species, such as trout, carp, and bass. Similarly in the marine environment, the accidental introduction of alien species in ballast water or on ships' hulls has resulted in a number of alien species occupying South African shores and coastal waters, in some instances displacing local species.

Despite the fact that there are fewer exotic animals than plants that threaten the natural biodiversity of South Africa, the legislative situation is not particularly different. The legislative and governmental structure responding to these threats is similarly fragmented and uncoordinated.

For example, the category "animal" is itself confusing. The Agricultural Pests Act 36 of 1983 (Agricultural Pests Act) defines "exotic animal" as any vertebrate member of the animal kingdom, which is not indigenous to the Republic of South Africa.[35] While the definition includes the eggs of such nonindigenous vertebrates, it does not include animals to which the Livestock Improvement Act 25 of 1977 (Livestock Improvement Act) applies, which can be any kind of animal or specified breed of animal declared by the Minister of Agriculture and Land Affairs under the terms of the Act.[36] Furthermore, the category of "exotic animal" under the Agricultural Pests Act does not include those animals defined as fish in the Sea Fishery Act 12 of 1988 (Sea Fishery Act). Such uncoordinated definitions clearly may result in confusion.

The Agricultural Pests Act regulates the importation of controlled goods into South Africa, and exotic animals are considered controlled goods. Exotic animals may only be imported if authorized by a permit or if the Minister of Agriculture and Land Affairs has determined otherwise by notice in the *Government Gazette*. The Minister, however, can import exotic animals of a specified kind, or pathogens or insects of a kind not indigenous to South Africa, if he or she believes that such importation is desirable to combat the occurrence of plants, pathogens, insects, or exotic animals of a specified kind.[37]

The Livestock Improvement Act established an Advisory Board for Animal Production to advise the Minister with regard to matters connected with inter alia the importation and exportation of animals, semen, ova, and eggs. However, the Act prohibits the collection, processing, packing, or storing of semen or ova, except by an officially registered person.[38] Furthermore, the importation and sale of semen or ova are prohibited in South Africa unless certain conditions are met. Contravention of this provision could result in a fine of ZAR8,000 and/or imprisonment for a period of two years.[39] In addition to these Acts, the Animal Health Bill,[40] aims to bring animal health legislation in line with the Constitution of the Republic of South Africa. The Bill seeks to replace the Animal Diseases Act 35 of 1984 (Animal Diseases Act). "Animal" is defined in the Animal Health Bill as:

> (a) any mammal, bird, fish, reptile or amphibian, which is a member of the phylum vertebrates, including the carcass thereof;
> (b) any invertebrate which is presumed as an animal for the purpose of this Act.[41]

The Animal Health Bill will have an effect on the transport industry in that amendments to import and export control mechanisms will be introduced. It aims to control animal disease and parasites and to provide for measures to promote animal health in general. It is highly probable that the Animal Health Bill will implement import controls, aimed at preventing the introduction of exotic animal diseases. This function is regulated at present by the Animal Diseases Act, which the Animal Health Bill seeks to replace.

The Marine Living Resources Act 18 of 1998 (Marine Living Resources Act) repeals the Sea Fishery Act. It defines "fish" as the living resources of the sea and the seashore, including any aquatic plant or animal—whether piscine or not, as well as any mollusc, crustacean, coral, sponge, holothurian or other echinoderm, reptile, or marine mammal, and includes their eggs, larvae, and all juvenile stages.[42] It does not include sea birds and seals. The Act aims to conserve marine living resources for both present and future generations as well as to preserve marine biodiversity. Ultimately, the Marine Living Resources Act regulates commercial, subsistence, and recreational fishing in South African Seas, but significantly, there are no provisions specifically to govern the import, introduction, or control of exotic fish into South African waters. The Act makes no distinction between exotic fish and indigenous fish.

As mentioned earlier, the Mpumalanga Nature Conservation Act completely restructures the law governing nature conservation in Mpumalanga. It deals comprehensively with exotic animals and fish. Not surprisingly, it has yet another definition of "exotic animal," which is any live vertebrate and its eggs, including birds and reptiles—but excluding fish—that belongs to a species, which is not a recognized domestic species and the natural habitat of which is not in the Republic of South Africa.[43] "Fish," in the Mpumalanga Nature Conservation Act, includes aquatic fauna generally, excluding mammals and birds, whether indigenous or exotic and whether alive or dead, and the ova or spawn thereof.[44] The Act also specifically deals with the hunting or catching of exotic animals and wild animals that are not considered game.

The Mpumalanga Nature Conservation Act prohibits any person from importing into the province or conveying or setting free therein a live exotic animal and from conveying, keeping, selling, or purchasing any exotic animal referred to in the Schedule to the Act, unless that person is the holder of a permit.[45] The Schedule includes all species of exotic tortoises, turtles, and terrapins; all exotic species of New World rats and mice; nutria; ferret; chukar partridge; all exotic species of newts and salamanders; and all exotic species of crustacean. With respect to fish, the Act prohibits any person from placing or releasing live fish, unless she or he is the holder of a permit, which authorizes him or her to do so.[46] Contravention of either of these provisions could result in a fine and/or imprisonment for a period not exceeding two years.[47] Provision is also made for regulations to be made concerning, inter alia, the hunting, control, importation into the province and exportation of, amongst other things, exotic animals and fish.[48] The remaining provinces are regulated by their independent ordinances.

In summary, the numerous definitions encountered in the provincial legislation are not uniform. In addition, the multiplicity of national and provincial Acts governing exotic animals results in many contradictions and inconsistencies.

GMOS

South African law dealing with GMOs is a recent area of concern. At present, the biotechnology industry in South Africa is relatively well developed, especially with regard to traditional technologies such as alcohol fermentation and bioleaching. Conventional and recombinant deoxyribonucleic acid (DNA) technologies for research purposes have also received considerable attention, although the commercial application of these technologies has not been developed to the same extent.

Several field trials have been permitted in South Africa. The commercial use of genetically modified cotton and maize seed from Monsanto was first approved in 1998. The first commercial experiment with genetically modified crops involved a few hundred hectares of genetically modified cotton, grown in KwaZulu-Natal province. According to press reports, the genetically modified maize, though also approved, is still being prepared for commercial distribution.

For the past couple of decades, biotechnology and genetic engineering have been regulated in South Africa by the South African Genetic Experimentation Committee (Sagene). Made up of ecologists, legal experts, and microbiologists, Sagene monitored and approved applications for genetic testing and the importation of transgenic seed (living organisms). But the new Genetically Modified Organisms Act 15 of 1997 (Genetically Modified Organisms Act) now governs the field of genetic testing. This Act established an advisory board to replace Sagene, although Sagene representatives were included on the board to ensure continuity. The need to regulate the industry and to minimize and avoid adverse impacts is widely recognized by both industry and other stakeholders. However, there is a crucial need to improve public awareness and open up the issue to wider debate.

The Genetically Modified Organisms Act defines GMOs as any organisms whose genes or genetic material have been modified in a way that does not occur naturally through mating or natural recombination or both.[49] The Act established an executive council made up of members from eight different government departments.[50] The council advises the Minister of Agriculture and Land Affairs on all aspects concerning the development, production, use, application, and release of GMOs, and ensures compliance with the Act. The council is empowered to require any applicant for a permit to use facilities involving GMOs or to release GMOs, to submit an assessment of the impact on the environment of such activity. All facilities involved in the contained use or the trial release of GMOs are required to be maintained in a register.

Provision is made for notification and inquiry in the event of an accident involving GMOs. An accident is defined as any incident involving an unintended release of GMOs that could have an immediate or delayed impact on the environment.[51] Furthermore, the executive council is empowered to advise the Minister on prohibitions, the authorization and exercise of the necessary control of imports, the authorization of trial or general releases, and any other matter with regard to GMOs.[52]

The Act also establishes an advisory committee, which is to be made up of knowledgeable persons in those fields of science applicable to the development and release of GMOs.[53] The purpose of the committee is to act as a national advisory body on all matters concerning or related to the genetic modification of organisms, including aspects relating to the introduction of GMOs into the environment as well as to the importation and exportation of GMOs. The Act grants extensive investigative powers to specified inspectors to ensure compliance with the provisions of the Act.[54] Furthermore, liability for damage caused by the use or release of a GMO is borne by the user. Users are obliged to ensure that appropriate measures are taken to avoid an adverse impact on the environment from GMOs.[55] Any person convicted of an offense under the Act is liable to a fine or imprisonment for a period not exceeding two years, for a first offense, and a fine or imprisonment for a period not exceeding four years for a subsequent conviction. Currently, there is no provincial legislation dealing with GMOs.

THE PROBLEM OF INVASIVE ALIEN ORGANISMS

One of the greatest obstacles facing the control of invasive species is public ignorance of the magnitude of the problem. Government departments are campaigning to educate people about the dangers and costs of invasive species and hopefully, in the process, to instill a sense of individual responsibility, particularly with regard to privately owned property.

Over the years, government departments have implemented projects to control specific invasive plants like the *Hakea* and the *Acacia* species. "Hack" groups as well as farmers have contributed to eradicating certain areas of invasive plants. The government's Working for Water Program, spearheaded by the Department of Water Affairs and Forestry, has the express purpose of dealing effectively with the problem of invasive alien plants.[56] The program works in conjunction with a range of partner organizations to control invading alien plants. The commitment of the government to this project is manifest in the budget allocated to the program, which has risen from ZAR25 million to a budget in 2001/2002 in excess of ZAR400 million.[57]

During the past 95 years, specialist institutes like the Botanical Research Institute and the Plant Protection Research Institute have built up a vast store of knowledge, not only about plant invaders, but also about the communities that they threaten and the environments in which they occur. Furthermore, institutions like the Soils and Irrigation Research Institute and the Weather Bureau have also made substantial contributions.[58] Nevertheless, weed data banks and the assessment of weed status remain in need of development and attention.

It is crucial to develop an awareness of invasive alien species as a problem, evaluate the damage or loss caused, carry out extensive research, enact effective legislation, and provide methods and finance for control. It is imperative to keep watch for new introductions, especially at likely ports of entry and wherever the veld is badly disturbed. All newly recorded plant species must be screened to see if they are known weeds in other countries and thus likely to become weeds in South Africa. The spread of such plants must be monitored regularly so that plant invaders can be recognized and destroyed while infestations are still limited.

CONCLUSION

It is evident from this examination of the laws dealing with invasive species that the legislation is rather fragmented and offers no comprehensive or holistic approach to deal with the problem of invasive species. The law is spread over a multitude of Acts and is therefore regulated by numerous government departments. Furthermore, the specific laws dealing with invasive plants, mammals, birds, fish, and GMOs are dispersed throughout legislation that deals with completely different areas of the law. Invasive species are dealt with separately on a national and provincial level, resulting in a legal framework that is difficult to access and understand, with no uniform definitions or terminology. Where one province may be adequately addressing the problem, another is completely lacking in any regulatory framework. The only workable solution to such a problem is a comprehensive law, which consolidates all of the laws in South Africa that deal with invasive species, whether on a national or provincial level.

Another disturbing feature of the situation is that penalties for noncompliance with provisions relating to the control of invasive species stretches over an enormous range. A comprehensive system is needed to deal uniformly with the problem through control and regulation. This could lead to a more efficient system whereby the laws could be implemented by a centralized institution and punishment could be imposed where necessary. To do this, sufficient resources would also be required. The level of awareness in government in South Africa is clearly increasing, and extensive funds have been allocated to the research and control of invasive species, as demonstrated by the immensely successful Working for Water Program, which has a substantial budget. As long as support continues to be granted to this type of project, it will be possible not only to maintain the work already being done, but also to implement follow-up programs that are crucially important for any long-term benefits.

The White Paper on the Conservation and Sustainable Use of South Africa's Biological Diversity aimed to consolidate the law and provide a more uniform approach. If the proposed policy is implemented, then many of the problems arising from the fragmentation of the law may be resolved.

Over the long-term, South Africa has no option but to apply more stringent and uniform laws and to educate the public about the magnitude of the invasive species problem. It is also imperative that the government commits itself to provide sufficient human and financial resources to enforce all legislation. While the control of invasive species seems to be a priority of environmental management, what remains now is the creation of an all-encompassing and efficient legal framework to accomplish this. The Biodiversity Bill is scheduled to be placed before the cabinet, prior to submission to Parliament, early in 2003. Enactment will occur within two years.

Although at the time of publication a draft of the bill was not in the public domain, it is expected to consolidate the law and provide a more uniform approach to the treatment of alien invasive species.

Perhaps the most promising light on the horizon is the New Partnership for Africa's Development (NEPAD), which is being spearheaded by President

Thabo Mbeki and his African counterparts. NEPAD proposes a continentwide initiative on invasive alien species and has already developed a framework for the initiative.

Chapter 2 Endnotes

1. Robyn Stein is a Corporate Legal Advisor in the Envirolaw Department at the firm Edward Nathan & Friedland (Pty) Ltd., where she is a Director. At the University of the Witwatersrand, South Africa, she obtained the degrees of B.A. (conferred in 1988) and LL.B. *cum laude* (conferred in 1990). In 1992, she obtained an LL.M. degree *with distinction* at the London School of Economics and Political Science. Ms. Stein is a Professor and teaches Natural Resources and Development Law at the Mandela Institute of the University of the Witwatersrand's School of Law on a visiting basis.

   The author would also like to express her appreciation to Amanda Anastassiades and Kerry Liebenberg for their help with this chapter.

2. National Water Act 36 of 1998, ch. 4, pt. 4.

3. 31 I.L.M. 818 (1992).

4. World Conservation Monitoring Centre (1992). Only Brazil and Indonesia surpass South Africa in biodiversity.

5. DR. JOHN HANKS, CONSERVATION IN THE NEW SOUTH AFRICA: OPPORTUNITIES FOR THE PRIVATE SECTOR (1999).

6. CONSTITUTION OF THE REPUBLIC OF SOUTH AFRICA, ch. 5, §85.

7. National Environmental Management Act 107 of 1998, ch. 7, §28(2).

8. *Id.* ch.7, §28(3).

9. Environment Conservation Act 73 of 1989, pt. V, §21.

10. Sections 4 and 5 of Regulation 1183 of September 5, 1997, which sets out the activities identified as having a substantially detrimental effect on the environment in terms of §21 of Environment Conservation Act 73 of 1989.

11. Environment Conservation Act 100 of 1982, pt. 3, §16(2).

12. 31 I.L.M. 818 (1992).

13. Constitution of the Republic of South Africa Act 108 of 1996, §§2, 231(4)-(5).

14. Government Notice No. R. 1095. Government Gazette 18163, July 28, 1997.

15. In South Africa, by way of democratic custom, a White Paper, once approved by the cabinet, constitutes a formal policy document, which, although not having the force of law, is used to determine legislative development and administrative activities relating to its subject matter.

16. White Paper on the Conservation and Sustainable Use of South Africa's Biological Diversity, ch. 3, goal 1.6, Government Notice No. R. 1095. Government Gazette 18163, July 28, 1997.

17. *Id.* ch. 2, goal 2.4.

18. CRAIG HILTON-TAYLOR, NATIONAL BOTANICAL INSTITUTE OF SOUTH AFRICA, RED DATA LIST OF SOUTHERN AFRICAN PLANTS (1996).

19. THE ENVIRONMENTAL IMPACTS OF INVADING ALIEN PLANTS IN SOUTH AFRICA, WORKING FOR WATER PROGRAM 8 (1998); BRIAN W. VON WILGA ET AL., VALUATION OF ECOSYSTEM SERVICES: A CASE STUDY FROM SOUTH AFRICAN FYNBOS ECOSYSTEMS, 46 BIOSCIENCE 3 (1996).

20. VON WILGA ET AL., *supra* note 19.

21. *Id.*

22. Conservation of Agricultural Resources Act 43 of 1983, §4.

23. *Id.* §2(3).

24. *Id.* §23.

25. *Id.* §5.

26. *Id.* §5(4).

27. Government Notice No. R. 1048, Government Gazette 9238, May 25, 1984. For requirements, Table 3 lists the plants considered in each category.

28. Regulations 17 and 18 of Government Notice No. R. 1048, Government Gazette 9238, May 25, 1984; Conservation of Agricultural Resources Act 43 of 1983, §16.

29. Mountain Catchment Areas Act 43 of 1983, §3.

30. National Water Act 36 of 1998.

31. *Id.* pt. 3.

32. Mpumulanga Nature Conservation Act, ch. 6, §80(3).

33. *Id.* §80(4).

34. *Id.* §80(5).

35. Agricultural Pests Act, §1.

36. Livestock Improvement Act, §2(1).

37. Agricultural Pests Act, §3(5).

38. Livestock Improvement Act, §§7(1)(a), 7(1)(b).

39. *Id.* §30(1)(iv)(aa).

40. Aug. 10, 2001.

41. Animal Health Bill, §1(1).

42. Marine Living Resources Act, §1.

43. Mpumalanga Nature Conservation Act, ch. 1, §1.

44. *Id.*

45. *Id.* ch. 2, §34(1).

46. *Id.* ch. 5, §62(1).

47. *Id.* ch. 5, §62(3).

48. *Id.* ch. 9, §86(1).

49. Genetically Modified Organisms Act, §1.

50. *Id.* §3(2).

51. *Id.* §1.

52. *Id.* §5(m).

53. *Id.* §10(1).

54. *Id.* §15(4).

55. *Id.* §17(1).

56. Department of Water Affairs and Forestry, *Working for Water Program, at* http://www.dwaf.gov.za/wfw (last visited Apr. 1, 2003).

57. WORKING FOR WATER PROGRAM, ANNUAL REPORT OF THE WORKING FOR WATER PROGRAM 2001/2002 (2002).

58. PLANT INVADERS: BEAUTIFUL BUT DANGEROUS 151 (C.H. Stirton ed., 1978).

CHAPTER 3:
INVASIVE ALIEN SPECIES: LEGAL AND INSTITUTIONAL FRAMEWORK IN ARGENTINA

by Maria E. Di Paola[1] and Diego G. Kravetz[2]

Despite some concern with and recognition of the threat of invasive species, Argentina's current legal and institutional framework to address this problem is dispersed, unsystematized, and incomplete. Since signing the Convention on Biological Diversity (CBD),[3] Argentina has designed and articulated a National Strategy on Biodiversity (NSB), which was approved in 2003 by an administrative regulation signed by the Federal Environmental Authority.[4] Regarding the implementation of the CBD to invasive species, Argentina is taking a few measures related to a few species of interest.[5]

According to the National Constitution, Argentine federal authorities regulate the introduction of exotic species into the country. But there are multiple regulations and authorities at the federal level, and jurisdiction varies depending on the class of species (wild or domestic), the category of species,[6] and whether control efforts lean toward sanitary or environmental aspects. The current regulations tend to emphasize sanitary measures and pest control, rather than invasive species. There is no single, unified invasive species law.

This situation is further complicated by the fact that Argentina is a federal state, but its natural resources belong to its provinces. Thus, there is a built-in potential for conflict and confusion between the federal government and provincial authorities, which is only exacerbated by a lack of interjurisdictional coordination.[7] A basic guideline clarifying this jurisdictional matter should be included in the implementation of current federal statutes on minimum standards for environmental protection and in the drafting process of future statutes on minimum standards for environmental protection. Finally, there is no complete official inventory of living species in Argentina, and this makes it particularly difficult to identify and monitor invasive species.

In this chapter, we examine Argentina's current legislative and institutional framework for addressing the threat of invasive species, and then conclude with some proposals to help systematize, streamline, and otherwise improve this framework.

ARGENTINA'S EXPERIENCE WITH INVASIVE SPECIES

South America was isolated from North America for millions of years. But species were still able to migrate back and forth, first across the islands that separated North America from South America, and then later across the Central

71

American land bridge. A large number of mammals now found in South American habitats entered the continent this way.

Spanish and Portuguese colonization, which began in the 16th century, produced a growing influx of dispersed, invasive flora and fauna brought to the continent by man.[8] The arrival of these new species, whether evident or hidden, exposed the ecological systems to new challenges. These systems as a whole were affected in diverse ways by the actions of these invasive species that had no history of harmonic development with the indigenous ecosystems. One example is the erosive devastation caused by ovine livestock to the Patagonian Plain.

In the late 19th and early 20th centuries, several invasions occurred because people with a *developing* bent intentionally introduced exotic species. Domingo F. Sarmiento,[9] for example, supported the introduction of the sparrow, which competed with indigenous species and eventually became a plague. There are, in fact, laws that address parasitic or harmful animal or vegetable invasions that date back to this period.[10]

Other, later invasions took place, like the beaver and the muskrat that were brought into the country for their fur. These species wreaked different types of havoc in Tierra del Fuego. The beaver built dams that led to the flooding of indigenous forests. These forests, unlike North American forests, were unable to withstand this and died.

Currently, the rate of invasion is assumed to be high because of increased and poorly regulated trade, which results in disordered transactions that ultimately vary the pathways of organisms. Although there is an ongoing project to inventory native forests and there is an inventory of implanted forests, research tools and monitoring mechanisms such as an official inventory of species including fauna species, and accurate statistics need to be implemented to improve decisionmaking with regard to invasive species in Argentina.[11]

THE NATIONAL CONSTITUTION

The inhabitants of Argentina, according to the National Constitution, are entitled to a healthy environment and have the duty to preserve it.[12] The authorities should guarantee the exercise of this right, but this is neither as straightforward nor as easy as it may at first seem.

For example, the Constitution assigns responsibility for natural resources to the provinces. Consequently, provinces have police jurisdiction over environmental issues.[13] Nevertheless, the Constitution also allows for certain exceptions to this provision by making the National Congress competent to enact legislation that addresses international, interprovincial and interjurisdictional commerce, as well as penal, civil, mining, and labor codes. The Congress is also competent to enact any legislation that relates to the harmonic growth of the nation.[14]

Furthermore, the Constitution requires the nation to set forth minimum standards for environmental protection.[15] The provinces can then complement these minimum standards with their own stricter regulations as they see fit. But the jurisdictional quagmire does not end here; the municipalities can also add their own layer of regulations to the management of local environmental issues.[16] Clearly, interjurisdictional problems impact Argentina's means of addressing invasive species.[17] Setting and enforcing minimum standards for environmental protection will encourage interjurisdictional coordination. At the end of 2002, the Congress enacted several statutes of minimum standards for environmental protection.[18] Although presently there is no minimum standard law on biodiversity or invasive species, there is a new General Environmental Law, which includes environmental principles, such as the precautionary one, and establishes a Federal Environmental System. This system includes the Environmental Federal Council (COFEMA), which groups the authorities of the nation, the provinces, and the city of Buenos Aires, and which is considered by the NSB as the appropriate framework to develop interjurisdictional coordination. In addition, Argentina has entered into international agreements like the CBD and the Convention on International Trade in Endangered Species (CITES)[19] as well as incorporated principles of soft law like the Rio Declaration on Environment and Development[20] into its internal legislation,[21] and recently approved its NSB.

Before looking more closely at the NSB and the improvements that will follow its enforcement, we want to look briefly at Argentina's current legal and institutional framework for the management of invasive species.

THE LEGAL FRAMEWORK

Argentina has a plethora of regulations that tangentially engage the issue of invasive species, but the majority of this legislation is primarily concerned with issues of sanitation and pest control.[22] The concept of alien invasive species was not adopted in Argentina until the signing of the CBD in 1994.[23] Before the adoption of the CBD, Argentina had focused on the protection of production systems, principally based on agriculture and forestry. Thus, sanitation and pest control legislation has a longer history and is more developed than invasive species regulations.[24]

Traditional sanitation and pest control tools may indirectly address invasive species, but the results tend to be incomplete. For example, an organism may be forbidden entrance into the country for sanitation reasons, but if that organism is also an invasive species, the effect of the prohibition will be positive with regard to the environment; that is, the sanitary prohibition will unwittingly prevent an adverse effect on the environment. The problems occur in the instances when an organism is not a sanitation concern, but is, in fact, an invasive species, a threat to ecosystems, habitats, or other species. In these cases, sanitation and pest control measures are clearly not restrictive enough to prevent the introduction of invasive species into the country.

Currently, the topic of invasive species is directly considered only in regulations that deal with wild fauna, though it is indirectly addressed to some extent in regulations related to aquatic hatcheries. The national regime for wild fauna[25] establishes requirements for importing animals that are in line with

CITES regulations.[26] There is a specific Environmental Impact Assessment Process required for the introduction of a new alien species.[27] The interested party has to present, along with an environmental impact assessment (EIA), proof of the alien species' conformity to the province where it will be located. The Secretariat of Environment and Sustainable Development, Department of Fauna, which is the national environmental authority, may consult the authorities of the neighboring provinces. Once the new exotic species is established in a particular province, transferring that species to another province requires a new EIA and proof of conformity to the new environment.

Thus, the movement of wild fauna inside Argentina is regulated by sanitary controls on the one hand, and by wild fauna transport regulations on the other.[28] Still, there are no tools to regulate the internal movement of wild fauna that pay specific attention to the issue of invasive species. There are also no specific regulations in place to detect or manage species that may already live in Argentina, yet may be potentially invasive.

The production of imported aquatic organisms[29] requires a permit, the application for which requires detailed references to the possible environmental impact of the species (whether indigenous or exotic).[30] But the regulations regarding aquatic organisms state that producers of first entrance exotic species cannot transfer them or their descendants to other aquaculture hatcheries, either in the province where they are initially settled or in other provinces. Nor can they sell juvenile specimens as ornaments, without the authorization of the National Department of Fishing and Aquaculture.

There is a lack of legislation pertaining to flora. Although forest legislation requires an EIA regarding the sustainability of a project that includes both native and alien species,[31] there is no flora legislation that addresses the introduction, control, or eradication of invasive species. There are specific regulations that address experimentation with and the release or marketing of genetically modified organisms (GMOs).[32] Consequently, GMOs are subject to a risk study prior to experimentation and release.[33]

THE INSTITUTIONAL FRAMEWORK

In addition to multiple and incomplete regulations, there are different federal authorities that are responsible for enforcement, depending on the class of species and its sanitary or environmental aspects.

The Secretariat of Environment and Sustainable Development (SAyDS) of the federal government is the enforcement authority for CBD, fauna, wild native forests, and flora. It includes the Office of Coordination of Biodiversity Conservation, and two key departments.[34] The Department of Fauna is the authority that regulates the introduction of wild fauna as new alien species and the requisite EIA process. The Department of Forests is the authority responsible for wild native forests. Although there is an ongoing project to develop a national inventory of all native forests and protected areas, there is no specific legislation that empowers this department to address the potential threat of invasive species in native forests.[35] As was pointed out above, there is no specific legislation pertaining to alien invasive species of flora.

For forestation projects that involve the introduction of native and/or non-native species into non-native forests, the SAyDS must work with the Secretariat of Agriculture, Livestock, Fishing, and Food (SAGPyA) of the federal government to develop criteria for an adequate EIA.[36] Besides this partial jurisdiction over non-native forests, the SAGPyA also includes several individual departments that monitor and regulate different charges of the Secretariat.

For example, the Department of Fishing and Aquaculture evaluates applications to introduce living aquatic organisms into land captive systems. This department can refuse any application if it determines that the introduction of said organism could cause alterations to the environment or affect other developing productions. Furthermore to register an aquatic hatchery, the department requires a detailed examination of the possible environmental impact of any introduction of species.[37]

The National Service of Health and Agri Food Quality (SENASA), another administrative body under the rubric of the SAGPyA, regulates and controls quality and sanitary aspects of livestock, fishing, and agriculture, as well as the application of the Food Code.[38] Consequently, sanitary controls on imported plants and animals (including quarantine measures), as well as interjurisdictional controls, depend on the SENASA. This body acts in coordination with the provincial sanitary authorities.

The federal Agricultural Biotechnology Advisory Committee (CONABIA) engages in experimentation with as well as regulation and release of animal and vegetable organisms that are the result of genetic engineering. Ultimately, the Secretariat authorizes the release of GMOs into the market, but it must first consult the CONABIA.[39]

Finally, to round out this somewhat confusing list of federal institutions, the Secretariat of Tourism and Sports of the federal government includes the Administration of National Parks. This regulatory body controls all aspects of the national parks throughout the country. In all protected areas, the introduction of alien species is forbidden. The authority is able to order the control or eradication of a species in a national park, though an environmental impact report is necessary to authorize commercial hunting of exotic species.[40]

ENFORCEMENT

Despite these varied authorities that each bear some specific responsibility for alien species, the SAyDS is, ultimately, the designated Enforcement Authority of the CBD. Therefore, it determines exactly which organisms fit the category of "invasive species."

Consequently, the Office of Coordination of Biodiversity Conservation has established strategic priorities in relation to three specific cases. Because there are no official statistics to guide it, the authority selected these cases based on its sense of each as a threat to indigenous species. In the first case—that of the European starling (*Sturnus vulgaris*) and the crested myna (*Acridotheres cristatellus*), birds introduced into the city and province of Buenos Aires—the agency has launched a joint campaign with the province of Buenos Aires and two nongovernmental organizations—Fundación Vida Silvestre and Ornitológica del Plata—to eradicate these species that it declared harmful and detrimental to productive activities by Resolution No. 974/98. Consequently, not only are national and provincial authorities authorized to carry out actions to eradicate these birds, but their interjurisdictional transit, export, or trade has also been prohibited.[41]

Wakame seaweed (*Undaria pinnaticida*), the second case, was introduced in the Province of Chubut. While the authority has designated this organism an invasive species and carried out several studies of its harmful environmental impact, it has yet to undertake any concrete measures to combat the threat the seaweed poses.

The third case—that of the beaver (*Castor canadensis*) introduced in Tierra del Fuego—poses a much more complicated problem because it involves both Argentina and Chile. The agency is working to encourage the interested sectors of both countries to carry out a joint project. For the moment, Tierra del Fuego has a provincial law that forbids both the introduction of alien species without prior authorization and the degradation of fauna and flora resources. Thus, the provincial authority currently permits the hunting of beavers throughout the year, but the province has not undertaken any specific eradication measures.

With the Argentine legal and institutional invasive species framework dispersed and unsystematized, the community lacks any real knowledge of the relevant regulations. This often inhibits appropriate implementation of regulations, and many times it affects the legal security of the individual and the community as a whole.

Furthermore, this incomplete framework can lead to jurisdictional questions. The federal regulations analyzed above are applicable to international and interprovincial situations, as well as to those that fall within federal jurisdiction as established by the National Constitution. These federal regulations are also applicable to situations that arise within a particular province, if that province has, in fact, ratified said regulations. But if in a particular province none of these suppositions are met, there could be regulations different from the national ones. This obviously creates a need for interjurisdictional coordination that many times does not exist. To complicate matters further, there are also different regulations related to invasive species in urban areas. The application of all of these regulations, whether federal, provincial, or urban, needs to be coordinated in such a way to prevent an invasive species from spreading to another part of the country.

The controls and precautions required by regulations, such as they are, demand human and economic resources that are not always available. Unfortunately, national and provincial budgets are often insufficient. This lack of economic support implies that the issue of invasive species is not a political priority in Argentina. In addition, the absence of public awareness—public understanding of invasive species issues, as stated above, is very weak—further inhibits the enforcement of laws. The government has failed to publicize the threat from invasive species, and commercial entities are, therefore, insensitive to the issue.

Yes, regulations have been enacted that attempt to address the harmful effects of alien species, but these regulations are clearly incomplete and unsystematized (existence of fauna regulations and lack of flora regulations are clear examples). Current problems caused by faulty administrative control of species coming from other countries, as well as the lack of a unified policy that applies to the whole country, cannot be ignored. However, a positive step toward a change regarding biodiversity conservation throughout the country is the recent approval of the NSB.

THE NSB

The Argentine NSB identifies several key requirements related to the country's institutional, legal, and management framework. Among the topics covered, the invasive alien species issue is specifically considered. The NSB establishes the following guidelines when implementing relevant action plans and policies:

- The Precautionary Principle should serve as the basis for all future policy and regulation, because the import or introduction of exotic species creates a potential danger to human beings, the environment, or both. This would require a ban on the introduction of all exotic species, unless a competent authority authorizes importation. Authorization would be manifest and taxonomically restrictive, and penalties and fines would apply in cases of illegal introduction of species.
- An [EIA] is a fundamental requirement, and must be undertaken previous to the introduction of exotic species from other countries or to the movement of species inside the country to areas that are different from their natural habitat. As an initial step, the enforcement authority could demand a determination of profitability expectations in an introductory application, thereby evaluating the interested party's ability to finance an environmental impact study of sufficient quality.
- In cases of deliberate introduction of species for investigation, production, or other use, the assessment of the socio-economic aspects should also be included in the environmental impact study, especially since the failure of the undertaking may lead to the release of the species. To prevent this, the NSB establishes that the legislation should require interested parties to post financial support to guarantee escape control and to cover damages to third parties in the event of a release and to cover costs of restitution. The implementation of a monitoring system to facilitate quick detection of new colonization and quick eradication is another measure under consideration.
- A regional approach, considering transboundary phyto- and zoo-sanitary control, whether international or between provinces, must be increased, especially with regard to the quarantine methods used. This will help prevent the entrance of species transported accidentally by ships.
- The country's legislation and institutional framework must be harmonized, and minimum standards for environmental protection of biodiversity must be enacted by the National Congress.
- A database of the precedents of native and foreign species that highlights those proven to be harmful, must be established; it is essential to develop appro-

priate policy that specifies responsibilities and sanctions.
- The threat of invasive species needs to be promoted to develop public awareness, and the production of indigenous species encouraged.[42]

Finally, the NSB quotes the 6th meeting of the Conference of the Parties to the CBD and Decision VI/23 on "Alien Species that threaten ecosystems, habitats or species,"[43] and considers that its principles are complementary to the NSB and help its development and implementation.

CONCLUSION

In Argentina, we currently find clearly separate regulations and authorities responsible for alien species, depending on the nature of the species (wild or domestic) and whether control is focused on environmental or sanitary aspects. Although the existence of federal authorities such as the SAyDS, the SAGPyA, and the Administration of National Parks seems to suggest that the problem of invasive species is under control, it is nevertheless important to realize that at present regulations and controls have yet to be elaborated in key areas such as the introduction of wild flora.

This situation becomes more complicated when one considers that Argentina is a federal state with three levels of government, but the federal, provincial, and municipal activities, institutions, and regulations are not yet coordinated.

In addition, most of the regulations related to alien species stem from sanitary measures and pest control and eradication measures. The topic of invasive species is clearly considered only in wild fauna regulation, though it is somewhat indirectly addressed in regulations related to aquatic hatcheries. Still, this limited consideration is clearly insufficient to deal with the potential threat.

Furthermore, there are no tools to regulate the internal movement of wild fauna from province to province, in terms of invasive species. There are also no specific preventions in place to detect or manage species that may already live in Argentina, but may be potentially invasive. The regulation of the internal movement of invasive species is a pending topic that deserves special attention, considering the expansion of the country and the different ecosystems that exist within its geography.

Finally, a positive sign is the recent approval of the NSB, a substantive point related to different core issues that we mention in this chapter, such as the need for appropriate statistics, harmonization of the legislation, and improved transboundary control.

PROPOSALS

First, Argentina needs to create a national inventory of species, as this is fundamental to any and all decisions regarding the control or eradication of invasive species.

Second, the National Congress needs to pass minimum standards regulation for biodiversity. As already mentioned, the National Congress enacted at the end of 2002 the Federal Environmental Law, which creates the Federal Environmental System including the Federal Council of the Environment, which groups environmental authorities of the nation, the provinces, and the city of Buenos Aires. Considering this basic framework, which would begin to close the jurisdictional and regulatory gaps between the different governmental authorities, we would recommend a minimum standard law related to biological diversity that directly addresses invasive species. Such legislation should include the following:

- Basic policies on the introduction of invasive species in the country (intentional-unintentional, Flora-Fauna);
- Basic policies on the movement of invasive species from one region of the country to another (Flora-Fauna); and
- Basic policies on eradication and control of invasive species.

Obviously, this is not the only way to address the problem. Provinces may enact stricter specific regulations regarding this issue.

Third, Argentina needs to establish interjurisdictional coordinated systems to facilitate better communication among the different governmental levels and authorities responsible for alien species, which will in turn improve the implementation of programs and the handling of emergency cases.

Fourth, the environmental authority should enforce the NSB, to ensure full and adequate compliance with the provisions of the CBD.

Finally, the dispersion of regulations related to alien and invasive species needs to be systematized. This will foster a more exact knowledge of the regulations and a greater understanding of the information on the part of the community.

Appendix 1

Issue	Regulation	Enforcement Authority	Definitions	Introduction	Control and Eradication
WILD FAUNA	Law 22.421, Law 22.344 (CITES), Regulatory Decree 666/97 and Regulatory Decree 522/97, Resolution ex-SRNyDS 376/97	SAyDS (Secretariat of Environment and Sustainable Development)	Wild Fauna	Requirements in line with CITES regulations Environmental Impact Process on the introduction of a new alien species into the country.	• The Enforcement Authority has to implement control and eradication plans. Hunting is considered as a measure with harmful species. • The party responsible for introducing alien species should implement a monitoring plan for early detection of escapes. In the case of existence of risk or eventual release, the immediate eradication of specimens should be achieved.
LIVING AQUATIC ORGANISMS	Resolution SAGPyA N° 987/97	SAGPyA (Secretariat of Agriculture, Livestock, Fishing, and Food), Federal Department on Fishing and Aquaculture		Production of living aquatic organisms: Import application with detailed references on the possible impact that the introduction of the species can cause.	• Imported organisms cannot be transferred to another hatchery without authorization. • First certificate is Temporary. Definitive Certificate is granted after the Enforcement Authority controlled the development of the activity. If the Definitive Certificate is not granted, the specimens of those species must be eradicated.
CULTIVATED FORESTS- FORESTATION	Law 25.080, Regulatory Decree 133/99	SAGPyA EIA: Co-ordination between SAGPyA and SDSyPA		Environmental Impact Study to assess forests' projects of native and exotic species.	
NATIVE FORESTS AND FORESTS WITH NO COMMERCIAL PURPOSES	Law 13.273, Law 19.995, Regulatory Decree 710/95	SDSyPA		Not regulated	

Appendix 1 (cont.)

Issue	Regulation	Enforcement Authority	Definitions	Introduction	Control and Eradication
PROTECTED AREAS	Law 22.351, Resolutions APN 16/94, 17/94 & 106/95	APN (Administration of National Parks)	Species Dominant species Threatened species Wild native or autochthonous species Wild exotic or introduced species Environmental Impact Assessment	Introduction of exotic species is forbidden.	• The Authority can permit hunting and fishing whenever there are biological, scientific, or technical reasons. Both activities can be used for control and eradication.
SANITARY CONTROL for ANIMALS and PLANTS	Law 2.268, Law 4.084 Regulatory Decree 4.238/69 and Several Resolutions by SAGPyA y SENASA	SENASA (National Service of Health and AgriFood Quality)		Introduction of animals and plants requires sanitary control.	• Quarantine measures for control.
PESTS	Law 11.843, Regulatory Decree 92.767/36 Law 4.863, Decree Law 6704/63 Regulatory Decree 8967/63 & 7466/65 Complementary SAGPyA resolutions	MS (Ministry of Health) SENASA	Pest can be defined considering different concepts of Law 6704/66	SENASA establishes specific regulations for each pest, hindering in certain cases the introduction of any species into the country. It determines quarantine protective areas.	• SENASA establishes mechanisms for control and eradication of pests and grants permits to the companies authorized to carry out them.
GENETICALLY MODIFIED ORGANISMS	Law 20.247 on seeds and phytogenetic creations Law 13.636 on veterinarian products, supervision, creation, and commercialization Resolution SAGPyA N° 656/92, 837/93, 226/97, 289/97 Disp. DNP y EAy F 4/99, 7/99, 8/99, 9/99	SAGPyA Advisory Entity: CONABIA (Federal Agricultural Biotechnology Advisory Committee)	Genetically Modified Organism	Risk Study before releasing into the market a GMO	• After the authorization for experimentation and releasing, the interested party must afford authority's periodic inspections.

Bibliography

1. Bertonatti, Claudio. *Invasiones Biológicas en la Argentina: Una Amenaza Para las Especies Autóctonas*. Resumen de la Exposición Presentada el 29/10/98 en el Ciclo de Charlas 1998 de la Fundación Vida Silvestre Argentina.
2. *Document on National Strategy of Biological Diversity*. Federal Government, UICN, INTA APN, GEF, PNUD-FEM, Buenos Aires, 1998.
3. Estrada Oyuela, Raúl A. y Zeballos de Sisto, María Cristina. *Digestos de Derecho Internacional, Evolución Reciente del Derecho Ambiental Internacional*. A-Z Editora S.A., Buenos Aires, 1993.
4. Glowka, Lyle. *Non-Indigenous Species Introductions: References in International Instruments, A Chart Distributed for Comments at the Norway/United Nations Conference on Alien Species*. Trondheim, July 1, 1996. IUCN Environmental Law Centre.
5. Plater, Adams. *Environmental Law and Policy, Nature, Law, and Society*. Corporation, St. Paul, Minnesota, 1992.
6. Sabsay D.–Onaindia, José. *La Constitución de los Porteños*. Editorial Errepar. Buenos Aires, 1997.
7. Sands, Philippe. *Principles of International Environmental Law. Volume I. Frameworks, Standards and Implementation*. Manchester University Press, Manchester, 1995.
8. Documents of the website of the SAyDS.
9. Documents of the website of the SAGPyA.

Chapter 3 Endnotes

1. Maria E. Di Paola is the Director of Research and Training for FARN. She is a member of the Environmental Law Commission of the IUCN. She received her LL.M. in environmental law from Pace University School of Law, and a specialist in natural resources legal regime from the University of Buenos Aires. She is an attorney at law and received her law degree from the University of Buenos Aires. She can be contacted at medipaola@farn.org.ar.

   The present chapter is based on the report *Invasive Alien Species: Argentina Country Report*, which the authors, in conjunction with Fundación Ambiente y Recursos Naturales (FARN), wrote for the Workshop on the Legal and Institutional Dimensions of Invasive Alien Species-World Conservation Union (IUCN) in 1999, and it was updated with the collaboration of María E. Alonso, Assistant of FARN Research and Training Area.

2. Diego Kravetz is an attorney at law, a specialist in environmental law, an Assistant Professor at the University of Buenos Aires, and a member of FARN. He can be contacted at diegokravetz@hotmail.com.

   Warmest thanks are due to the following people: María Inés Nicolini, María Pía Franchi, Diego Santamaría, Fernando Kravetz, Gustavo Gonzalez Acosta, Mariano Jagger, Daniel Forselli, Daniel Ryan, Daniel Sabsay, Javier García Fernandez, Juan Rodrigo Walsh, Victoria Lichtschein, and the FARN Information Center Staff: Julia Otamendi and Patricia Aizerstein.

3. 31 I.L.M. 818 (1992).

4. Resolution Secretaría de Ambiente y Desarrollo Sustentable (SAyDS) 91/2003 (B.O. 02/24/03). With the signing of the CBD, the issue of invasive species has acquired singular institutional importance in Argentina. The NSB was prepared by the federal government, in conjunction with the Argentine Committee, which included members of the IUCN. The project received financial support from the Global Facility for the Environment. The NSB aims to implement the CBD appropriately throughout the country. Thus, development of the strategy involved a number of different participants, including the public and private sectors as well as local communities. The design of the NSB was carried out first at the regional level and then at the national level.

5. *See* Ministerio de Desarrollo Social y Medio Ambiente, Secretaría de Desarrollo Sustentable y Política Ambiental, Argentine Country Report to the Secretariat of the Convention of Biological Diversity: Segundo Informe Nacional a las Partes (2001), *available at* http://www.medioambiente. gov.ar/documentos/acuerdos/convenciones/cdb/2infnac_partes_CDB.pdf (last visited Feb. 28, 2003); Informe de Especies Acuáticas (2001), *available at* http:// www.medioambiente.gov.ar/documentos/acuerdos/convenciones/cdb/TEMespexot infnac_partes_CDB.pdf.

6. Categories include fauna, aquatic organisms, genetically modified organisms, etc. *See* Appendix 1.

7. For example, if the federal government wants to combat an invasive species in provincial territory, it must request prior permission from the affected province to carry out the procedure.

8. With the settlers came their plagues. Bovine, ovine, and equine livestock; wheat; dogs; cats; hens; domestic geese; ducks; and doves, as well as other domestic or "useful" animals were accompanied by ticks, lice, fleas, the black rat, the Norwegian rat (and *rodent ectoparasites*, including the transmitters of the bubonic pest), and domestic cockroaches, as well as other coleopterans that arrived in the wood of furniture or other objects.

9. Domingo F. Sarmiento, President of Argentina, 1868-1874.

10. In 1888, laws referring to cattle imports and quarantine already existed. For example, Law 2,268 forbids importing cattle affected by contagious diseases or any reproducing animal with inherited organic malfunctions. It also establishes import requirements like a mandatory veterinary examination. Law 4,863, which was passed in 1905, establishes agricultural requirements that extend throughout the territory and attempt to guard against parasitic or harmful animal or vegetable invasions. This law takes effect whenever any organism becomes a pest, due to spreading, invasive, or disastrous characteristics, or mere presence in a province or territory from which it may affect agricultural products.

11. In December 2002, the First National Native Forest Inventory was presented by the Federal Environmental Authority (it is an ongoing project). In addition, the Secretary of Agriculture, Livestock, Fishing, and Food (SAGPyA) implemented in 1997 an inventory of implanted forest and published a completed inventory at *Forestacion, at* http://www.sagpya.mecon.gov.ar/0-0/index/forestacion/index_forestacion.htm (last visited Feb. 28, 2003).

    In addition, there is a project initiated in 2002 by the academia called the "Inter-American Invasives Information Network," developed by Universidad del Sur, Bahía Blanca, province of Buenos Aires, and financed by the U.S. Geological Survey and the U.S. Department of State. *See Inter-American Biodiversity Information Network, at* http://www.uns.edu.ar/inbiar/i3n.htm (last visited Feb. 28, 2003).

12. NATIONAL CONSTITUTION §41.

13. Argentina has a federal system, under which the provinces retain the power that has not been delegated to the nation. NATIONAL CONSTITUTION §§1, 5, and 121. In accordance with National Constitution §124, natural resources' domain belongs to the provinces.

14. *See* NATIONAL CONSTITUTION §75. In the same section, the National Constitution acknowledges the ethnic and cultural preexistence of Argentine indigenous peoples. It attributes to the Congress the power to assure, concurrently with the provinces, indigenous participation in the administration of the natural resources and other interests that may affect them.

15. *See* NATIONAL CONSTITUTION §41.

16. The Municipalities are autonomous entities, and are therefore empowered to issue their own regulations with "range and content in the institutional, political, administrative, economic, and financial order" that the provincial government establishes. NATIONAL CONSTITUTION §123. According to National Constitution §129, the city of Buenos Aires is an autonomous administration. This autonomy is in transition, which implies the coexistence of national and local powers in the same city.

17. The cases of the European starling, the crested myna, the Wakame seaweed, and the beaver that we consider below, provide several examples of the impact of jurisdictional complexity on the problems of managing invasive alien species.

18. *See* The General Environmental Law 25.675 (B.O. 11-21-2002).

19. 27 U.S.T. 1987, T.I.A.S. No. 8249, 993 U.N.T.S. 243 (1973). Besides the CBD and CITES, Argentina has entered into the following international conventions that are directly or indirectly related to sustainable use of biological diversity and invasive species: International Convention to Prevent Pollution Caused by Ships MARPOL 73/78; Convention on Wetlands of International Importance, Especially as Waterfowl Habitat, Ramsar, Iran (1971); United Nations Convention to Fight Against Desertification, Paris, France (1994); Convention on the Conservation of the Migratory Species of Wild Animals, Bonn, Germany (1979); Convention on the Protection of Natural and Cultural Patrimony, Paris, France (1972); United Nations Convention on the Law of

84

the Sea, Montego Bay, Jamaica (1992); Decision No. 6/96 of the Mercosur CMC, that approves the World Trade Organization Agreement on the Application of Sanitary and Phytosanitary Measures, Marrakesh (1994); International Plant Protection Convention, Rome, Italy (1951); and the Antarctica International Documents: Antarctic Treaty, Protocol to the Antarctic Treaty on Environmental Protection, Convention on the Conservation of Antarctic Marine Living Resources, Canberra, Australia, Apr. 7, 1982, T.I.A.S. 10240; Convention on the Conservation of Antarctic Seal, London (1972).

20. Rio Declaration on Environment and Development, U.N. Conference on Environment and Development, U.N. Doc. A/CONF.151/5/Rev. 1, 31 I.L.M. 874 (1992).

21. Soft Law and Technical Guidance: Rio Declaration on Environment and Development. Agenda 21; IMO Resolutions A.774/A. 686: Those resolutions have been introduced in the national legislation by the Bylaw (Ordenanza) No. 7/1998 of the Argentinean Coast Guard (Prefectura Naval Argentina- Dirección de Protección del Medio Ambiente).

22. *See* Appendix 1.

23. Ratified by Law No. 24.375, 9/7/1994.

24. *See* Appendix 1: Sanitary Control for Animals, Plants, and Pests.

25. *See* Appendix 1: Wild Fauna.

26. The wild fauna protection and conservation law is regulated by Decree 666/97, which establishes the following requirements for the importation of live wild animals:

    a. A Certificate issued by the official administrative authority responsible for wild fauna in the country of export;

    b. A dispatch, corresponding to the Federal Administration of Customs without detriment to the sanitary authority requirements; and

    c. The import permit foreseen by CITES, if necessary.

Importation will always be denied in the following instances:

    1. In the case of species that are included in Appendix I of CITES, unless they are considered in the exceptions of the Convention;

    2. In the case of species, not included under the previous point, but protected in the entire region of their natural habitat. This section states that "it is equally forbidden to introduce external products and by-products, manufactured or not, of those species of the indigenous wild fauna whose hunting, trade, possession and transformation are forbidden in the whole region of their natural habitat without previous permission of the national Enforcement Authority," *see* Section 7 Law 22.421;

    3. In the case of organisms that are live specimens of harmful or detrimental species;

    4. In the case of live animals, spoils, their products, by-products or derived products, that could somehow be harmful to commercial, agricultural activities, or that are prohibited by other competent national organizations; and

    5. In the case of live specimens, semen, embryos, eggs, larvae, etc. of species that can alter the biological balance or affect economic activities according to that foreseen in section 5 of the Law.

    This list does not exclude the denial of imports for other causes derived from the application of the CITES Convention. These regulations are complemented by Resolution SRNyDS No. 376/97, which regulates the introduction into the country of specimens of new exotic species.

27. An environmental impact assessment (EIA) for the introduction of a new exotic species requires the following:

a. Objectives and justification of the project;

b. Description of the work or project and the different alternatives to consider, which must include at least the following: site or location, nature of the project, abandonment of the project, no project; any feasibility plan must include a previous, compulsory experimental phase with a duration of at least one year;

c. The influenced area and a description of the environment, which will contain the following information: geographic location, environmental details, topography and natural barriers, type of soil, water-bodies and drainage network, vegetation, fauna, jeopardised species, soil use (map), productive systems, and road networks, as well as rural, urban, industrial, and tourist areas. If this information is incomplete, the interested parties must generate it. For species imported as pets, the enforcement authority will ask for specific parts of this information to be determined on a case-by-case basis;

d. A potential impacts assessment that includes the following aspects: loss or change in biodiversity, human zoonosis problems, economic and productive risks, genetic pollution, animal or plant sanitation risks, and pests. Impacts should be classified according to their characteristics: impact magnitude, duration or persistence, sign, reversibility;

e. Impact prevention, mitigation and neutralisation measures that must, at least, foresee the following: safety measures, sanitation measures, and harm mitigation measures;

f. An environmental vigilance plan designed to guarantee the fulfilment of corrective measures. The responsible import party also has to propose and finance a regular monitoring plan for the early detection of accidental environmental escapes; and

g. A contingency plan that takes into account possible faults in the impact prediction process.

These studies cannot exceed 50 pages and must be presented in terms that are easily understandable. Furthermore, during the five days following the presentation of the impact study, the Department of Wild Flora and Fauna will form an ad-hoc Assessing Committee to review and revise the study. This committee, made up of five prestigious members with expertise in the study of the particular species, must then present an environmental impact statement to the authority within a 30-day term.

28. *See* Appendix 1.

29. *Id.*

30. *See* Resolution No. 987/97 SALFF. The import application form for aquatic organisms requests the following information:

(a) The affiliation of the corresponding person or society, duly registered in the competent organism, that intends to carry out the introduction;

(b) Registration in national fiscal and social security organizations;

(c) A photocopy of the social contract, name, last name, number, type of document, and evidence of the legal representative;

(d) Common scientific name/s;

(e) References about source and origin of the import;

(f) Approximate date of the import; and

(g) Provincial authorization of introduction issued by a competent authority.

The aquatic hatchery registration, on the other hand, requests detailed references about the possible environmental impact that the species may cause.

31. In an EIA previous to forestation of native or exotic species, the interested party must present a report that includes the following information: the potential positive and negative environmental effects the project may cause, the mitigating measures of detrimental impacts, and a plan for a vigilance and environmental control during the performance and useful life of the project.

32. *See* Appendix 1: GMOs.

33. *Id.*

34. The SAyDS is a branch of the Ministry of Social Development of the federal government. *See* Decrees 1300/02, 2213/02 & 2742/02.

35. The legal framework classifies forests in five types: (a) protecting; (b) permanent; (c) experimental; (d) special woods; and (e) forests for production. The experimental forest is most closely related to the topic of invasive species. According to §8 of Decree 710/95, experimental forests are: (a) those intended for forestry research on indigenous species; and (b) artificial forests assigned to accommodation, acclimatization, and naturalization of indigenous or exogenous species. To the present date, this section has not been regulated.

36. Law 25.080.

37. *See* Appendix 1. Resolution 987/97 regulates production of living organisms, whether indigenous or exotic. This resolution defines an aquatic production facility as any setting within a limited geographical area where aquatic organisms for re-population of aquatic environments, sport fishing, or other projects, are cultivated, grown, or maintained. Accordingly, this definition encompasses production carried out at aquatic systems, in cage systems, enclosures, torches, long-lines, rafts, or other existing or later developed methodologies and that involve total or partial exploitation under human control.

38. *See* Food Code Law No. 18.284/69.

39. As pointed out in Appendix 1, diverse resolutions of the SAGPyA refer to the risk study that should be carried out before the enforcement authority releases a GMO or microorganism into the market. According to the CONABIA, a negative precedent exists regarding a large-scale release of rapeseed (*Colza o canola*). It is important to acknowledge that the authority had granted the release of rapeseed into the market for small-scale projects before.

40. Resolution Administración de Parques Nacionales, Secretaría de Turismo y Deportes de la Nación 16/94. *See* Appendix 1.

41. Resolution No. 974/98 SAyDS B.O 27/11/98.

42. *See* PREVENTION AND CONTROL OF EXOTIC AND INVASIVE SPECIES ch. VIII (2002), *available at* http://www.medioambiente.gov.ar/mlegal/biodiversidad/res91_03.htm (last visited Apr. 2, 2003).

43. *See* Annex I "Decisions adopted by the Conference of the Parties to the Convention on Biological Diversity at Its Sixth Meeting," Hague, 7-19 Apr. 7, 2002, *available at* http://www.biodiv.org/doc/decisions/cop-06-dec-en.pdf (last visited Apr. 2, 2003).

CHAPTER 4:
INVASIVE NON-NATIVE SPECIES IN GERMANY: BIOLOGICAL, LEGAL, AND INSTITUTIONAL DIMENSIONS

by Ingo Kowarik[1] and Lothar Guendling[2]

In Germany, the issues of invasive alien species are addressed in both federal and state (Laender) legislation. The Federal Nature Conservation Act requires a permit for the release or installation of alien animal or plant species. Similar provisions are included in Laender Nature Conservation Acts, which implement the Federal Nature Conservation Act at the Laender level. Administrative responsibilities for nature conservation rest with the Laender authorities. Generally, intermediate (regional) authorities issue licenses, while lower (local) authorities are responsible for control.

Biological invasions are a prominent issue in both public and scientific debates in Germany.[3] The Federal Nature Conservation Act does provide legal measures to prevent the release of alien species, but if non-native species are already established, the act includes them in the general scope of conserving the historically evolved biological diversity. This is somewhat confusing, as the term "indigenous" (*heimisch*) includes both native and established non-native species, while the term "alien species" is not defined at all.

German nature conservation law does not explicitly regulate the monitoring, control, or eradication of invasive alien species, but there are some general control and enforcement mechanisms, including the duty to provide information and the rights of authorities to enter premises,[4] that do apply. Still, the lack of specific regimes to monitor, control, or eradicate invasive species indicates serious gaps in German legislation. Issues of migration, accidental (nonintentional) release, and liability for damages resulting from the introduction of alien species are not addressed either. All of these gaps are further emphasized when German legislation is assessed in light of Germany's commitments to international agreements.

Problems also exist with regard to agriculture and forestry, because regulations addressing alien species do not apply to them. Furthermore, laws and regulations concerning the control of invasive alien species are applicable only to open areas; residential areas, gardens, and parks are not included. Release of genetically modified organisms (GMOs) is regulated by the Federal Genetic Engineering Act, which implements relevant directives of the European Union (EU). Sectoral legislation, particularly that concerned with hunting and fishing, also requires a license for the release of alien species, but no comprehensive regimes are established. This reflects the general assumption that the problem of alien species is an issue under control in Germany.

THE BIOLOGICAL PERSPECTIVE

Non-Native Species in the German Flora and Vegetation

Unlike other parts of the world, most central European landscapes have been strongly influenced by humans since the neolithic period. For several thousand years, this process coincided with both deliberate and unintentional introductions of non-native plant and animal species, whether in the context of early migrations, trade, or the evolution of agricultural practices. An estimated total of some 12,000 plant species have been brought to central Europe either by humans or with indirect human help. Though there is remarkable regional variation, invasions have led to an increase in species diversity, as demonstrated by the floral changes in one area of northern Germany, which are shown in Figure 1.[5] This process, which started about 3200 B.C., accelerated with industrialization and the globalization of trade that began in the 19th century.[6] In many central European countries, the introduction and establishment of non-native species have been documented in detail since the mid-19th century.[7] In addition, the use of archeobotanical methods has helped elucidate the history of early arrivals. This wealth of floristic data provides a basis to assess the number of new plant species recently introduced, as well as the dynamics and success of their dispersal.

Because of the impoverished flora and fauna in post-glacial Europe, the number of new species introduced by humans was relatively high compared to North America or to tropical and subtropical regions. Table 1 illustrates the role of non-native species in the German flora. A total of 22.4% of the present flora consists of established non-native species, among them 275 species established before 1500 A.D., and 412 established after. This gain of 687 species significantly exceeds the loss of 47 extinct species.[8]

There is also abundant information about invasions of terrestrial, freshwater, and marine ecosystems by non-native animal species.[9] The primary vectors of animal invasions include voluntary releases, mainly of mammals, birds, amphibians, and fish; deliberate introductions through imported goods or ballast water; and canals, which link otherwise isolated river systems. Currently, 1,123 non-native animal species were reported, making up roughly 2.4% of the German fauna.[10] Of these 1,123 species, 262 are permanently established in Germany.[11]

Figure 1: Development of Species Richness in Mecklenburg Under the Influence of Biological Invasion (changed from Fukarek 1988)

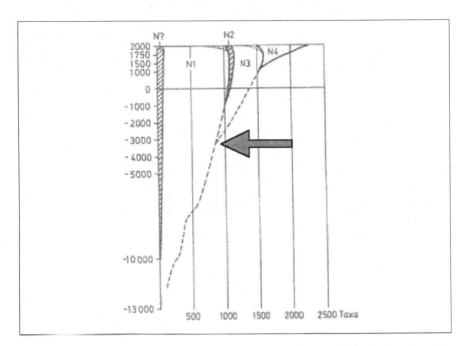

Note: Mecklenburg is located in Northeast Germany under the influence of biological invasions. The arrow marks the start.of biological invasions (ca. 3200 A.D.). N1 are native species; N2 to N4 are non-native species, including species established in natural vegetation (N2), species established in anthropogenic vegetation (N3), and casuals (N4); N? are undifferentiated species; and the dotted lines indicate the decline of established species.

Table 1: Role of Non-Native Plant Species in the German Flora[12]

	Number of Plant Species	%
(a) Flora of Germany	**3,062**	**100%**
• native species	2375	77.6%
• non-native species	687	22.4%
▸ established before 1500 A.D. (archeophytes)	275	9.0%
▸ established after 1500 A.D. (neophytes)	412	13.4%
• extinct species	47	1.5%
(b) Established non-native species	**687**	**100%**
• established in natural/near natural vegetation	277	40.3%
• subject to specific control (without agricultural weeds)	30	4.4%
(c) Assumed number of introductions	**12**	**100%**
• established non-native species	687	5.7%
• established in natural/near natural vegetation	277	2.3%
• subject to specific control	30	0.3%

Non-native plant species have invaded, with varying abundance, almost every type of ecosystem in Germany. A high level of both human and natural disturbance enhances a species' successful establishment. Thus, a large proportion of non-native species is typical of agricultural and urban-industrial ecosystems. For example, analysis of the Berlin region shows that almost one-half—49.8%—of the local flora in downtown Berlin consists of alien species. This percentage decreases with distance from the city center, to about one-fifth—20.7%—in the region of the Spreewald Forest.[13] Floodplain vegetation, an example of naturally disturbed vegetation, is also rich in alien species. But relatively undisturbed natural types of vegetation such as forests and wetlands are, in contrast, generally characterized by a predominance of native species, though individual alien species may occur under natural conditions. *Impatiens parviflora* from central Asia is the most abundant non-native herb in central European forests,[14] and the North American black cherry (*Prunus serotina*) may cause severe impacts in Pine and Larch plantations.[15] In total, 40.3% of the established non-native species are able to invade natural vegetation.[16] The frequency and abundance of most of these species is, however, higher in the anthropogenic vegetation.

Assessing Plant Invasions: The Need for Differentiation

The impacts of non-native plant species differ in the pathways of their establishment. Roughly, three overlapping cases can be differentiated: (1) establishment by integrating into existing communities; (2) establishment by forming new communities that result from the colonization of new anthropogenic sites; and (3) establishment by out-competing a significant part of the existing vegetation to form a new community.

In Germany, the first case, that of integration, tends to be tolerated. The second, colonization, is often recognized as a beneficial response to human induced environmental changes. This holds also for non-native species that perform as invasives on urban-industrial or other sites that have been strongly altered by humans. Thus, invasive alien species are not generally equated with problematic alien species, mainly due to the beneficial role they may have on man-made sites. The establishment of older immigrants is generally appreciated as an enrichment of the flora.

Red Data Books often do not distinguish between native and alien species that were introduced before 1500 A.D. (archeophytes). Recently, though, neophytes have been included in the Red Data Books if they comply with two conditions: their populations must be declining, and the species had to have been permanently established before the decline started. Following this approach, which resulted from a controversial debate about how to assess non-native species in nature conservation, native and non-native species are now treated equally in Red Data Books.[17]

This attitude is in accordance with the Federal Nature Conservation Act, which in §10(2) (No. 5) equates established non-native species with native species by using the German term *heimisch*, or indigenous, for both. The targets of

92

the general conservation of species, whether established non-native or native species, are all indirectly defined as *heimisch* plant and animal species. This reflects the long history of human impact on flora, fauna, and habitat conditions in Germany. But while the use of *heimisch* in the Federal Nature Conservation Act is clear in theory, it nevertheless causes much terminological confusion in practice, due to its similarity to the term *einheimisch*, which is used exclusively to refer to native species. The difference in meaning is subtle, with *heimisch* meaning indigenous in the sense of to settle down or to become established, while *einheimisch* means indigenous in the sense of endemic or homegrown. Despite these important differences in meaning, these terms are often perceived as synonyms, and this leads to confusion about the general goals of the law with respect to the treatment of native and non-native species.

The general acceptance of non-native species, which is expressed by the definition in Federal Nature Conservation Act §10(2) (No. 5), holds also for those species that form new communities by out-competing a significant part of the existing vegetation. But non-native species belonging to this group may, however, cause severe ecological impacts that are often also of high economic relevance.[18]

The following species may cause far-reaching changes in abundance patterns, species composition, and ecosystem functions: *Campylopus introflexus* and *Rosa rugosa* in coastal dunes, *Spartina x townsendii* in the Wadden Sea, *Heracleum mantegazzianum*, *Impatiens glandulifera*, *Fallopia japonica*, *F. sachalinensis*, *F. x bohemica*, *Solidago canadensis*, *S. gigantea* and *Helianthus tuberosus* in river banks and floodplains, *Elodea canadensis* and *E. nuttallii* in still and flowing waters, *Solidago canadensis*, *S. gigantea*, *Heracleum mantegazzianum*, *Lupinus polyphyllus*, *Bunias orientalis*, *Robinia pseudoacacia*, *Prunus serotina* and *Pinus nigra* in dry or wet grassland, *Vaccinium corymbosum* x *angustifolium* and *Prunus serotina* in wetlands, *Acer negundo*, *Populus* x *euramericana* and *Solidago gigantea* in floodplain forests, *Prunus serotina*, *Robinia pseudoacacia*, *Pseudotsuga menziesii*, *Pinus strobus* and *Quercus rubra* in other forest types, and *Pinus strobus*, *Pseudotsuga menziesii* and *Quercus rubra* on rocky outcrops. In addition, some 20 non-native species are controlled specifically by herbicides in agricultural systems.

Taking into account those species that are specifically subject to control, about 30 non-native species (not including non-native agricultural weeds) can be listed.[19] As Table 1 shows, these problematic species represent only a small percentage—0.3%—of total introduced species and less than 5%—4.4%—of the group of established non-native species. This small group of problematic non-native species, however, has been the main source of conflict in an emotionally charged public debate during recent years. A characteristic feature of this debate has been a lack of differentiation. Many authors argue simply *pro* or *contra* alien species, failing to acknowledge the various performances of non-native species already roughly delineated in the above named three groups of cases and in the numbers presented in Table 1. The number of nonharmful alien species, including many with beneficial effects, far exceeds that of noxious non-native species.

On the other hand, the small group of problematic alien species does cause far-reaching problems, as a 1998 inquiry has revealed.[20] Asked to what extent they are faced with problems caused by plant invasions, a majority—72%—of local authorities in northern Germany (nature conservation, forestry, water management, coastal protection, and urban green) confirmed extensive invasion problems in their area of responsibility—80% in forestry, 88% in nature conservation. More than one-quarter—27%—of 592 specified cases of invasion were related to economic conflicts, 6% to health problems (mostly ascribed to *Heracleum mantegazzianum*), and the rest to conservation conflicts in a broad sense. The conflicts were ascribed to a total of 31 species. More than 80% of the reports concerned nine taxa.[21] The impacts of single species out of the group of about 30 problem species vary regionally in Germany.[22]

There is no commonly accepted rule about how to define a problematic non-native (or native) species in Germany. But the extreme variation in the performance of non-native species nevertheless presents the task of differentiating between harmful and nonharmful non-native species.

How to Respond to Problematic Invasions

Most strategies to avoid negative invasion impacts have two components: regulation of the first introduction of a species and control of the unwanted species in a later stage of the invasion process. The latter is usually of poor success, as the results of a 1998 inquiry in northern Germany show.[23] One-half of all invasion events—49%—that have been assessed as problematic were subject to control, but in only 23% of these controlled events were the measures described as successful. This poor success rate was due to one or more of the following: the application of unsuitable methods, inaccurate performance, or the temporal and spatial limitations of control. In consequence, priority should be given to prevention.

Rigorous risk assessments preceding the first introductions of non-native species are necessary, but not sufficient. Most of the problematic invasive species were introduced to central Europe more than 100 years ago. Studying the invasion process over longer periods of time has revealed a surprisingly high lag phase between the first introduction and the outbreak of subsequent invasions. For example, in Brandenburg, a part of eastern Germany, lag phases have been reconstructed for 184 non-native woody species. On average, invasions started 147 years after the first introduction (170 years for trees, 131 for shrubs).[24] Thus, with the large number—approximately 3,100—of non-native woody species that were most likely introduced into Germany, coupled with the inherent unknowns and inadequacies of predictions, including the time lag between introduction and invasion, it would have been virtually impossible not only to predict the invasions of these many species, but also, and more importantly, to prevent negative invasion impacts by regulating their first introductions.

While regulating imports is important, e.g., to prevent non-native species dispersed by ballast water or introduced through crops and other goods, measures that restrict secondary transfers or releases within the borders of Germany have to be enforced as well. The Federal Nature Conservation Act, in §41(2), does require a permit for the release or installation into the wild of non-native animal or plant species. But this legal instrument is rarely used in practice. Besides a lack of public awareness of the threats posed by the release of non-native species, there is also, in fact, no established method to implement the permit provisions included in the Federal Nature Conservation Act. However, a code of practice will be proposed in 2003. The Federal Environmental Agency, in a survey of state (Laender) licensing practices and administrative controls, found that only a few applications for licenses were filed, mostly to support research purposes. The majority of reported cases that involved administrative controls concerned animals already installed in the wild, escaped into the wild, or released into the wild, mainly fish, turtle, or bird species. The practice of authorities was characterized as being restrictive, sometimes involving conflicts. No court cases were reported. The administrative reactions, in a few cases, did consist of cleanup orders, but authorities tended to react to the majority of cases simply by providing information about the risks of alien species with the hope of preventing future releases.[25]

An inquiry in Niedersachsen revealed that 75% of the problematic populations of non-native plant species were established directly by human actions like planting, seeding, and distributing garden waste or soil depositions.[26] Thus, only one-quarter of the problematic cases that were studied resulted from "classic" invasion processes.[27] These results stress the necessity to regulate secondary transfers and unlicensed releases of non-native species—and to enhance the implementation and improvement of the existing legal instruments.

A number of German case studies have indicated that invasions by non-native plant and animal species, as well as microorganisms, may lead to far-reaching ecological, evolutionary, and economic consequences. Some pathways and impacts of invasions are well known, while others still need more research. Most non-native species, however, are not harmful. Thus, differentiation is necessary. Because of the general failure of eradication programs, priority should be given to prevention. This holds for both first introductions and secondary releases within Germany. A 1998 conference in Berlin recommended the following steps:

> (1) An inventory of alien species, including an assessment of the ecological, economic, and sanitary consequences of their dispersal;
> (2) The implementation of a monitoring program targeted at alien organisms in terrestrial, freshwater, and marine ecosystems;
> (3) The development of methods of risk assessment;
> (4) An examination of legal regulations regarding alien organisms; and
> (5) The development of adequate measures and action plans both to reduce the spread of alien organisms and to encourage the exchange of information.

Furthermore, there is a need for additional research into the ecosystemic integration of alien species. Besides taxonomic investigations, identifications, and surveys to monitor alien organisms, particularly microorganisms, which have been neglected until now, research should also explore competition and other interactions between native and non-native organisms, as well as the integration of alien organisms into food webs, and the modification of habitat structures, and its consequences.[28]

LEGAL AND INSTITUTIONAL DIMENSIONS

Institutional, Administrative, and Legal Framework Relevant to Invasive Species

Control of alien species in Germany is regulated by a variety of legal instruments, including nature conservation legislation and sectoral legislation on forestry, hunting, and fishing.[29] There are also laws and regulations that only indirectly concern the control of alien species, such as plant protection legislation, animal disease control legislation, and animal protection legislation. These laws establish their own rules, procedures, and institutional responsibilities, which may lead to major coordination problems, possibly exacerbated by the federal structure of Germany.

Nature conservation in Germany is addressed in both federal and state (Laender) law. The German Federation has enacted the Federal Nature Conservation Act, which is a framework law that is implemented by individual Laender Nature Conservation Acts. The Federal Nature Conservation Act regulates the control of alien species in §41(2) as follows:

> Alien animal and plant species may be released or installed in the natural environment only with the permission of the authority responsible under Laender law. This does not apply to the cultivation of plants in agriculture and forestry. The permission shall be denied if the risk of contamination ("Verfälschung") of the animal and plant world ("Tier- und Pflanzenwelt") or risks for the stocks and the occurrence of wild living animal and plants species or for populations of such species cannot be ruled out.[30]

According to the definition in Federal Nature Conservation Act §10(2) (No. 3), the term species includes "species, subspecies, or parts of populations of species or subspecies." By referring to the population level, the term species also includes the genetic variation within species.

Section 41(2) is included in Chapter 5 of the Act, which is entitled: "Protection and management of wild animal and plant species." It defines the terms and the scope of "species protection" regulated in Chapter 5 as follows:

- [T]he protection of animals and plants and their populations against impact by man, particularly through taking;
- the protection, management, development and restoration of biotopes of wild animal and plant species as well as ensuring their other conditions of life; [and]
- the installment of animals and plants of displaced wild species in appropriate biotopes within their natural areas of occurrence.[31]

Definitions are included in §10(2) of the Federal Nature Conservation Act, including the definition of the term "native species," which refers to any animal or plant species that has or previously had its area of occurrence or regular migration in Germany or that is spreading in Germany by natural means. As mentioned above, the definition also covers non-native animal and plant species that have reverted to the wild state or have become naturalized by human influence and have maintained populations in the natural environment for several generations without human support.

The Laender authorities have institutional responsibility for administering alien species legislation as laid down in the Federal Nature Conservation Act. Power to issue licenses is in some of the Laender given to the ministries of environment—as in Thuringia and Hessen—or to the intermediate level of government (regional level). Powers to control and enforce are vested in the lower level of government at the district and municipal levels.

Other, more specific sectoral laws and regulations apply in addition to the Nature Conservation Acts of the Federation and the Laender, e.g., Hunting Acts, Fishery Acts, and Forest Acts. Hunting and Fishing Acts not only usually require licenses for releases of species into the wild, but also normally provide lists of species that may be released. Where hunting or fishing laws do not require licenses for release of species, the requirements of nature conservation legislation apply. Competent authorities are the Laender hunting and fishing authorities. While hunting and fishing laws provide control measures that aim not at conserving biodiversity but rather at protecting those animals that may be harvested, these laws may nevertheless make a considerable contribution to conserving biodiversity.

The Forest Laws of the Federation and the Laender do not explicitly regulate alien species, but general principles of public nuisance do apply. These public nuisance principles, which require that forests be managed to ensure that damages do not occur, include the prevention of damages to indigenous species. A specific provision, which may be relevant for forests, is included in §3(1) (No. 17) of the Federal Plant Protection Act. It empowers the Federal Minister for Food, Agriculture, and Forestry to regulate the marketing and use of animals, plants, or microorganisms to combat certain pests. Such regulation may require licenses for marketing and use of animals, plants or microorganisms.

Other laws and regulations, like the Federal Plant Protection Act, which is the German Pesticide Control Law, the Animal Diseases Control Act, and the Animal Protection Act, are not explicitly but indirectly relevant to the control of alien species. The conservation of nature is not the primary objective of these laws, but by protecting animals and plants against pests, they still serve the purpose of controlling alien species. The competent authority established by the Federal Plant Protection Act is the Federal Biological Agency, while the Animal Diseases Act and the Federal Animal Protection Act are both enforced by the competent Laender authorities.

For example, the Federal Plant Protection Act as amended in 1998 serves the following objectives: (1) the protection of plants, in particular cultivated plants, against pest organisms; (2) the protection of plant products against pests; (3) the prevention of risks from the use of pesticides; and (4) the implementation of EU legislation.[32] Plant protection must be carried out according to "good professional practice," which is defined as serving the health and quality of plants or plant products through preventive measures, including measures to prevent the introduction of pests.[33] Section 4 of the Act, which deals with the prevention of pest introduction, empowers the Federal Minister for Food, Agriculture, and Forestry to regulate the import of pests and products carrying pests. Regulations enacted by the Minister may require permits, notification tests, or documentation of tests. The Regulation on Plant Inspection was enacted on 10 May 1985.[34]

GMOs released into the natural environment fall under the Federal Genetic Engineering Act, which implements the two relevant EU directives.[35] Section 16 of the Act requires a license for deliberate release of GMOs into the natural environment. The power to issue the license lies with the Robert-Koch-Institute, which has to consult with the Federal Biological Research Center of Agriculture and Forestry, the Federal Environmental Agency, the Federal Institute of Virus Diseases of Animals, and the Central Commission on Biological Safety.

Overview of Germany's Environmental Legislation and Management System

Germany is a federation consisting of 16 states called Laender. Powers and responsibilities for policy and law making as well as law enforcement are shared between the Federation and the Laender. The local governments established at the district and municipality level develop, implement, and enforce policies and regulations within the framework provided by the constitution and the statutory law.

Legislative powers in Germany are shared between the Federation and the Laender according to a tripartite scheme of exclusive powers, concurring powers, and "framework powers" (powers to enact framework legislation). Exclusive federal powers exist in a limited number of areas such as customs, trade harmonization, shipping agreements, and external payments. In most areas, though, federal powers are concurring powers, meaning that the Federation may exercise these powers under certain requirements.[36] The exercise of concurring powers precludes the Laender from acting only to the extent that the Federation has exercised its authority, which implies that even if the Federation has exercised certain powers there may still be room for the Laender to act. Matters of concurring powers include private law, penal law, the court system, judicial procedure, economic law including mining, industry, energy production, commercial activities, internal trade, banks, the insurance system, nuclear energy production, agriculture, forestry, fisheries, coastal protection, land tenure, food security, plant and animal protection, placing on the market of seeds, shipping on the coastal and high seas, federal roads, federal rail roads, dumping of wastes, air pollution control, noise control, state liability, and genetic engineering.

The Federation has exercised its powers in most of the areas enumerated above, so federal laws and regulations do exist. But there are cases where federal laws and regulations do not exhaust the matter, and the Laender have, in turn, implemented their own regulations to complement and extend the federal rules. This practice sometimes gives rise to controversies, as the division between federal and Laender powers becomes blurred.

In several areas, including nature conservation, hunting, distribution of land, land use planning, and water resource management, the Federation exercises framework legislative powers, enacting a basic outline for regulation that the Laender then complement with additional specific legislation that follows and fleshes out the federal framework. The Federation does not enact detailed or set rules that are directly applicable in the Laender. In the areas mentioned above, the Federation has enacted framework laws like the Federal Nature Conservation Act that are then implemented in detail by laws in each of the 16 Laender.

Enforcement of environmental legislation, whether federal or Laender, is mainly the responsibility of the Laender, which in principle decide on the establishment of authorities and administrative procedures. Harmonization of administrative procedures is ensured either through procedural provisions in the federal laws and regulations themselves or by the Federal Administrative Procedure Act. Laender enforce most of the laws in their own jurisdiction, which means that control by federal authorities is limited to ensuring that laws are complied with (legal control only, no control in substantive and technical matters). In a few areas, Laender enforce the federal laws "on behalf of the Federation," thus giving federal authorities stricter legal and substantive control powers. This is the case, for example, with nuclear energy production and federal road administration. Federal authorities do exist to regulate the foreign service, federal finances, federal railroads, the federal postal service, and federal waterways and shipping.

An important aspect of German environmental policy and law is Germany's membership in the EU, which adopts environmental policy and law through either directives binding the Member states or regulations applicable directly in the Member states. The EU has adopted directives and (a limited number of) regulations in almost all areas of environmental law. For example, in the area of nature conservation, there are the 1979 Directive on the Protection of Birds and the 1992 Directive on the Conservation of Natural Habitats and of Wild Fauna and Flora. EU directives concerning genetic engineering have been mentioned already.[37]

Germany's federal constitution, which is called Basic Law, provides a particular legal guarantee to local governments vested in municipalities and districts. Local governments have the fundamental right to regulate in their own jurisdiction and within the framework of the law all matters of concern for the local community.[38] Therefore, local governments adopt and enforce local regulations, which may concern nature conservation wherever federal and Laender laws leave room for local government powers. In addition, local authorities in their respective areas of jurisdiction serve as enforcing agencies for federal and Laender legislation.

Environmental legislation in Germany may be characterized generally as follows: numerous laws and regulations following different regulatory approaches co-exist. Laws and regulations concerning ecosystems (nature conservation, forestry, fisheries, wildlife) and environmental media (air, water, soil) co-exist with laws and regulations concerning hazardous substances (chemicals, wastes, GMOs) and dangerous activities (nuclear energy production). A few laws and regulations concern general issues such as environmental impact assessment, environmental information or environmental auditing. The major problem today is harmonization of environmental legislation. For several decades, efforts have been made to prepare proposals for an environmental code, including a commission established by the federal government, which has submitted a draft presently under consideration. A formal proposal prepared by the federal government will be the next stage. In the draft Environmental Code (Umweltgesetzbuch), the commission proposed both a general section to regulate cross-cutting issues, as well as several specific sections to regulate major areas of environmental legislation such as nature conservation, air pollution, waste management, etc.

Finally, it should be noted that Germany's environmental policy and law are governed by "classical" principles like the polluter-pays principle, the precautionary principle, and the principle of coordination. The principle of coordination is understood in Germany as requiring all actors both in government and in the private sphere to cooperate in solving the problems of environmental management. The principle of cooperation, therefore, is the basis for public participation, including nongovernmental organizations and the private sector, in environmental decisionmaking.

INTERNATIONAL LEGAL AND INSTITUTIONAL APPROACHES/TOOLS

International Conventions Relating to Invasive Species

Germany has ratified most of the international conventions, whether global or regional, related to biodiversity, including the Convention on Biological Diversity (CBD),[39] the Convention on International Trade in Endangered Species (CITES),[40] the Convention on Migratory Species (CMS, Bonn Convention),[41] the Convention for the Conservation of European Wildlife and Natural Habitats (Bern Convention),[42] the Convention on the Protection of the Alps,[43] the Protocol on the Conservation of Nature and Landscape, and the United Nations (U.N.) Convention on the Law of the Sea (UNCLOS).[44] Germany is also not only a party to the 1980 Convention on the Conservation of Antarctic Marine Living Resource[45] and the 1991 Protocol to the Antarctic Treaty on Environment Protection, but also bound by the International Plant Protection Convention of 1951.[46] Germany is a Member of the International Maritime Organization (IMO), of the Council of Europe, of the International Council for the Exploration of the Sea (ICES), of the U.N. Food and Agricultural Organization (FAO), of the Organization for Economic Cooperation and Development (OECD), and of the World Conservation Union (IUCN), thereby making the recommendations, codes and measures adopted by these organizations relevant to Germany as well.

Germany, as a Member of the EU, is also bound by the relevant directives and regulations, namely the 1979 Directive on the Protection of Birds; the 1992 Directive on the Protection of the European Flora, Fauna, and Their Habitats; and the 1997 Regulation on the Protection of Wild Animal and Plant Species Through the Control of Trade. Furthermore, Germany is bound by EU directives that concern GMOs (see above), as well as the EU Directive on Plant Protection[47] and the Directive on Aquaculture Animals.[48]

Finally, Germany has subscribed to a number of "soft law" requirements, including Council of Europe recommendations on the introduction on non-native species into the national environment, on the prohibition of the introduction of the American cottontail, and on the reintroduction of species[49]; as well as IMO guidelines to prevent the introduction of undesirable organisms in ballast water or in sediments carried by ships[50] and an ICES 1973/1994 Code of Practice to reduce risks caused by the introduction of non-native marine species.

Measures Taken to Implement International Conventions and Legal Instruments

Existing legislation in Germany, in particular the Federal Nature Conservation Act and the Nature Conservation Acts of the Laender, covers most of the obligations and commitments required by the international conventions and legal instruments mentioned above. Some qualifications, however, may be noted. For example, while many of the commitments included in the CBD are basically fulfilled, Germany's nature conservation legislation still does not provide an explicit obligation to restore degraded ecosystems; consequently, it establishes no explicit obligation to remove alien invasive species where they damage indigenous ecosystems. This legislative gap also affects compliance with the Bonn Convention, which requires the control, curtailing, or removal of non-indigenous species if they threaten certain endangered species. According to the Bonn Convention, which only applies to animals, Germany may be required to establish an explicit regulation to remove alien invasive species under certain conditions.

Both the Bern Convention and the Protocol on the Conservation of Nature and Landscape under the Alps Convention are sometimes said not to be fully implemented in German legislation, in particular where they require the promotion of the reintroduction of indigenous species.[51] However, §39(1) of the Federal Nature Conservation Act defines the term "species protection" as including "the installment of animals and plants of displaced wild species in appropriate biotopes within their natural areas of occurrence." This provision does come close to an obligation to reintroduce indigenous species.

The Protocol under the Alps Convention may require further implementation with regard to the obligation to base the decision whether or not to reintroduce particular species on scientific knowledge. Such an obligation is not explicitly included in German nature conservation legislation at this time.

The Protocol is also interesting because it calls for a general prevention of the release of alien species and accepts releases only as a matter of exception. But

German law may be considered less restrictive than the Protocol. Furthermore, the Protocol requires that the release of alien species serve some specific purpose, which is also stricter than German law.

Germany has, for the most part, implemented EU legislation with regard to alien invasive species. Further implementation measures may, however, be necessary because of EU requirements for consultation with the European Commission, scientific assessments that include the experiences of other countries, and consultations with local and concerned people when releasing alien species or reintroducing indigenous species.

In March 1998, the German federal government submitted its National Report on "Biological Diversity," which was required under the CBD. The report does not address the issue of invasive alien species. At present, a National Biodiversity Strategy is being prepared. To what extent it will deal with the issue of invasive alien species is not yet clear.

National Laws and Institutions Addressing Introduction, Eradication, and Control of Invasive Species

German law governing alien invasive species does not provide specific objectives, but Federal Nature Conservation Act §41(2) does establish a permit requirement for the release and installation of alien species. This permit requirement and its specified criteria indirectly suggest the objective of protecting indigenous animal and plant species. Section 39(1) of the Federal Nature Conservation Act contains a definition of "species protection," which includes the conservation and management of animal and plant species in their natural and historically grown biodiversity, as well as the reinstallation of displaced indigenous species.

Section 41(2) of the Federal Nature Conservation Act requires a permit for the release and installation of alien species. The Federal Nature Conservation Act also includes the option to prohibit the possession or sale of animals and plants, which are qualified in a regulation by the Federal Ministry for the Environment, as dangerous to the animal and plant world or to other animal and plant species.[52] But specific regulation has not been developed yet, which may be considered a serious gap.

There are no provisions in German law for the eradication of alien invasive species. The Federal Law on Plant Protection, however, allows the Minister of Food, Agriculture, and Forestry to regulate the cultivation of certain plant species. The Minister's authority to prohibit or restrict cultivation may be applied to alien plant species, but specific regulation has yet to be developed.[53]

German law does not provide an explicit requirement for authorities to reintroduce indigenous species. While reintroduction is stated as an objective in the Federal Nature Conservation Act,[54] it is not complemented by a corresponding duty.

German law, both federal and Laender, fails to define "alien species." In the Federal Nature Conservation Act, "alien" seems to be understood as "alien to a region" or "non-local" (*gebietsfremd*). The term "indigenous" (*heimisch*), as discussed above, refers to animal and plant species which have or had in the past their area of distribution or regular migration wholly or partly in Germany or which spread by natural means into Germany.[55] A wild animal or plant species is also considered "indigenous" if animals or plants of this species have reverted to the wild state or have become naturalized by human influence and have maintained populations in the natural environment for several generations without human assistance.

The Federal Nature Conservation Act defines the term "animals" as including "wild, captive, or bred animals including those which have not escaped to the wild, as well as dead animals belonging to wild species and eggs, larvae, pupae, and other forms of animals belonging to wild species."[56] The Act also defines the term "plants" as including "wild, cultivated, and dead plants belonging to wild species and seeds, fruits and other forms of plants belonging to wild species."[57]

Interestingly, fungi, which are not plants or animals, and microorganisms are generally covered by the Federal Nature Conservation Act, though they are not explicitly mentioned. GMOs are regulated in a specific statute, the Genetic Engineering Act. The genetic variation below the species level (ecotypes, geographical races, provenances) is covered by the term "species" that includes "species, subspecies, or parts of populations of species or subspecies."[58]

The terms "release" and "installation"[59] are not defined in the Act at all. But in practice, there is a consensus that "release" refers to setting free without any control or management measure while "installation" means setting free with control or management measures. "Accidental/nonintentional introduction" is not defined (and not regulated) in the Act either. Nonintentional introduction may be qualified as "release," but the "release" provision,[60] which requires a permit and formal procedure, clearly cannot be applied to an unintentional action.

Basic Legal and Institutional Tools and Mechanisms That Address the Control, Monitoring, or Eradication of Invasive Alien Species

The permit required by the Federal Nature Conservation Act §41(2) for the release or installation of alien species is the basic mechanism of control in German. Similar provisions are also found in the Laender Nature Conservation Acts.[61] Legislation in several Laender, including Sachsen, Berlin (animals only), Bremen (animals only), Hamburg (animals only), and Schleswig-Holstein, also specifically prohibits certain alien (in the sense of non-local) species of animals and plants. For example, Thüringen not only prohibits, as a matter of principle, the release of alien (non-local) animals and plants, but also requires the monitoring of all alien species,[62] perhaps the only Laender to do so.

The requirements for issuing a permit are fairly strict. A permit must be denied if the risk of contamination of the animal and plant world flora and or risk to the stock or distribution of wild living animal and plant species "cannot be ruled out."[63] Thus, if there are any indications that such may occur, the permit must be refused. This is a consistent but rigorous application of the precautionary principle, placing a heavy burden on the applicant. The applicant must prove that there is no risk of contamination of the animal and plant world and no risk to the stocks and occurrence of wild living animal and plant species or the populations of such species. The provision also raises difficult questions of interpretation: What precisely is "contamination"? Any change of the respective ecosystem? Or major changes or damages? Furthermore, when can we speak of a risk to the stocks, occurrence, or populations of wild living species? There is certainly room for different interpretations. It is clear, though, from the wording of Federal Nature Conservation Act §41(2) that any release or installation of alien (in the sense of non-local) species requires a permit, and as a consequence, this would seem to apply to the release or installation of a displaced or extinct indigenous species of animal or plant.

The release of a GMO requires a permit under the Genetic Engineering Act. The Act allows the issuance of a license as long as there are no risks to human, animal, or plant health, or threats to the environment or private property. Furthermore, the operator must be reliable, and the project leader and the security expert must have the necessary competence.[64] The requirements for the license are comprehensive and strict, but if they are fulfilled, the license must be given; there is no discretion to refuse it.

Why Current Legal and Institutional Approaches Do and Do Not Work

Several major problems in Germany's approach to the threat of invasive species can be identified, including the following:

- Important terms are not clearly defined, in particular "contamination of the animal and plant world";
- The term "indigenous species" is clearly defined, but the wording leads to confusion;
- It is uncertain whether or not the definition of "species" includes genetic diversity within species, but consequences for the regulation of non-local provenances or geographical races of native species are still lacking;
- The implementation of the permit requirement mostly fails, for methodological reasons; and
- There is no duty to control invasive alien species.

Furthermore, the prevention and control systems are rudimentary, including the following, which are not covered:

- The regulation of accidental introductions and releases;
- The regulation of migrating alien species which may create risks to wild living species;
- The duty to monitor alien species; and
- The duty to control or eradicate alien invasive species if there are risks to wild living plants or animals.

CONCLUSIONS AND RECOMMENDATIONS

With regard to alien species, German law needs to be revised and adapted to international conventions to provide a comprehensive and consistent system of control. Of primary importance is to complement existing mechanisms that require permits for deliberate releases or installations only, with duties to monitor and eradicate alien species if they create serious risks to indigenous species of animals and plants.

The major terms need to be defined ("alien species," "contamination") or redefined ("indigenous species," "non-local species"). Objectives need to be clearly spelled out. The exceptions to the permit requirement (agriculture and forestry) need to be reconsidered. The introduction of new plants and animals that were never indigenous to Germany may be subject to stricter requirements. Accidental, unintentional introduction as well as introduction by negligence need to be addressed.

Chapter 4 Endnotes

1. Dr. Kowarik is a Professor at the Institute of Ecology at the Technical University of Berlin where he is the head of the Section of Ecosystem Science/Plant Ecology. He received his diploma in Landscape Planning from the Technical University of Berlin in 1982 and his Ph.D. from the Technical University of Berlin in 1988. He also completed a thesis in 1992 on invasion biology in Germany.

2. Dr. Lothar Guendling is an attorney at law in his own law firm, specializing in environmental law, nature conservation law, and natural resources law. He carries out environmental law consultancies in countries around the world, with a focus on supporting preparation of environmental and nature conservation legislation. Formally, he has been associated with the World Conservation Union (IUCN) Environmental Law Center (ELC) in Bonn, coordinating the legal assistance projects of the ELC. Before joining the ELC, Dr. Guendling was a fellow at the Max-Planck-Institute of Comparative Public Law and International Law in Heidelberg, Germany, responsible for research in international and comparative environmental law, European Union (EU) environmental policy, and the law of the sea. He is author of books and essays on international, comparative, and European environmental law, including publications on legal issues of biodiversity conservation and sustainable use.

3. Major magazines such as *Der Spiegel* and *Natur & Kosmos* published feature stories. DER SPIEGEL, Jan. 4, 1999; NATUR & KOSMOS, June 1999, at 44ss.

4. Federal Nature Conservation Act §50.

5. F. Fukarek et al., 16 GLEDITSCHIA 69-74 (1988).

6. E.J. Jäger, Möglichkeiten der Prognose synanthroper Pflanzenausbreitungen, 180 FLORA 101-131 (1988).

7. L. Trepl, *Research on the Anthropogenic Migration of Plants and Naturalization: Its History and Current State of Development*, in URBAN ECOLOGY, PLANTS, AND PLANT COMMUNITIES IN URBAN ENVIRONMENTS 75-97 (H. Sukopp et al. eds., 1990).

8. INGO KOWARIK, BIOLOGISCHE INVASIONEN. NEOPHYTEN UND NEOZOEN IN MITTELEUROPA. ULMER, STUTTGART (2003).

9. For an overview, see Gebietsfremde Tierarten. Umweltforschung in Baden-Württemberg., ecomed, Landsberg (H. Gebhardt et al. eds., 1996); Changes in Fauna and Flora as a Result of Watercourse Development—Neozoans and Neophytes–Texte 74/96 (Federal Environmental Agency ed. 1996); Exotic Invaders of the North Sea Shore—Helgoländer Meeresuntersuchungen 52: 217-400 (K. Reise ed., 1999); O. GEITER & R. KINZELBACH, STATUS AND ASSESSMENT OF NEOZOANS IN GERMANY. FEDERAL ENVIRONMENTAL AGENCY TEXTE 25/02 (2002).

10. GEITER & KINZELBACH, *supra* note 9.

11. *Id.*

12. KOWARIK, *supra* note 8.

13. Ingo Kowarik, *On the Role of Alien Species in Urban Flora and Vegetation*, in PLANT INVASIONS: GENERAL ASPECTS AND SPECIAL PROBLEMS 85-103 (P. Pysek et al. eds., 1995).

14. L. Trepl, Über *Impatiens parviflora* DC. als Agriophyt in Mitteleuropa., 73 DISS. BOT. 1-400 (1984).

15. U. Starfinger, *Introduction and Naturalization of* Prunus Serotina *in Central Europe*, in PLANT INVASIONS: STUDIES FROM NORTH AMERICA AND EUROPE 161-72 (J.H. Brock et al. eds., 1997); H. Schepker, Wahrnehmung, Ausbreitung und Bewertung von

Neophyten—Eine Analyse problematischer nichteinheimischer Pflanzenarten in Niedersachsen. ibidem-Verlag, Stuttgart 246 (1998).

16. *See* Table 1. *See also* W. Lohmeyer & H. Sukopp, *Agriophyten in der Vegetation Mitteleuropas*, 25 SCHRIFTENREIHE VEGETATIONSKDE 1-185 (1992).

17. Ingo Kowarik, Berücksichtigung von nichteinheimischen Pflanzenarten, von "Kulturflüchtlingen" sowie von Vorkommen auf Sekundärstandorten bei der Aufstellung "Roter Listen," 23 SCHRIFTENREIHE VEGETATIONSKDE 175-90 (1992); D. Korneck et al., *Rote Liste der Farn- und Blütenpflanzen* (Pteridophyta et Spermatophyta) *Deutschlands*, 28 SCHRIFTENREIHE VEGETATIONSKDE 21-187 (1998).

18. Ingo Kowarik, *Neophytes in Germany. Quantitative Overview, Introduction and Dispersal Pathways, Ecological Consequences, and Open Questions, in* ALIEN ORGANISMS IN GERMANY: DOCUMENTATION OF A CONFERENCE ON "LEGAL REGULATIONS CONCERNING ALIEN ORGANISMS IN COMPARISON TO GENETICALLY MODIFIED ORGANISMS" TEXTE (Federal Environmental Agency ed. 1999).

19. KOWARIK, *supra* note 12.

20. Ingo Kowarik & H. Schepker, *Plant Invasions in Northern Germany: Human Perception and Response, in* PLANT INVASIONS: ECOLOGICAL MECHANISMS AND HUMAN RESPONSES 109-20 (U. Starfinger et al. eds., 1998).

21. The nine taxa are: *Prunus serotina, Heracleum mantegazzianum, Fallopia* (including *Fallopia japonica, F. sachalinensis, F. bohemica*), *Impatiens glandulifera, Elodea* (including *E. canadensis, E. nuttalii*, and *Vaccinium corymbosum x angustifolium*).

22. For southern Germany, see E. Hartmann, H. Schuldes, R. Kübler & W. Konold. (1995): Neophyten. Biologie, Verbreitung und Kontrolle ausgewählter Arten. ecomed, Landsberg, 301 (1995); and Gebietsfremde Pflanzen. Auswirkungen auf einheimische Arten, Lebensgemeinschaften und Biotopie, Kontrollmöglichkeiten und Management. ecomed-Verlag, Landesberg 215 (R. Böcker, H. Gebhardt, W. Konold & S. Schmidt-Fischer eds. 1995).

23. Kowarik & Schepker, *supra* note 20.

24. Ingo Kowarik, *Time-lags, in Biological Invasions, in* PLANT INVASIONS: GENERAL ASPECTS AND SPECIAL PROBLEMS 15-38 (P. Pysek et al. eds., 1995).

25. U. Doyle et al., *Current Legal Status Regarding Release of Non-Native Plants and Animals in Germany, in* PLANT INVASIONS: ECOLOGICAL MECHANISMS AND HUMAN RESPONSE 71-83 (U. Starfinger et al. eds., 1998); *see also* Die Aussetzung gebietsfremder Organismen—Recht und Praxis Texte 20/99 (Federal Environmental Agency ed. 1999).

26. Schepker, *supra* note 15; Kowarik, *supra* note 18.

27. *Id.*

28. U. Doyle, *Alien Organisms in Germany: Results of a Conference at the Federal Environmental Agency in March, 1998, in* ALIEN ORGANISMS IN GERMANY texte 18/99 1-11 (Federal Environmental Agency ed. 1999).

29. This description of the legal aspects of invasive non-native species in Germany uses and to some extent is based on two research projects of the Federal Environmental Agency (FEA). *See* ALIEN ORGANISMS IN GERMANY texte 18/99 (1999); Die Aussetzung gebietsfremder Organismen—Recht und Praxis texte 20/99 (1999).

30. Original of the above, and the legislative provisions quoted in the following text, in German; translations by the second author unless indicated otherwise.

31. Federal Nature Conservation Act §41(2).

32. Federal Plant Protection Act §1.

33. *Id.* §2(a)(1) (No. 1).

34. Federal Gazette vol. I, 905.

35. 90/219/EEC and 90/220/EEC on contained use and release, respectively.

36. Such requirements include equal conditions throughout Germany and preservation of legal and economic unity.

37. 90/219/EEC and 90/220/EEC.

38. Article 28 Basic Law.

39. 31 I.L.M. 818 (1992).

40. 27 U.S.T. 1987, T.I.A.S. No. 8249, 993 U.N.T.S. 243 (1973).

41. Bonn Germany, June 23, 1979.

42. Bern, Switzerland, Sept. 19, 1979, 1284 U.N.T.S. 209.

43. Salzburg, Germany, Nov. 7, 1991, 31 I.L.M. 767.

44. Montego Bay, Jamaica, Dec. 10, 1092.

45. Canberra, Australia, Apr. 7, 1982, T.I.A.S. 10240.

46. Rome 1951.

47. Directive 77/93 as amended by Directive 91/683.

48. Directive 91/67.

49. R(84)14, R(85)14 and R(85)15.

50. Res. A774(18).

51. *Cf.* Die Aussetzung gebietsfremder Organismen, 45.

52. Federal Nature Conservation Act §52(4).

53. Federal Law on Plant Protection §3, No. 10.

54. Federal Nature Conservation Act §39(1).

55. *See id.* §10(2) (No. 5).

56. *Id.* §10(2) (No. 1).

57. *Id.* §10(2) (No. 2).

58. *Id.* §10(2) (No. 3).

59. *Id.* §41(2).

60. *Id.*

61. *See* the corresponding Nature Conservation Acts of Brandenburg, Sachsen-Anhalt, Baden-Württemberg, Bayern, Hessen, Niedersachsen, Nordrhein-Westfalen, Rheinland-Pfalz, and Saarland.

62. *See* Thüringen Nature Conservation Act §31(IV).

63. Federal Nature Conservation Act §41(2).

64. *See* Genetic Engineering Act §§1, 13, 16.

CHAPTER 5:
THE POLISH INVASIVE SPECIES EXPERIENCE, LEGISLATION, AND POLICY

by Grazyna Krzywkowska[1]

Polish environmental law recognizes the problem of invasive species, but it remains a marginalized concern. Part One of this chapter provides a short introduction to the Polish legal system. Part Two then evaluates the invasive species problem in Poland, discussing both listed and nonlisted harmful plants and animals and their effect on biological diversity.

Part Three examines several of Poland's international obligations, including the Convention on Biological Diversity (CBD)[2] and the Convention on International Trade in Endangered Species of Wild Fauna and Flora (CITES).[3] Due to constraints of space and specificity of topic, some of Poland's obligations, like the international conventions that address the Antarctic environment, are not examined in this chapter.

Part Four explores the Polish legal instruments relevant to invasive species, including the National Strategy and Management Plan for Protection and Sustainable Use of Biodiversity, followed by an examination of the institutional framework for possible invasive species management. One should bear in mind that in Polish environmental law there are no specific acts or even specific sets of provisions within particular acts that directly address invasive species per se. Part Five briefly assesses the potential funding available for invasive species management needs.

After examining the issues of Polish environmental law and policy that either have an impact on invasive species or provide possible guidelines for this sphere of environmental law, the chapter concludes with some general observations on invasive species regulation.

BACKGROUND INFORMATION

Poland is a civil law country. The national government has three specific divisions: the Parliament (the legislative body made up of the Sejm and the Senate); the Council of Ministers; and the President. The Ministry of Environment, including among others the Department of Environmental Protection and the Department of Forestry Nature Conservation and Landscape Protection, bears primary responsibility for environmental protection and nature conservation, though the Ministry of Agriculture and Rural Development also bears some responsibility for the control, management, and eradication of invasive species.

Poland is divided into provinces (voivodships), counties, and townships. There are environmental protection and nature conservation officials at each level of government, with their responsibilities and powers stated in law. Article 5 of the 1997 Constitution of Poland establishes environmental protection as an obligation of the state. Moreover, Article 74 of the Constitution also makes sustainable use of the environment an element of policy and a duty of state authorities. The Constitution not only grants public access to environmental information, but also obliges the state to support public activities for the protection and improvement of the environment. Ultimately according to Article 86 of the Constitution, everybody is responsible for the protection of the environment and liable for damages to it as specified in law.

Despite the attempts of Polish environmental law and the National Strategy for Protection and Sustainable Use of Biodiversity[4] to address the issue of invasive species, it is still a marginalized concern. This is due partly to a lack of both financial resources and public awareness and partly to the many pressing environmental issues that must be addressed before accession to the European Union (EU). Protecting biodiversity may be at the heart of the Polish Environmental Law of April 27, 2001, as well as a significant factor in other environmental laws, but the specific threat of invasive species is not addressed systematically in Polish environmental law.

Invasive species appear in Polish law, policy, and strategy purely as a result of international obligations and efforts to harmonize the country's environmental protection standards with those of the EU. The 1992 CBD[5] triggered the preparation and determined the content of the National Strategy. CITES[6] paved the way for better management of invasive species by strengthening customs officials and expanding the scope of the Ministry of Environment. Nevertheless, the legislative and institutional regime lacks detail, as far as invasive species are concerned.

POLISH EXPERIENCE WITH INVASIVE SPECIES

A positive list of organisms harmful to plants and plant products can be found in Annex I to the Executive Act of the Ministry of Agriculture and Food Management of February 6, 1996. To some extent, this list illustrates Poland's experience with invasive species. The list contains weed species like *Acroptilon repens, Ambrosia spp., Cenchrus tibuloides*, and *Iva spp.*, and parasitic plant species like *Arceuthobium spp., Cuscuta spp.*, and *Orobanche spp.* They are all harmful and subject to quarantine provisions.[7] By putting pressure on indigenous species, these invasive plants and animals can limit biodiversity and increase the retreat of some species.[8] The invasiveness of species has been identified in Poland in a random way, and this is still the case with invasive species management performance.

One foreign invasive plant species, which is not on the quarantine list, has started to cause problems in some parts of Poland. Sosnovsky hogweed, which reaches up to 4.5 meters in height, originally comes from the Caucasus. Beginning in the 1950s, it was farmed in the former Soviet Union to produce foodstuffs and was later intentionally introduced to Poland. It was cultivated on both state-owned and private farms in Poland throughout the 1960s and the 1970s. Seed plantations were established and cultivation was popularized following official orders. But the hogweed irritated farmers' skin, and animals did not like ensilage made from it. Farmers began to realize that it was extremely difficult to farm other plants on former hogweed plantations. The hogweed became a weed, which spread beyond the plantations and pushed out other species. Its cultivation was stopped in the middle of the 1980s, but the invasion continued.[9]

The hogweed has had harmful effects, according to local officials, on indigenous flora in southeastern Poland near the Tatra Mountains National Park and in the Pieniny Mountains National Park territory, where it can be seen growing on the banks of streams and mountain rivers. The hogweed is subject to eradication actions that have, unfortunately, been minor with rather short-lived effects. In 1994, the Department of Forestry Nature Conservation and Landscape Protection of the Ministry of Environment invited the Botanical Institute of the Polish Academy of Science in Cracow to produce a study that examined the prevalence of Sosnovsky hogweed in Poland and the environmental threat it posed.[10] Besides documenting the previously mentioned invasions in forests adjacent to the Tatra mountains, near the places were it was originally farmed, and in the Pieniny mountains, the study highlights damage the Sosnovsky hogweed has done to the precious Niepolomice Forest wetlands as well as the threat it poses to the Ojcowski National Park and the Masurian Lake district in the North of Poland.

In addition, some of Poland's experience with invasive animal species can be mentioned here. Prussian carp from southern Europe was introduced into the Polish environment at the beginning of the 20th century, though not for fish farming purposes, as was the case in Russia and Byelorussia. There is no available research on the effect that Prussian carp might have had on the population of indigenous crucian carp.[11] But, as A. Szczerbowski of the Institute of the Inland Fishery of the Academy of Agriculture in Olsztyn has suggested, there has not really been any research at all that examines the effect of invasive species on fish in Poland.

American mink was introduced into Poland both from farms in the former Soviet Union (now Russia and Byelorussia) and from farms in Poland that were established as early as 1928.[12] A very flexible animal well established in Poland, American mink supposedly suppress the populations of birds and even beavers (because they are competitors) in the Masurian Lake district, but again there is no research to substantiate this. Until the end of 1996, they were on the list of beasts of the chase issued by the Ministry of Environment, but because they are not on the latest list, American mink can no longer be hunted. American mink likely replaced European mink by simply filling the ecological niche that opened after European mink became extinct at the beginning of the 20th century.[13]

Raccoon dog, also originally farmed for its fur, invaded Polish territory after Soviet farms were destroyed during World War II. Though found in Poland as early as 1963, it is still quite rare, but expansive nonetheless.[14] Unfortunately once again, there is no research that examines the influence of the raccoon on the Polish environment. The muskrat colonized Poland in a mere 30 years. It was first spotted in the country in 1924, and it became common in the 1950s, inhabiting some 74% of all mountain territory, except for the Tatra Mountains National Park.[15]

The introduction of invasive species is in many cases incidental. For example, *Elodea canadensis*, which moved across the Atlantic Ocean in wood shipments of the 1850s, invaded natural ecosystems at once, including Poland. It was expansive in the 1860s and 1870s, though it is not so at present. Typically, invasive plants are first seen near households and then slowly some of them move to natural ecosystems. This was the case in Poland with such invasive plants as *Bidens frondosa* and *Xanthium strumarium*, both of American origin, and *Anaphalis margaritacea* of Canadian origin. Roughly 117 invasive plant species were introduced into Poland during the period beginning in the 16th century and ending in the 1960s.[16] As of 30 years ago, already 22.5% of the species in the protected Bialowieza Forest in eastern Poland were foreign and potentially invasive.[17]

INTERNATIONAL OBLIGATIONS

Poland signed the CBD in 1992 and ratified it in 1996. A national strategy and action plan for the protection and sustainable use of biological resources was prepared in 1998. According to the First National Report to the Conference of the Parties at the CBD in 1997, Polish legislation addresses all the conventional obligations of national authorities.[18] Polish obligations to the CBD are covered under a number of different acts and provisions, including the Environmental Law of 2001, the Act on Nature Conservation of 1991, the Environmental Impact Assessment regulation of 1998, the Forestry Act of 1991, the Act on Environment Protection Inspection of 1991, and the Act on Plant Protection of 1998. While these acts reflect Polish obligations under the CBD, most of them were, in fact, enacted and have been executed mainly as a result of the process of accession to the EU.

Poland, as a contracting Party to CITES, has established a system of permits for import, export, and re-export of endangered plants, animals, or their parts. There are 19 CITES coordinators in customs bureaus around the country. As the designated management authority under the treaty, the Ministry of Environment is responsible for the issuance of permits for import, export, and re-export of species that are covered by CITES. The National Council for Nature Conservation is the CITES scientific authority in Poland. In addition, veterinary border control checkpoints were established by the Executive Act of December 10, 1997.[19]

Poland is also a party to the Convention on the Conservation of Migratory Species of Wild Animals (CMS) of 1979, and to the 1971 Convention on Wetlands of International Importance, Especially as Waterfowl Habitat, which is commonly known as the Ramsar Convention.[20]

Ballast Water Issue

Marine invasive species can be introduced by ballast water dumping. A species can be easily transported by ship to any part of the world, due in part to the speed of modern ships and the suitable environment created by a ship's ballast water. Therefore, ballast water should be cleaned before being dumped, regardless of where dumping takes place, whether in territorial waters or the open sea. The ballast water problem is indirectly dealt with in the regional Convention on the Maritime Environment Protection of the Baltic Sea of March 22, 1974,[21] to which Poland has been a contracting Party since 1979.[22] Poland is also a Party to the United Nation's (U.N.'s) Law of the Sea Convention of 1982, which requires states to "take all measures necessary to prevent, reduce and control . . . the intentional or accidental introduction of species, alien or new, to a particular part of marine environment, which may cause significant or harmful changes thereto."[23] Unfortunately, there were no provisions adopted to implement this provision. The 1954 International Maritime Organization (IMO) Convention for the Prevention of Pollution of the Sea by Oil was superseded by the International Convention for the Prevention of Pollution From Ships of 1973 (MARPOL),[24] which was ratified by Poland in 1987.[25] MARPOL does not cover dumping of all waste in the sea. However, there is a Protocol to MARPOL of November 7, 1996. The protocol's intention is to supersede MARPOL, but only 4 of its acceptance documents have been received, with 26 such documents needed for the protocol to become binding. The protocol represents a precautionary approach and the polluter-pays principle for the dumping of all kinds of waste, including organic material of natural origin. Poland waits until the protocol takes effect before introducing standards and regulations on ballast water treatment.[26]

THE LEGAL SYSTEM OF ENVIRONMENTAL PROTECTION AND NATURE CONSERVATION

As mentioned above, except for Article 42 of the Nature Protection Act, there is neither a separate set of provisions nor a specific act to address invasive species in Polish environmental law. There are, however, many other provisions of environmental law that could be applied to this issue. These include provisions in the Forestry Act of 1991. Unfortunately, this presumption is rarely if ever put into practice.

Article 1 of the Environmental Law of 2001 highlights the main principle of environment protection: the principle of sustainable development. The key ideas behind "sustainable development" are that the durability limits of the environment should not be exceeded, and biodiversity should be preserved. Clearly, this notion of environmental protection implies the control and prevention of invasive species.

Both the national as well as local governments preparing for spatial development have to consider the strictures of environmental protection, including the principles of sustainable development, ecological balance, and rational protection of the environment and landscape.[27]

The Nature Conservation Act of 1991

The most important environmental protection and nature conservation acts in the Polish legal system that could be used to address invasive species are the Environmental Law of 2001, the Nature Conservation Act of 1991 and the Forestry Act of September 28, 1991 as amended.[28] The introduction and movement of foreign or non-native animals or plants and their reproductive forms are prohibited by law, subject to exceptions provided by the Ministry of Environment as agreed to by the minister responsible for agriculture and after consultation with the National Nature Protection Council.[29] Article 42 also applies to species introduced before the Act entered into force. However, significantly, there is no official system for the introduction, control, or eradication of invasive species in any of this legislation.

The Act on Nature Conservation of October 16, 1991,[30] establishes the relevant authorities for and the goals and forms of nature conservation, as well as the specific obligations of both citizens and officials. Protecting biodiversity and maintaining sustainable use are key elements of nature conservation.[31] The relevant authorities are the Ministry of Environment and the individual governors (voivods) who perform their duties through the Superior Nature Conservator nominated by the Prime Minister and voivodship nature conservators nominated by the voivods.

National Parks are managed by independent directors, who have local powers within the park like those of the voivod. The Nature Conservation Council, voivodship, and park nature councils are advisory bodies to these authorities, with council members nominated by nature conservation authorities. The authorities establish special protection for designated territories and decide on the method of environment protection, in accordance with the National Strategy of Nature Conservation. The National Park Service can check people's documents, impose monetary penalties, control means of transport, and perform search and seizure of objects that are the subject or tool of an incriminating act.[32] National parks, nature reserves, and landscape parks draft plans for nature conservation. The Ministry of Environment then confirms the nature conservation plan for the national parks, and all such plans should be binding during preparation of spatial plans.

The Forestry Act of 1991

The Forestry Act of 1991 outlines principles for the conservation, protection, and management of forests. Again, these principles may be interpreted as including invasive species management. Principles include maintaining the biodiversity of forests and conserving their genetic resources through specific forest management plans set out for each individual forest.[33] According to Article 13 of the Forestry Act, owners of forests have to maintain them and secure their continuous use. Protection against invasive species, which are a threat to the use of the forest, may be understood under this obligation. Forest owners have the responsibility to detect and prevent invasions of harmful species when possible, and to eradicate harmful species if they become invasive.[34] When invasive species are detected, the government representative on the district level, known as the starost, establishes the obligations of private forest owners. This administrative decision can be reviewed first by the voivod and then, if necessary, by the administrative court.

If a harmful organism threatens the durability of a state forest, the forest inspector executes protection means. He or she can apply to the starost of the relevant district for a decision to undertake such means. A starost can, as with private forests, make decisions about state forests without application from the forest inspector. It is, however, difficult to imagine an invasion that would threaten the very existence or continuous use of forests in Poland.

The state authority, Lasy Panstwowe,[35] regardless of the legal ownership of the forest, evaluates the state of the forests, monitors changes in their ecosystems, and maintains a database on the subject.[36] A 10-year forest management plan is prepared for every state forest, while simplified plans covering the same time span are prepared for forests that are not state-owned. Private forests, or those which are broken up into many small parts, are not covered by management plans, but individual management tasks are subject to decisions by the local starost.[37] Management plans consist of a program of nature conservation prepared by specialists,[38] the selection of which has been determined by the Ministry of Environment in a special executive act.[39] Forest management plans are subject to public review, and the owners of forests must be informed about the display of plans in the township. Those whose legal interests or authority are infringed upon by a proposed plan have 14 days from the date of display to object to it. Such an objection is subject to a fact-based legally reasoned decision by a local government council, which can then be appealed to an administrative court. On the other hand, anyone in the community can raise objections to the plan during the 14-day period, but such a protest is subject to a local government decision, which does not have to be reasoned and cannot be taken to an administrative court.

The Ministry of Environment makes a forest management plan into law by executive decision; similarly, the voivod accepts a simplified forest management plan after consulting the forest inspector, who is responsible for the forest in question. The forest inspector has 30 days to contest the simplified plan. The Ministry of Environment supervises the preparation of plans for state-owned forests, and for forests that are part of the State Agriculture Ownership Resources. The Ministry has outlined in an executive act the requirements for the preparation of a forest management plan, a simplified forest management plan, and a forest catalogue.[40] The starost of a county supervises preparation of simplified plans for nonstate-owned forests. If the forest owner does not fulfill the obligations established by the simplified forest management plan or a starost's decision, the starost can order the execution of the obligations and tasks in his or her decision.

The Forestry Act of 1991 establishes the forest fund.[41] Activities concerning forest management, most probably including invasive species management, can be funded from the forest fund means.

Harmful Organisms of Quarantine Concerns

The following discussion of quarantine and phytosanitary regulations and authorities is only indirectly relevant to the regulation and management of invasive species. But in a country of scarce financial resources like Poland, these regulations, despite their original intent, should be employed as much as possible to deal with the invasive species problem.

The Act on Protection of Cultivated Crops of July 12, 1995[42] is designed to protect plants against harmful organisms, but it does not specifically mention invasive species. The Ministry of Agriculture and Food Management publishes the positive list of species subject to quarantine. Furthermore, nature conservation officials at the voivod level can order the eradication of harmful organisms or other entities or foodstuffs infected with harmful organisms at state expense if they pose a serious threat to cultivated plants or if such actions are required by international agreement. Owners are required to inform nature conservation or local government officials of any invasion of harmful organisms on the Ministry list. Unfortunately, the Act does not specify the way such notification should be carried out.

State nature conservation authorities maintain statistics of all harmful organisms found in Poland. All imported plants, foods, and means of transport for plants should be free from harmful organisms. All imported plants and plant products must have a phytosanitary certificate, issued by the authorities in the state of origin, which guarantees that no harmful organisms enter Poland with the imports. Plants on the Ministry of Agriculture and Food Management list cannot be imported.[43] Anyone who imports such plants faces either a monetary penalty or detention, as well as plant seizure. The list includes such microorganisms as fungi and bacteria.

The phytosanitary certificate obtained in the state of origin has to be issued no more than 14 days before the date of planned import to Poland. Coffee, tea, cacao, herbal spices, packed herbs, aquarium plants, dry plants, fresh fruit and vegetables, cut flowers, single-potted flowers, and European plant bulbs not for sale do not have to have a phytosanitary certificate. All plants and foodstuffs are inspected on the border except those in closed containers. If the inspection results are not satisfactory, the nature conservation official can place the subject of the inspection under quarantine or adequately manage the organism. If the shipment does not have a phytosanitary certificate it can be stopped at the border or put under the quarantine. The nature conservation authority in each voivod also issues phytosanitary certificates for plants that are being exported from Poland.[44]

Inspection officials can enter private property and inspect means of transporting plants and the places of their storage. They can take samples of plants and foodstuffs for research purposes, interrogate people, and control all adequate documents. While on duty, an inspection officer must wear a uniform. Obstructing the actions of inspectors is a petty crime that can be punished by detention or fines. The inspectors have to cooperate with local government and keep it informed as to the state of plant protection in its territory.

Quarantine provisions are justified only by the threat of the spread of disease and possible economic disadvantages from the introduction of harmful foreign species. The protection of biodiversity and nature conservation should be added to this list of quarantine justifications. Moreover, the lack of public education about the invasive species problem is a decisive factor in the incidental introduction of species because of a lack of due care.

Polish National Strategy for the Protection and Sustainable Use of Biodiversity

On May 10, 1991, the Polish Parliament enacted a resolution, which required that sustainable development become a regular consideration in Polish development. On January 19, 1995, Parliament passed another resolution, which required the integration of ecological concerns into Polish politics and economic strategy. In 1998, the National Environment Protection Foundation, in cooperation with the U.N. Environment Program and the Ministry of Environment, produced the Polish National Strategy and Management Plan for Protection and Sustainable Use of Biodiversity, which was based on the Strategy of Natural Resources Protection written by the Polish Academy of Science in 1991. Financed by a grant from the Global Environmental Fund, the strategy fulfilled the conditions and implementation requirements set out in Article 6 of the CBD. The newest version of the strategy of January 17, 2002, was open for public comments until August 15, 2002, and is currently being re-drafted.

Ratification of the CBD has changed some aspects of nature protection in Polish law. For example, all species are covered by a conventional definition of biodiversity; therefore, all species are worthy of protection, not just the rare ones. All aspects of biodiversity, including the landscape and cultural diversity, should also be protected.[45] However, entities threatened by invasive species should be under strict protection. The National Strategy mentions limiting invasions of foreign species as an element of biodiversity protection, though the category of "foreign species" is not defined. One can assume that these are not present or are recently present in Poland.

Foreign Species in the National Strategy and Management Plan for Protection and Sustainable Use of Biodiversity

The National Strategy recognizes the problem of "foreign species" and calls for research of invasion vectors and paths. It calls for adoption and implementation of the program of invasive species eradication by 2005. It does not allocate any financial resources to its implementation but indicates Ministry of Environment as the authority responsible for it, in cooperation with Ministry of Agriculture, National Forests, Polish Hunting Association, national parks, botanical gardens, scientific institutes, and nongovernmental organizations (NGOs).

Besides improved monitoring, the National Strategy also makes an updated record of invasive species and their eradication an ongoing priority. Foreign species are generally labeled in the National Strategy as the ones that reduce biodiversity. Hopefully, the National Strategy when adopted will lead to the introduction of specific legislation regulating the introduction, control, and eradication of invasive species, as well as provisions that establish emergency response plans.

A number of government lists are directly or indirectly relevant to the invasive species issue, including the positive list of protected plants,[46] the list of protected animals,[47] the list of hunted animals,[48] and the list of protected fish.[49]

The strategy includes efforts to improve nature conservation in nationally protected areas. According to the Polish Main Statistics Office, special protected territories make up 26% of the land in Poland. These territories include nature reserves, national parks, landscape parks, protected landscape territories, and other specially protected sites.

The Control and Use of the Environment With Focus on the Environmental Inspection

Responsible authorities monitor and control the use of the environment within the bounds of law. The Minister of Environment is responsible for the interpretation and enforcement of the Environmental Protection Act of 1980. The National Environmental Council is the Minister's expert and advisory body. NGOs can educate the public about environmental protection, and initiate public actions regarding such protection. They can initiate authorities' actions with regard to the removal of threats to the environment. Authorities have to consider such initiatives and inform the NGOs about the way they are settled. Responsible authorities can enter property with specialists or needed machinery, do research or other supervisory acts, demand oral or written information and explanations needed to establish facts, and require documents and the display of data regarding the scope of control in question. The responsible authorities then prepare a control protocol.[50] The NGOs are competent to initiate suits to stop damaging actions, to recover a former state, and to redress existing damage. NGOs can also be a party to administrative proceedings regarding environment protection.

The Act on the Establishment of the State Inspection for Environmental Protection (PIOS) of June 20, 1991[51] establishes the General Environmental Inspector as the highest state authority responsible for environment law compliance. The Inspector's tasks include monitoring both the state of the environment and the progress of environmental research. Besides the General Environmental Inspector and the General Environmental Inspectorate, each voivod has an environmental inspector with an environmental inspectorate. These voivod inspectors cooperate with local government, county, and voivodship councils, formally hearing information about the state of the environment in their territory at least once a year as well as any other time they wish to have it submitted. They set the agenda for their individual inspectorates with regard to the best ways to improve the state of the environment in their voivod. Moreover, local government can direct inspectorates in the event of an emergency or grave threat to the environment.[52]

Environmental inspectors, in accordance with Article 9 of the Act on the Establishment of the State Inspection for Environmental Protection, have the authority to do the following:

(1) enter the premises of any enterprise;
(2) demand information (oral or in writing) and summon persons;
(3) demand documents or data submission;
(4) collect samples of material needed for research; and
(5) evaluate the operation of any equipment for environment protection.

The first four competencies here are important for preventing or controlling the introduction or invasion of foreign species.

After an inspection, an administrative decision may be issued based on the provisions of law. The decision can include an obligation to remove the environmental threat, impose a monetary penalty or order a stop to actions that are not in accordance with the requirements of environmental protection.[53] The decision can also initiate administrative proceedings against state or local government authorities or intervene in the course of such proceedings. Inspectorates disseminate information pertaining to their jurisdiction to other state and local government authorities, and they consider all applications to initiate control procedures. The polluter pays the cost of these control procedures.[54]

The Inspectorate of Plant Protection, which was established by the Executive Act of the Ministry of Environment on the Statute of the Inspectorate of Plant Protection and the Act on Voivodship Inspectorates of Plant Protection Organization of December 28, 1998,[55] deals with the protection of cultivated plants. The Voivodship Plant Protection inspectorates issue information on the state of plant protection in their territory, including phytosanitary certificates for plants being exported. In the event of an introduction of an invasive or listed species, any person can sue for damages or redress in a civil court in accordance with the Civil Code of 1964, under Article 322 of the Environmental Law of 2001.

Access to environmental information and public participation in procedures relating to environmental protection are regulated in Chapters IV and V of the Environmental Law of 2001 and by the Act on Access to Information on the Environment and Its Protection and on Environmental Impact Assessment of November 9, 2000.[56] The Act is accompanied by ministerial regulations on costs of access to environmental information, modes of such access, and a public registry of documents containing such information.

INVASIVE SPECIES PROJECT FUNDING

The resources of the National Environmental Fund, voivodship environmental funds, county environmental funds and township environmental funds are all spent on environmental protection in an effort to achieve sustainable development. The funds are collected from penalties and fees for using and misusing the environment. Invasive species management could be financed with township environmental funds as an environmental protection task necessary to achieve sustainable development. Voivodship environmental funds can finance some nature conservation tasks involving invasive species, and the National Environmental Fund can support invasive species research, pilot and education programs, and regional and co-regional sustainable development and environment protection programs. The National Environmental Fund can directly include in its plans allocations to finance foreign or invasive species projects. The same applies to voivodship, county, and township environmental funds.

CONCLUSION

Despite the general ban on the introduction of "foreign species" that is included in the Nature Conservation Act of 1991, there are still no definitions for the terms, "invasive species," "foreign species," "alien species," "non-indigenous species," and "non-native species," as well as invasive species introduction, and reintroduction. There is no reference to the eradication of such species; nor are there guidelines to address exceptions to the ban on the introduction of "foreign species." There are no specific provisions regarding the possibility of the intentional introduction of such species either. Moreover, activities that may contribute to the unintentional introduction of invasive species are not identified by law. There are no specific provisions at all for control and eradication of invasive species, nor are there emergency plans or direct funding sources provided for such activities. There are no sanctions for the introduction of such species directly stated, either. Public education and awareness in this field is very poor. This situation is most probably caused by the fact that there has not been a severe invasive species problem in Poland, especially one that has been widely publicized. Nevertheless, the National Strategy for Protection and Sustainable Use of Biodiversity of 2002 recognizes the threat of foreign species and the need for action plans to eliminate that threat.

Chapter 5 Endnotes

1. Grazyna Krzywkowska is the Project Coordinator of the SEE Initiative for the Environmental Policy Program at the Regional Environmental Center for central and eastern Europe in Szentendre, Hungary.

2. 31 I.L.M. 818 (1992).

3. 27 U.S.T. 1987, T.I.A.S. No. 8249, 993 U.N.T.S. 243 (1973).

4. "Krajowa strategia ochrony i zrównowaæonego uæytkowania róænorodnosci biologicznej", draft of January 17, 2002, Ministry of Environment, *at* http://www. mos.gov.pl/1prace_legislacyjne/inne_documenty/strategia/strategia1.html.

5. 31 I.L.M. 818.

6. 27 U.S.T. 1987, T.I.A.S. No. 8249, 993 U.N.T.S. 243.

7. *Acroptilon repens* (from the cornflower family), which was accidentally introduced, is established on several sites, but it was still not settled and had not yet invaded farms as of 1998. An Asian weed species that can be found in Afghanistan, Armenia, Australia, Azerbaijan, Canada, China, Georgia, Iran, Iraq, Kazakhstan, Kyrgyzstan, Syria, Tajikistan, Turkmenistan, Turkey, the United States, and Uzbekistan, as well as in Russia and the Ukraine, this farm and garden weed grows along rivers, drains, and roads. Several species of *Ambrosia L.* (the ragweed family) are found in Poland. They are farm, garden, and pasture weeds that can also grow on the edges of forests, though they are not persisting there. Of North American origin, *Ambrosia L.* is also found in Africa (in Madagascar and Madeira), Asia (in Azerbaijan, Georgia, Japan, Kazakhstan, and Korea), Australia, Europe, and in South America. Species of *Iva L.* (the sallow family) are weeds of North American origin that occur in Australia and in Europe. They are weeds of corn, pastures, and meadows, but in Poland they occur near households and on the wasteland only. *Iva xathiifolia Nutt.* was found here in 1931.
   The parasitic plant species *Arceuthobium spp.* (a non-European species of mistletoe) is not found in Poland, but some *Cuscuta L.* (the dodder family), a parasite plant species of North American origin, are found in the south. The *Cuscuta epilinum Weihe* species of this family of Eurasian origin is occasionally found in eastern Poland; it is not only invasive, but also poisonous. *Cuscuta epithymum L.* is also poisonous and widely established in Poland. *Cuscuta europea L.* is common in the lowlands of Poland and near the mountains. The dodder family of plants is parasitic on pasture and meadow plants, grain plants, red pepper, tobacco, potato, flax, willow, lentil, broad bean, pea, herbs, bushes, and trees. *Orobanche L.* (broomrape) of Eurasia origin is parasitic on roots of other plants and can cause immense agricultural waste. It is quite rare in Poland.

8. L. Kucharski, *The Plants of American Origin That Invaded Water Bodies and Wetlands in Poland*, Lódzkie Towarzystwo Naukowe, Lódz 17, 18 (1992).

9. Sosnovsky hogweed produces some 40,000 seeds per plant and can grow in very poor soil. It spread easily beyond the original fields because, among other reasons, its parts were not properly destroyed. The Ministry of Environment issued an official information leaflet on possible harmful effects of Sosnovsky hogweed in August 1995, after several articles appeared in the press. The information was based on some research and scientific expertise. In 1994, the Department of Forestry Nature Conservation and Landscape Protection of the Ministry of Environment issued an official letter to all county (voivodship) nature conservation officials inquiring about Sosnovsky hogweed sites and the state of its invasion. The Ministry of Environment also sent a letter to the Ministry of Agriculture and Rural Development asking about possibilities for eradicating the hogweed. The county nature protection officials were asked about Sosnovsky hogweed sites in the counties and its possible harmful effects on indigenous flora. Be-

fore the changes in Polish local government of 1998 there were 49 voivodships in Poland and Sosnovsky hogweed was reported in 21 of them, in southeastern and northern Poland.

10. J. Guzik, *Ocena stopnia zagrozenia rodzimej flory polski oraz niebezpieczenstwa jakie moze stwarzac dla czlowieka barszcz Sosnowskiego (Heracleum Sosnovsky Manden.)*, Polish Academy of Science, Cracow (1994). Guzik concluded that Sosnovsky hogweed is a rare and nonharmful plant, that its sites are mostly near its old agriculture sites, along roads and streams, and that it poses no threat to general indigenous flora. Moreover, the author found that none of the foreign species introduced in Poland caused direct harm to the Polish environment and its biodiversity. Such plants include *Polygonum cuspidatum, Solidago gigantea, Solidago canadensis* (golden rot family), *Rudabeckia lacinata* (rudbeckia), *Impatiens glandulifera, Impatiens parviflora* (touch-me-not), *Helianthus tuberosus* (Jerusalem artichoke), *Eschinocystis lobata* and *Bidens frondosa* (bur marigold). But Guzik admits that the Sosnovsky hogweed, once introduced, creates monocultures on its sites and thus eliminates some rare species, especially those that once inhabited wetlands. The hogweed expands because it is so big that it takes away all the sunlight, minerals, and water available in a site. Following the 1994 study, the Ministry of Environment pledged to organize hogweed eradication. Unfortunately, there has been no follow-up to this promise. Extermination of Sosnovsky hogweed can be handled by the County Plan Protection and Quarantine Stations with financial support of the County and National Environmental Funds, budgeted from their financial means for nature conservation. According to this author's survey, no entity turned to the National Environment Fund for financial support for this need. There were no such cases in the Olsztyn voivodship (Masurian Lake district), either. Following the conclusions of the expertise, the Department of Forestry Nature Conservation and Landscape Protection underlined that Sosnovsky hogweed can limit biodiversity where it is abundant. Prof. T. Korniak and M. Sroda, Ph.D., of the Agricultural Academy in Olsztyn believe that its sowing has to be limited systematically. The weeds continue to grow until its two- or three-year life cycle is finished. Cutting the plants will only trigger the alternative way of the Sosnovsky hogweed reproduction, from its underground parts. The plant is also resistant to herbicides and diseases, and has no natural enemies.

11. *See* J.A. Szczerbowski & A. Szczerbowski, *Karasie*, Olsztyn (1996), *at* http://www.infish.com.pl/ksiazki_pliki/karasie.html and Personal Communication with A. Szczerbowski, Ph.D. (Nov. 1999).

12. P. Janiszewski, Lowca Polski No. 3 (1999).

13. M. Brzezinski & J. Romanowski, *Norka amerykanska*, Lowca Polski No. 4 21 (1996).

14. G. Jamrozy, *Nieproszeni goscie*, Lowca Polski No. 3 9 (1995).

15. *Id.* at 8.

16. J. Kornas, *Prowizoryczna lista nowszych przybyszów synantropijnych (kenofitów) zadomowionych w Polsce* (1968).

17. J. B. Falinski, Antropogeniczna roslinnosc Puszczy Bialowieskiej 184 (1966). The author could not find any current research material dealing with invasive species in the Bialowierza Forest.

18. *See* relevant provisions of the CBD, 31 I.L.M. 818.

19. *See* Dziennik Ustaw (Dz. U.) 97.150.996. The Executive Act of December 10, 1997, is based on Art. 14(6) of the Act on Fighting Against Infectious Animal Diseases, Animal and Meat Examination, and Veterinary Inspection of 24 April, 1997. *See* Dz. U. 97.60.369.

20. The Ramsar Convention, which focuses on the wise use of wetlands, was the first convention to deal with the wise use of biological resources. Prevention of invasive species introduction to wetlands ecosystems should be considered as an element of the prudent use of the wetlands.

21. Dz. U. 80.18.64.

22. The convention does not specifically address the issue of invasive species, but the definition of "dangerous substance" covers any substance that creates a threat of pollution after being released into the sea. Ballast water could be treated as a dangerous substance that causes a threat of pollution because it potentially harbors invasive species. "Pollution" in turn means human introduction of substances into the marine environment that endanger the living resources of the sea. The Contracting Parties are obliged to provide legal measures to protect the Baltic Sea against pollution originating from the land and in the open sea by substances stated in the convention. Unfortunately, organic polluted water is not stated as such a substance in the convention. The authorities will strive to adopt common criteria for dumping of any such substances. Such dumping can take place only in accordance with the state authority's permission. The Commission on Maritime Environment of the Baltic Sea established by the convention works on pollution control requirements and tasks to reduce it. Annex IV of the convention is concerned with prevention of the pollution of the Baltic Sea from ships. However, in the case of the ballast water the concern is its pollution by the oil or other stated substances. Ballast water that is clean or kept separate from oil tanks can be released to the sea. Ballast water clean from substances mentioned in the convention but full of invasive species is considered to be safe.

23. Ratification document of July 2, 1998 (Dz. U. 98.98.609).

24. 12 I.L.M. 1319 (1973), as amended by 1978 Protocol (MARPOL 73/78) 17 I.L.M. 546.

25. Dz. U. 87.17.101.

26. Personal Communication with A. Dunikowski of the Polish Registry of Ships, Gdansk, Poland (Nov. 1999).

27. *See* Art. 71 of the Environmental Law of 2001.

28. Dz. U. 91.101.444; Dz. U. 92.21.85; Dz. U. 92.54.254; Dz. U. 94.1.3; Dz. U. 94.127.627; Dz. U. 95.141.692; Dz. U. 95.141.713; Dz. U. 96.91.409; Dz. U. 97.54.349; Dz. U. 97.54.349; Dz. U. 97.121.770; Dz. U. 98.106.668.

29. *See* Article 42 of the Act on Nature Conservation of 1991 (consolidated text in Dz. U. 2001.99.1079).

30. Dz. U. 200199.1079.

31. *See* Article 2 of the Act on Nature Conservation of 1991.

32. *Id.* art. 18(2).

33. *See* Forestry Act of 1991, arts. 6(6)-(7) and art. 7(1) (consolidated text in Dz. U. 2000.56.679 as amended).

34. Forestry Act of 1991, art. 9.

35. Lasy Panstwowe is the state entity, but not the legal entity, representing fiscus. *See* Forestry Act of 1991, art. 32(1).

36. Forestry Act of 1991, art. 13a.

37. However, for forests up to 10 hectares which are broken into many parts and are owned by the State Agriculture Ownership Resources such management tasks are outlined by a forest inspector.

38. *See* Forestry Act of 1991, arts. 18(4), point 2a, 19(5).

39. Executive Act of the Ministry of Environment of May 28, 1998 (Dz. U. 98.69.452).

40. The Executive Act of the Ministry of Environment of December 28, 1998 (Dz. U. 99.3.16).

41. *See* Forestry Act of 1991, arts. 56-58.

42. Dz. U. 95.90.446.

43. *See* Act on Protection of Cultivated Crops of July 12, 1995, arts. 7-9.

44. *See* Act on Protection of Cultivated Crops of July 12, 1995, as amended, arts. 3-12.

45. National Strategy and Management Plan for Protection and Sustainable Use of Biodiversity, Warsaw 2 (1998).

46. Ministry of Environment Act of Apr. 6, 1995, Dz. U. 95.41.214.

47. *Id.*, Dz. U. 95.13.61.

48. Ministry of Environment Act of Dec. 6, 1996, Dz. U. 97.01.05.

49. Act of the Ministry of Transport and Maritime Economy of Mar. 12, 1997, Dz. U. 97.39.247.

50. *See* arts. 9(2) and 11 of the Act on the Establishment of the State Inspection for Environmental Protection.

51. Dz. U. 91.77.335.

52. *See* Act on the Establishment of the State Inspection for Environmental Protection, art. 8a-8b.

53. *See id.* art. 12.

54. *See id.* arts. 17-18.

55. Dz. U. 98.166.1250.

56. Dz. U. 2000.109.1157.

CHAPTER 6:
THE PARADOX OF U.S. ALIEN SPECIES LAW

by Marc L. Miller[1]

N on-indigenous species (NIS) have increasingly come to be recognized in scientific and popular arenas as one of the most significant threats to biodiversity. That recognition has yet to extend to law and policy, which, in the United States, remain fractured and incomplete. This chapter surveys the most significant of the many bits and pieces of U.S. federal law that relate to prevention and control of NIS, and argues that a more coherent and powerful legal framework is needed to address the NIS problem.

INTRODUCTION

U.S. law addressing NIS presents a paradox.

The best way to summarize U.S. NIS law is to say that there is very little statutory law, and for important dimensions of the NIS problem, including identifying new NIS invasions, tracking the impact of known harmful invasive species, and responding to emerging threats, there is none. Some federal laws have responded to threats from particular invasive species, or threats from particular pathways for alien species (such as ballast water as a source of aquatic NIS). But no federal law has ever responded directly to the general problem of prohibiting, preventing, screening, identifying, attacking, and understanding NIS.

The law of the various U.S. states is even easier to summarize: with a few interesting exceptions, including NIS legislation in Hawaii and Minnesota, most U.S. states at best offer a weak echo of the general aspects of federal statutory law.

Oddly, the second best way to summarize U.S. NIS law is to say that there is a ton of it, and that no report has yet done it justice. Indeed, there is so much law, of so many kinds, that there is no way this chapter can do it justice. A comprehensive summary would point to the many dozens of federal statutes that are relevant, or might be relevant, to NIS issues. It would point to the dozens of federal agencies and hundreds of state agencies that have responded to alien species issues under various kinds of legal authority, including general organic acts for the supervisory agency and annual appropriations bills.

High on the list of evidence supporting the view that invasive species have a broad presence in U.S. law would be two presidential Executive Orders, a quirky species of law, that have addressed NIS issues directly, first in a 1977 Executive Order issued by President Jimmy Carter, and then, in an Executive Order issued by President William J. Clinton on February 3, 1999. Indeed, the first piece of evidence in support of the view that the United States has broad le-

gal coverage of invasive species issues would be the creation of a National Invasive Species Council staffed by cabinet-level officers and the promulgation,
in January 2001, of a National Invasive Species Management Plan.

To complicate matters still further, to the extent that law reflects culture and
popular understanding, there has been a dramatic increase in coverage of NIS
issues in the popular press, and to some degree in scientific and legal materials.
An increasing flood of news stories has focused on particular invaders and their
economic, social, aesthetic, and ecological costs.

One way to resolve the paradox is to shift the terrain of the question from:
"what laws apply to NIS?" to "what legal authority should exist to deal with
harmful NIS, and what purposes would a new or different set of NIS laws
serve?" In other words, the proper question is not whether a lawyer or policymaker might be able to find a basis in current legal authority to defend a specific
action, but whether a biologist or policymaker would say that the law adequately guides and mandates appropriate government and private actions, and,
more generally, that it responds to the costs and threats imposed by NIS.

From the perspective of coherent law and policy, it is relatively easy to identify the gaps in U.S. federal and state law. It is harder to explain whether and
how those gaps should be filled. If government agencies can respond to NIS
problems under their current authority, and if increasing public awareness of
threats from harmful NIS makes it more likely that agencies will try to deal with
NIS issues, then why should anyone care about the absence of clearer, explicit
legal authority on NIS issues?

Part I of this chapter summarizes the increasing awareness of the importance
and seriousness of NIS issues in the United States in popular, scientific, and legal literature. Part II describes current federal legal authority, focusing first on
the limitations of the existing federal statutory law regarding NIS, and then on
an unusual legal animal—the presidential Executive Orders—at the heart of
modern U.S. legal history regarding NIS. Part III considers the legal authority
regarding NIS in the U.S. states, with a special emphasis on the law of Hawaii
and Minnesota.

Part IV addresses the need for new statutory provisions in U.S. federal and
state law. The chapter concludes that current U.S. statutory law leaves essential
aspects of the NIS problem unaddressed. Moreover, as a social and political
matter, NIS pose a sufficient threat to justify their separate recognition in positive law, including the structural, substantive, public, and funding issues that
such legal identification would generate. At a minimum, as a matter of coherent
law and policy, a single, organic NIS law should be articulated, and that model
then used to assess gaps in actual current legal authority.

ALIEN AWARENESS IN THE UNITED STATES

Any evaluation of the adequacy of current law must have some metric against
which to test its success or failure. In other words, there must be some sense of a
social problem or situation that calls for a governmental response. If the values
against which the law is being tested are not stated explicitly, or are not clear

and compelling, then any critique of current law must stand or fall based on materials or facts not presented with the legal analysis.

Moreover, any assessment of the adequacy of current law must also encompass or reflect some theory of law—what role law plays in society, what subjects are the legitimate and proper domain of regulation (in contrast to private discourse and markets), and how laws work, including both the likely efficacy and the likely costs of any proposed regulation, i.e., a theory of regulation.

The present analysis rests on the assumption that invasive alien species pose a major economic, ecological, and social threat that is not being dealt with adequately. This section provides an overview of the scope of the NIS problem in the United States, and the level of public and professional awareness of that problem. The legal analysis that follows assumes that the multidimensional case for responding to NIS has been more than adequately made elsewhere by ecologists and economists.

Though increasingly outdated, the best overview of the NIS problem in the United States remains the 1993 report *Harmful Non-Indigenous Species in the United States*.[2] The Office of Technology Assessment (OTA), a now-defunct research arm of the U.S. Congress (eliminated in 1995),[3] produced a 400-page report that for a decade has been the standard reference for the scope of the NIS problem in the United States.

The OTA scientists, after reviewing the literature, concluded that "[a]t least 4,500 species of foreign origin have established free-living populations" in the United States.[4] The OTA summary of the estimated numbers of NIS in the United States appears in Table 1. Other scientists have estimated much higher numbers,[5] and all assessments, including that by the OTA, emphasize the lack of knowledge in this area, and the likelihood that for many kinds of organisms, the counts are probably much higher.

The OTA notes the variety of harms from NIS, including economic, ecological, and aesthetic harms. The report captures the difficulty in adequately describing the scope of harm in the following summary paragraphs:

> Approximately 15[%] of the NIS in the United States cause severe harm. High impact species—such as the zebra mussel, gypsy moth, or leafy spurge (*Euphorbia esula*) (a weed)—occur through the country. Almost every part of the United States confronts at least one highly damaging NIS today. They affect many national interests: agriculture, industry, human health, and the protection of natural areas.
>
> The number and impact of harmful NIS are chronically underestimated, especially for species that do not damage agriculture, industry, or human health. Harmful NIS cost millions to perhaps billions of dollars annually. From 1906 to 1991, just 79 NIS caused documented losses of $97 billion in harmful effects, for example. A worst-case scenario for 15 potential high-impact NIS puts forth another $134 billion in future economic losses. The figures represent only a part of the total documented and possible costs—that is, they do not include a large number of species known to be costly but for which little or no economic data were available, e.g., non-indigenous agricultural weeds. Nor do they account for intangible, nonmarket impacts.
>
> Harmful NIS also have had profound environmental consequences, exacting a significant toll on U.S. ecosystems. These range from wholesale ecosystem

changes and extinction of indigenous species (especially on islands) to more subtle ecological changes and increased biological sameness. . . .[6]

It is easy to list harmful NIS that do not seem to be included in the cumulative economic and ecological assessments. For example at the turn of the last century, chestnut blight—a non-indigenous disease—appeared in the United States and decimated eastern forests by wiping out the American chestnut. The American chestnut was the most important hardwood species in eastern forests[7] and constituted 25% of the trees and a substantial portion of the biomass in those forests. The blight is estimated to have killed as many as one billion trees.[8] Any estimate of economic harm from chestnut blight is likely to be highly speculative, and it is not clear that this harm was included in the OTA estimates.

Table 1[9]

Table 1 [OTA Table 1-1] Estimated Numbers of Non-Indigenous Species in the United States[a]		
Species with origins outside of the United States		
Category	Number	Percentage of total species in the United States in category
Plants	>2,000	[b]
Terrestrial vertebrates	142	=6%
Insects and arachnids	>2,000	=2%
Fish	70	=8%[c]
Mollusks (non-marine)	91	=4%
Plant pathogens	239	[b]
Total	4,542	
Species of U.S. origin introduced beyond their natural ranges		
Category	Number	Percentage of total species in the United States in category
Plants	[b]	[b]
Terrestrial vertebrates	51	=2%
Insects and arachnids	[b]	[b]
Fish	57	=17%
Mollusks (non-marine)	[b]	[b]
Plant pathogens	[b]	[b]

[a] Numbers should be considered minimum estimates. Experts believe many more NIS are established in the country, but have not yet been detected.
[b] Number or proportion unknown.
[c] Percentage for fish is the calculated average percentage for several regions. Percentages for all other categories are calculated as the percent of the total U.S. flora or fauna in that category.

Other reports, popular and technical, have tried to capture the scope of harm from NIS in the United States, and have concluded that the impact is even greater than the OTA report suggests. A 1999 Congressional Research Service (CRS) report cited an unpublished study estimating NIS costs at $123 billion annually.[10] Another study concluded in 1998 that NIS are second only to habitat destruction as a cause of modern extinction.[11]

Reports on the harm from NIS are equally dramatic when focused on specific areas and specific invaders. For example, among the best state-level evaluations of general NIS issues is a 1992 report by the Nature Conservancy of Hawaii and the National Resources Defense Council (NRDC) titled *The Alien Species Invasion in Hawaii: Background Study and Recommendations for Interagency Planning*.[12] This report found significant financial impact on Hawaii's $1 billion annual agriculture industry; ecosystem degradation, especially of watershed forests; financial harm to housing from an introduced termite; harm to rangeland; and threats to human health. The report also found that "[t]he primary cause of [ecosystem changes], and the greatest single threat to native species, is predation or competition by non-native weeds and animal pests."[13]

Breathtaking economic and ecological impacts leap from the pages of various reports that begin with a focus on one area or problem. An excellent 1999 report on NIS in the Great Lakes suggests the scope of alien species issues at regional scales:

> Harmful exotic aquatic organisms (aquatic nuisance species) do economic damage in the range of several billion dollars per year, damage native fishery resources, and cause irreplaceable loss to the biodiversity of the planet. Some of the past invaders of the Great Lakes include the sea lamprey, purple loosestrife, the alewife, furunculosus, Eurasian watermilfoil, protozoan fish parasites, European ruffe, the Asiatic clam, and the zebra mussel. The threat includes organisms throughout the taxonomic scale, from fish and macroscopic plants to bacteria and viruses. The majority of current aquatic invaders of the Great Lakes enter through ballast water of transoceanic commercial shipping. Other major vectors of concern are commercial transportation of aquatic organisms across large ecological zones for use as aquaculture, bait, and aquarium or ornamental pond fish. Genetic modification of native species for use in aquaculture is also a matter of concern.[14]

Both technical and policy literatures reveal widespread agreement that the NIS problem in the United States is substantial on economic, ecological, and aesthetic dimensions. The problems are so substantial and so varied, both in cause and in impact, that they are difficult to frame in policy and research terms. In other words, descriptions of the harm from specific invasive species often show a concreteness and specificity that aggregate descriptions lack. But I have found no serious (or for that matter, nonserious) statement suggesting that modern scientific concerns with NIS are overblown.

Despite this consistent view in the scientific and policy literature about NIS, general concern for NIS has only recently begun to attract much popular—or political—attention. Indeed, until recently, only a handful of NIS had received widespread recognition for the harm they caused. Even the OTA report recognizes that only a handful of economically significant species led to Congress' request for this report. These species include the zebra mussel and Asian clam, the gypsy moth, and leafy spurge. The list might easily and fairly be expanded to include another dozen organisms. However, it would be fair to say that general NIS threats, as opposed to species or location-specific concerns, are much more an emerging phenomenon.[15]

But, as Bob Dylan noted some years back: "There's a battle outside, and it is ragin' . . . for the times, they are a-changin'."[16] Over the past several years, there has been a dramatic increase in the number of news stories that address the potential harm from NIS. Increasingly, the popular media highlights invasive species beyond the handful that have achieved statutory responses and widespread recognition. For reasons that are not hard to understand, news stories tend to focus on invasive species with substantial economic impacts or other impacts on human enjoyment. For example, Africanized honeybees have received widespread coverage, as have concerns about the spread of fire ants. In both cases, the direct impact on peoples' lives may help sell the stories.

News stories have been expanding, in number and scope, to include a wider range of invasive species with a wider range of impacts. Chart 1 illustrates the trend toward increasing coverage of NIS issues in the U.S. media.[17] Illustrations of U.S. media coverage of invasive species issues can be found on the National Invasive Species Council web site.[18]

Chart 1

NIS U.S. News Stories, 1980-2003

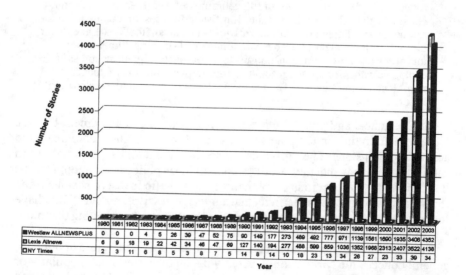

	1980	1981	1982	1983	1984	1985	1986	1987	1988	1989	1990	1991	1992	1993	1994	1995	1996	1997	1998	1999	2000	2001	2002	2003
■ Westlaw ALLNEWSPLUS	0	0	0	4	5	26	39	47	52	75	90	149	177	273	489	492	777	971	1139	1561	1690	1935	3405	4352
▨ Lexis Allnews	6	9	18	19	22	42	34	46	47	69	127	140	194	277	488	599	859	1036	1352	1968	2313	2407	3522	4138
▢ NY Times	2	3	11	6	8	5	3	8	7	5	14	8	14	10	18	23	13	34	26	27	23	33	39	34

Year

The increase in popular attention to NIS issues is reflected in books and magazines as well. The best illustration of this trend may be the 1998 book *Alien Invasion: America's Battle With Non-Native Plants and Animals*.[19] This volume, written by science writer Robert Devine, was published by the National Geographic Society, and appeared with an introduction by then-Secretary of the Interior Bruce Babbitt. Another current popular overview of NIS issues appears in the 1998 book *Life Out of Bounds: Bioinvasion in a Borderless World*.[20]

The scientific literature addressing invasive species has been growing steadily, and one journal—the *Journal of Biological Invasions*[21]—is devoted to the topic. The legal literature devoted to invasive species is far more sparse, but even among legal scholars there seems to be some increasing attention to NIS issues.

NIS have a substantial presence in scientific discourse, a growing popular recognition, and a small but growing presence in legal literature. But to what extent are they part of our laws? The answer, oddly, is a lot, and a little.

U.S. LEGAL AUTHORITY

The most important point about U.S. NIS law is that there is very little, and yet, in another sense, there is a lot. There are a small number of U.S. federal laws that address specific NIS issues directly, but there are a huge number of U.S. federal laws that grant authority and funding to agencies that might be used to deal with NIS problems. Moreover, there are two dramatic presidential Executive Orders directly addressing NIS issues, the first issued by President Carter in 1977 and the second by President Clinton in February 1999. Finally, there are a host of regulations and practices in federal agencies and less formal working groups that also address NIS issues.

This paradox—the essential absence and, at the same time, the abundance of relevant legal authority—is the major puzzle that this chapter tries to solve. To do so, I first present summaries of current law, and then suggest the limits of available law to serve as a foundation for a general legal framework to deal with harmful NIS. Finally, given the indirect and odd nature of much of the available legal authority, I point out what does not yet exist—what is missing from this seemingly rich legal bouillabaisse.

The first part of this section describes the federal legal authority that exists, summarizing explicit federal NIS statutory authority and then noting, in passing, the general authorizing legislation for relevant government agencies. It then describes general federal governmental powers under environmental legislation not designed primarily (and perhaps at all) with NIS in mind. The second and more detailed part of this section evaluates the two presidential Executive Orders. In a very direct way, these presidential Executive Orders test the combined powers of all available laws since they rely on those collective powers to direct federal agencies to act.

Federal Statutory Authority

The first question regarding current federal statutory authority is whether current law directly addresses the general issue of harmful NIS: it does not. A more interesting question with regard to current authority, however, is whether enough partial and indirect authority exists that, when read expansively, would allow current federal agencies to act appropriately to deal with harmful NIS.

No one has yet published a full accounting of U.S. legal authority that might be applicable to government responses to harmful NIS. The OTA report concluded that "[t]he current Federal effort is largely a patchwork of laws, regulations, policies, and programs. Many only peripherally address NIS, while others address the more narrowly drawn problems of the past, not the broader emerging issues."[22] An April 1999 CRS report titled *Harmful Non-Native Species: Issues for Congress*, concluded that "[f]ederal law concerning non-native species is scattered. No laws focus on the broad problems of non-native species, their interception, prevention, and control across a variety of industries and habitats."[23] At another point, the CRS report summarized U.S. federal law this way:

> [I]n the century or so of congressional responses to harmful, non-native species, the usual approach has been an ad hoc attack on the particular problem, from impure seed stocks, to brown tree snakes on Guam. A few attempts have been made to address specific pathways, e.g., contaminated ballast water, but no current law addresses the general concern over non-native species and the variety of paths by which they enter this country.[24]

The CRS report did provide a list of relevant federal laws, but none of the discussions of any one law, even the most relevant, extended more than a few paragraphs. The OTA report made reference to a number of federal laws, but did not analyze any of those laws in detail. The OTA was primarily interested in what federal and state agencies were doing (under whatever authority) and what such agencies might do, rather than in specifying the precise limits on government power under current statutes and regulations. Indeed, some of the assertions about federal law in the OTA report seem open to challenge.

The reasons that a comprehensive survey of U.S. law on invasive species has not been done is partly practical, but more importantly the challenges are conceptual and functional. The practical challenge arises because of the immense number of minor legal provisions that might be used to justify policy responses to invasive species. Such provisions would include appropriations and spending bills for relevant agencies, and many pieces of legislation with no obvious link to invasive species, such as the organic acts (the initial, general authorization and authority) for the many relevant government agencies.[25] Thus, practically, a complete listing of all potentially relevant U.S. legal authority would be a dreary project, and it would produce a ponderous product.

More importantly, even an exhaustive survey of potentially relevant statutory authority would not produce a determinate answer to the abstract question "what legal authority might be used to support invasive species policies." The full answer, if there is ever to be a full answer, would come in light of judicial, executive, or legislative challenges to particular policy initiatives. Moreover, a catalog of all potentially applicable legal authorities would not be especially revealing, since it would be unlikely to answer the most immediate and important questions about how either the federal or state governments are responding, or how they should respond, to harmful NIS.

Providing a comprehensive review of U.S. law might be necessary in defense of some government action that is alleged to be lawless (or less dramatically, beyond current authority). Indeed, it is fair to say that for most conceivable federal government actions with respect to NIS there would probably be a reasonable claim that authority exists, should such actions be challenged in court. But such a study of the plausible outer reaches of the law is not necessary or even useful to answer the question of what general legal authority is currently used in responding to harmful NIS, or whether additional legal authority (and responsibility) would be useful.

While it is useful to consider whether the current authority might be stretched to cover new policy initiatives, the very need to imagine creative readings and understandings of current authority highlights the most important point: most aspects of the harmful NIS problem are not clearly addressed in current law. Moreover, examining the minutiae of the mass of legal authority that might be brought to bear on the problem of harmful NIS could also obscure the important virtues—from the standpoint of efficiency, funding, coherent policy, and public understanding—of designing laws to address serious problems directly.

Explicit Federal Statutory NIS Authority

"Black List" and "Exclusion" Acts

> "There is a compensation in the distribution of plants, birds, and animals by the God of nature. Man's attempt to change and interfere often leads to serious results."
>
> Rep. John Lacey (R-Ind.)
> 33 Cong. Rec. 4871 (1900)

The recognition that NIS might cause harm has been evident in U.S. federal law at least since the Lacey Act, first enacted in 1900 and substantially revised in recent years.[26] It was originally enacted for a range of purposes anchored to the idea of protecting native wildlife, especially birds that were being commercially harvested for their feathers. A particular place of concern was the Everglades. The sponsors were not only aware of the lack of controls on commerce in wild species among the states, as well as between nations, but they also recognized that alien species could harm native species and ecosystems (though, of course, Representative Lacey and his colleagues did not use the term "ecosystems"). Harms from sparrows and starlings that had been introduced in the latter half of the 19th century were noted in the legislative history.[27]

The Laccy Act currently provides the federal government with authority to ban the import, export, or transportation of "any fish or wildlife" or "any plant" that is made illegal by "any law, treaty[,] or regulation" of the United States or of any individual state.[28] The Act provides for both civil penalties of a modest nature, e.g., knowingly or negligently violating the Act may result in a penalty of "not more than $10,000 for each such violation,"[29] and criminal penalties, up to five years in prison and a $20,000 fine for each violation.[30]

The Lacey Act seems to provide broad authority to the government to ban harmful NIS. There are other aspects of the Lacey Act that also have this sweeping character. For example, the Act provides enforcement authority to the Secretary of the Interior, the Secretary of Transportation, and the Secretary of the Treasury.[31] The Act also explicitly leaves U.S. states free to make or enforce laws "not inconsistent" with the federal provisions.[32]

The problem with relying on the Lacey Act's general authority to ban animal and plant species is that these powers only apply to animals and plants that are made illegal under federal or state law. The key provision of the Lacey Act that establishes the authority to specify which organisms should be excluded is substantially more restrictive than the general enforcement powers, which relate to organisms identified not only under the Lacey Act, but also under other federal and state laws. Title 18, §42 provides the following:

> The importation into the United States ... or any shipment between the continental United States [and Hawaii, Puerto Rico, U.S. territories or possessions] of the mongoose of the species Herpestes auropunctatus; of the species of so-called flying foxes or fruit bats of the genus Pteropus; of the zebra mussel of the species Dreissena polymorpha and such other species of wild mammals, wild birds, fish (including mollusks and crustracea), amphibians, reptiles, brown tree snakes, or the offspring of eggs of any of the foregoing which the Secretary of the Interior may prescribe by regulation to be injurious to human beings, to the interests of agriculture, forestry, or to wildlife or the wildlife resources of the United States, is hereby prohibited.[33]

There are three major limitations that prevent the Lacey Act from being or becoming a general harmful NIS law.[34] First, while the Lacey Act provides the Secretary of the Interior the power to exclude several species of particular concern, as demonstrated above, as well as some other animals, it does not provide for the exclusion of plants, seeds, or plant pests.[35] This gap in the Lacey Act is partially closed by a host of federal statutes that, together, provide federal officials with power to exclude many kinds of harmful plant pests, seeds, and noxious weeds. These acts are the Plant Pest Act,[36] the Plant Quarantine Act,[37] the Federal Noxious Weed Act of 1974,[38] and the Federal Seed Act.[39] In May 2000, Congress passed the Plant Protection Act, which consolidated and revised the Plant Quarantine Act, the Plant Pest Act, the Federal Noxious Weed Act, aspects of the Department of Agriculture Organic Act, and several less prominent acts.[40]

Second, the Lacey Act focuses on identifying harmful species with the purpose of limiting their importation. But introduction of new NIS, or harmful NIS, is only one aspect of the NIS problem. Many NIS have already been introduced, many have already caused great harm, and even the most stringent barriers to introduction of known harmful NIS will not keep some harmful NIS, known and unknown, from entering the country. A complete law regarding harmful NIS would address not only the identification of potentially harmful NIS, but also the review of proposed introductions not known to be harmful, and the proper response to harmful NIS already in place. In addition, a comprehensive legal response to NIS would address various education and research efforts to address the cultural and scientific aspects that contribute to expanding or limiting the NIS problem.

The third major problem with the Lacey Act as the foundation for a complete strategy to deal with harmful NIS is that it authorizes the creation of a list of forbidden animals—a "black list" or "exclusion list"—but it does not authorize the exclusion of animals whose threat is unknown.

Laws that are passed for a particular purpose or based on a specific understanding often change over time in light of shifts in knowledge or culture, yet they may still grant sufficient legal authority for government to respond to the newer demands and conceptions. Could the Secretary of the Interior simply declare that all species of animals and plants not previously approved are disapproved, and thus convert the "black" list to a "white" list?

Probably not. Both the text of 18 U.S.C. §42 and the history of the Lacey Act suggest that Congress requires the Secretary of the Interior to make a particular finding that a particular species is "injurious to human beings, to the interests of agriculture, forestry, or to wildlife or the wildlife resources of the United States."[41] The Secretary of the Interior has issued regulations that appear to limit the importation of any live wildlife or eggs under the Lacey Act, but this broad assertion of authority has not been tested.[42] Even if a court were to uphold this broad reading of the Lacey Act, the limitations of the Act as a general foundation for harmful NIS law would remain.

The May 2000 Plant Protection Act shows clear signs of Congress' increasing awareness of the importance of NIS issues and the need for more coherent legislative responses. The Plant Protection Act provides a unitary framework for dealing with plant pests and noxious weeds. While the statement of findings recognizes that plant pests and noxious weeds threaten "the agriculture, environment, and economy of the United States,"[43] and noxious weeds are defined to include "any plant or plant product that can directly injure or cause damage to . . . the natural resources of the United States . . . or the environment,"[44] it is nevertheless apparent that the principal focus of the Act is to protect against agricultural and other economic harms, since the environment is not a prominent concern in the remainder of the Act.[45]

The 2000 Plant Protection Act suggests the importance of mere reorganization and simplification of laws that relate to harmful invasive species. However, the Plant Protection Act does not merely reorganize existing law. It expands the regulatory and enforcement powers over plant pests and noxious weeds, including new civil penalty structures.[46] The Act also encourages a steady use of science,[47] the wide involvement of experts and stakeholders in policymaking, consideration of "systems approaches," the development of integrated management plans on the basis of geographic and ecological regions, and the authorization of new types of classification systems. While some of these systematic concepts were evident in prior law, the new act joins them to regulatory and enforcement mechanisms and thus offers the hope for more effective, efficient, and informed federal plant pest and noxious weed policies.

Several provisions, however, plant their own substantial seeds for mischief. For example, the Act encourages the use of biological pest controls, finding that "biological control is often a desirable, low-risk means of ridding crops and other plants of plant pests and noxious weeds."[48] Biological controls are themselves invasive species—additional biological pollution.[49] Congress does not seem to have considered this fact, or the very mixed record of biological controls over the past century.[50]

Congress chose to create a strong federal preemption of state efforts to regulate plant pests and noxious weeds.[51] States and political subdivisions are forbidden to regulate "any article, means of conveyance, plant, biological control organism, plant pest, noxious weed, or plant product" in an effort to control, eradicate, or prevent the introduction of plant pests, noxious weeds, or biological control organisms.[52] States and local subdivisions are also barred from regulating the interstate commerce of these kinds of organisms when there are already federal regulations regarding these organisms.[53]

Given the varied needs of different states, most notably those with highly unique and susceptible ecosystems, such as Hawaii, these are extraordinary and unwise preemption provisions that go far beyond prior law. Whether or not these preemption provisions prove to be harmful will depend on how courts and agencies interpret the provision that allows regulation of interstate commerce when regulations "are consistent with" federal regulations, and how sympathetic and wise the Secretary of Commerce will be in response to state requests for waivers based on "special need."[54]

Some federal laws promote harmful NIS, and make it difficult or impossible for federal or state authorities to deal with important aspects of the harmful NIS problem. One example is the Wild Free-Roaming Horses and Burros Act, which protects some feral horses and burros from elimination or control.[55] A less clear but perhaps more important example is the sum of trade laws and international agreements that may place limits on the kinds of inspections and regulations the United States and its states can create for detection of harmful NIS.

What other federal laws might be used to fill in the requirements for a general law that responds to harmful NIS?[56]

National Invasive Species Act: Big Name, Narrow Scope

If awards were given for act titles, then anyone concerned with the threat from harmful NIS would give the grand prize to two federal statutes: the National Invasive Species Act (NISA) of 1996[57] and the Alien Species Prevention and Enforcement Act of 1992.[58]

NISA reauthorized a 1990 federal statute with a less encompassing but more accurate title: the Non-Indigenous Aquatic Nuisance Prevention and Control Act (NANPCA) of 1990.[59] The NANPCA focused on one place (the Great Lakes), on one pathway (ballast water), and was driven by concerns about one NIS (zebra mussel). It was a statute designed to organize state and federal forces against the zebra mussel and other NIS that had been, and might be, introduced through ballast water. The Act directed the U.S. Army Corp of Engineers to develop a research program for the control of zebra mussels.[60] (Clearly, Congress understood the invasion metaphor in this specific context.) The NANPCA created a federal interagency Aquatic Nuisance Species Task Force to reduce risk from harmful NIS. The task force was charged with assessing aquatic nuisance species threats to "the ecological characteristics and economic uses of U.S. waters other than the Great Lakes."[61]

In 1996, NISA expanded the focus of the NANPCA to mandate regulations to prevent introduction and spread of aquatic nuisance species.[62] In NISA, Congress encouraged the federal government to negotiate with foreign governments to develop an international program for preventing NIS introductions through ballast water. The geographical scope of the Act was expanded as well, to include funding authorization for research on aquatic NIS in the Chesapeake Bay, San Francisco Bay, Honolulu Harbor, and the Columbia River system.[63]

As of March 2003, a bill to reauthorize NISA has been introduced in the U.S. Senate and referred to committee.[64] The NISA of 2003 proposes to require mandatory ballast water regulations, and to encourage both further development of ballast water treatment and the use of best available technologies by the shipping industry, though with substantial lag time for adoption.[65] Sen. Susan Collins (R-Me.) introduced the bill with the following observations:

> As with national security, protecting the integrity of our lakes, streams, and coastlines from invading species cannot be accomplished by individual States alone. We need a uniform, nationwide approach to deal effectively with invasive species . . . .
>
> The [NISA] of 2003 is the most comprehensive effort ever to address the threat of invasive species. By authorizing $836 million over 6 years, this legislation would open numerous new fronts in our war against invasive species. The bill directs the [U.S.] Coast Guard to develop regulations that will end the easy cruise of invasive species into U.S. waters through the ballast water of international ships, and would provide the Coast Guard with $6 million per year to develop and implement these regulations.
>
> The bill also would provide $30 million per year for a grant program to assist State efforts to prevent the spread of invasive species. It would provide $12 million per year for the U.S. Army Corps of Engineers and U.S. Fish and Wildlife Service to contain and control invasive species. Finally, the Levin-Collins Bill would authorize $30 million annually for research, education, and outreach.
>
> The most effective means of stopping invading species is to attack them before they attack us. We need an early alert, rapid response system to combat invading species before they have a chance to take hold. For the first time, this bill would establish a national monitoring network to detect newly introduced species, while providing $25 million to the Secretary of the Interior to create a rapid response fund to help States and regions respond quickly once invasive species have been detected. This bill is our best effort at preventing the next wave of invasive species from taking hold and decimating industries and destroying waterways in Maine and throughout the country.[66]

NISA may well be a good piece of legislation for responding to threats from aquatic invasive species introduced in ballast water; if a version anything like the proposed reauthorization is enacted the legislation will be even better.[67] The increase in authority and scope from the NANPCA to NISA in 1996 suggests an increasing awareness on the part of Congress about the complexity of NIS issues, even in the focused context of the ballast water pathway. The proposed expansion of authority in 2003 and the range of bipartisan sponsorship for the bill suggests that Congress is likely to further expand the mandates and authorities with regard to aquatic invasive species, with a particular emphasis on regulating the introduction of NIS through ballast water.

But NISA fails to suggest a general model for responding to harmful NIS. The 1996 version demonstrates that Congress did not then recognize the NIS problem to be the serious problem that its own research agency, the OTA, had described only three years earlier in its path-breaking report. The reauthorization of NISA in 2003, if it succeeds, will be evidence of Congress' awareness of the nature and scope of one slice of the NIS problem (aquatic species).

The second linguistically promising federal statute is the Alien Species Prevention and Enforcement Act (ASPEA) of 1992.[68] Unfortunately, the major (and useful) purpose of this act, despite its grand title, was simply to confirm the authority to make illegal the shipment through the mail of otherwise illegal organisms, including those species identified under the Lacey Act, the Plant Pest Act, and the Plant Quarantine Act. ASPEA does not itself create any new categories of organisms that are illegal to ship, nor does it create any presumptions or institutions to help in responding to harmful NIS.

Individual members of Congress have shown increasing awareness of threats specific to their jurisdictions and especially agricultural, commercial, and industrial interests with strong concerns about harm from invasive species. Thus, in the first session of the 108th Congress alone, Congress passed the Nutria Eradication and Control Act of 2003[69] and introduced the Tamarisk Research and Control Act of 2003,[70] the Salt Cedar Control Demonstration Act,[71] and the Noxious Weed Control Act of 2003.[72]

General Environmental Policy Acts

There are at least two major federal environmental policy statutes and a set of public lands statutes that might apply to harmful NIS in some situations. The National Environmental Policy Act[73] (NEPA) requires federal government agencies to assess the environmental impact of their actions through the promulgation of an environmental impact statement (EIS). Yet many actions of the federal government that seem as if they could or should trigger EIS requirements, in fact, do not, due to both statutory and regulatory interpretations that limit NEPA to "major" government actions that "significantly" affect the quality of "the human environment."[74]

Claimants have argued that the federal government has failed to take account of the impact of invasive species under NEPA.[75] But even an expanded interpretation of NEPA to apply to as many federal actions as possible regarding NIS would cover only a modest portion of the full range of harmful NIS issues.[76] NEPA is primarily directed at the actions of federal agencies, and therefore would not apply to the myriad actions of individuals relevant to harmful NIS, or to the actions of state and local authorities. Moreover, NEPA assumes the possibility of expertise in recognizing and assessing future environmental harms from present actions. In the case of potentially harmful NIS, this kind of information and expertise may not be present, and the policy issue will then turn on legal presumptions and risk preferences in the face of great uncertainty. More importantly, even when NEPA applies, it only requires analysis of environmental impacts, but does not itself impose substantive barriers, preferences, or limits on government action.[77]

A second major federal environmental statute with some possible application to harmful NIS issues is the Endangered Species Act (ESA).[78] The ESA might apply whenever a government or private action threatens an endangered species. The ESA might also lead to direct actions against harmful NIS in the development of recovery plans for listed species. Since harmful NIS have been identified as a significant source of ecosystem change (which may lead to pressures on rare or endangered species), and in some contexts as a direct extinction threat through predation, competition, or displacement, the ESA might bar some introductions or lead to some efforts at removal.

The situations where the powerful effects of the ESA apply, however, are likely to be few. If the ESA applies at all in terms of introductions, it will most likely apply only to intentional introductions of NIS, and only to those introductions where a nexus can be found between the NIS and a listed species. Perhaps a creative argument under the ESA could focus on the risk of introducing harmful NIS that could have a substantial impact on a listed species. Thus, a claim might be made that particular activities (such as use of wood packing materials or whole log imports or release of ballast water) provide a sufficient risk to a listed species to come within regulation under a recovery plan or a voluntary habitat conservation plan (HCP), but courts might well find such links too distant to support such policies.[79] More directly, a recovery plan for a species listed under the ESA can involve control of existing harmful NIS. While control of NIS is apparently a common feature of recovery plans according to the OTA report, implementation of recovery plans, at least with respect to components related to harmful NIS, has been poor.[80]

In at least one prominent case the federal courts have several times upheld an order to the Hawaiian Department of Land and Natural Resources to remove non-indigenous goats and sheep that threatened the endangered palila bird. The unlikelihood of the ESA and recovery plans becoming a major mechanism for control of harmful NIS is suggested not only by the limited numbers of species listed under the ESA, but by the very caption of the federal case: *Palila (Psittirostra bailleui), an endangered species v. Hawaii Department of Land & Natural Resources*.[81] Thus, while the ESA creates government obligations and provides government powers beyond other statutes, for the general range of harmful NIS these obligations and powers are in practice fairly limited.

Another broad class of federal laws that provide authority to federal agencies that have at times been used for regulation and policy with respect to harmful invasive species are the federal public lands laws, especially the Multiple Use Sustained Yield Act of 1960,[82] the National Forest Management Act of 1976,[83] and the Federal Land Policy and Management Act of 1976.[84] These acts, and related historical and contemporary legislation governing grazing, timber, and other uses of federal lands, provide a broad array of authorities and responsibilities with respect to public lands. Similar legislation aimed at the governance of smaller federal land units includes the National Wildlife Refuge System Administration Act.[85] In addition, the powers granted under these sweeping public land laws may be magnified further still, and extended to some activities on state and private lands, under the expansive interpretation of the U.S. Constitution's "Property Clause," which provides that "[t]he Congress shall have power to . . . make all needful rules and regulations respecting the Territory or other property belonging to the United States."[86]

In addition to these major federal environmental statutes, a host of more focused environmental and nonenvironmental laws also have some relevance to harmful NIS. For example, the Wild Bird Conservation Act of 1992[87] regulates the importation of some wild birds, and thus might limit both the introduction of birds that pose a special risk of becoming harmful NIS should they escape, and might as well reduce the chance of accidental introduction of bird diseases through careless importation of wild birds.[88] Other pieces of legislation, seemingly utterly unrelated to NIS issues on their surface, include a handful of odd provisions, some with very direct relevance. For example, the Violent Crime Control and Law Enforcement Act of 1994 includes a provision authorizing the U.S. Attorney General to convene a multiagency, federal, and state "law enforcement task force in Hawaii to facilitate the prosecution of violations of Federal laws, and laws of the State of Hawaii, relating to the wrongful conveyance, sale, or introduction of non-indigenous plant and animal species."[89]

At this point in our review of federal U.S. authority relating to harmful NIS, a reader might ask why analysis of any additional laws is necessary. If the most direct federal legislation (the various black list acts) and the most grandly titled legislation (NISA and ASPEA) and the most sweeping environmental legislation (NEPA and ESA) together leave enormous gaps in terms of government authority to respond to harmful NIS, then why look at less direct laws? Why not declare analytic victory and substantive defeat and move on to an assessment of what kinds of new legal authority might be appropriate?

If only the analytic task were so easy! Tables 2 and 3, taken from the OTA report, suggest one reason why considerable additional analysis is required to understand the federal U.S. NIS legal picture. These tables show 21 different federal agencies that deal with some aspect of harmful NIS. This multitude of government actors suggests (though alone it does not prove) that there must be far greater legal authority to deal with NIS than is described by the handful of statutes dealing explicitly with narrow aspects of the NIS problem. This long list of federal government actors also suggests that perhaps the sum of federal legal authority to deal with NIS may be great enough to respond to most NIS problems after all.

Table 2 – Areas of Federal Agency Activity Related to NIS [OTA Table 6-2]

Agency[a]	Movement into U.S. — Restrict	Movement into U.S. — Enhance	Interstate movement within U.S. — Restrict	Interstate movement within U.S. — Enhance	Regulate product content or labeling	Control or eradication programs	Fund or do introductions	Federal land management — Prevent eradication or control	Federal land management — Introduce or maintain	Fund or do research — Prevention control eradication	Fund or do research — Uses of species	Fund or do research — Aquaculture development	Fund or do research — Biocontrol development
APHIS	✓		✓	✓		✓	✓			✓	✓		✓
AMS	✓		✓		✓								
FAS		b											
USFS						✓	✓	✓	✓				
ARS		✓		✓						✓	✓	✓	✓
SCS		✓		✓						✓			
ASCS							✓						
CSRS										✓	✓	✓	✓
FWS	✓		✓		✓	✓	✓	✓	✓	✓	✓	✓	✓
NPS						✓		✓	✓	✓	✓		✓
BLM						✓		✓	✓	✓	✓		✓
BIA						✓			✓				
BOR				✓		✓			✓	✓			
NOAA	✓				✓					✓	✓	✓	✓
DOD	✓									✓			
EPA	✓							e	e	✓	d		
PHS	✓		c							✓			
Customs	✓												
USCG	✓									✓			
DOE									e				
DEA	✓												

[a] Acronyms of Federal Agencies: Department of Agriculture—Animal and Plant Health Inspection Service (APHIS); Agricultural Marketing Service (AMS); Foreign Agricultural Service (FAS); Forest Service (USFS); Agricultural Research Service (ARS); Soil Conservation Service (SCS); Agricultural Stabilization and Conservation Service (ASCS); Cooperative State Research Service (CSRS); Department of the Interior—Fish and Wildlife Service (FWS); National Park Service (NFS); Bureau of Land Management (BLM); Bureau of Indian Affairs (BIA); Bureau of Reclamation (BOR); Department of Commerce—National Oceanic and Atmospheric Administration (NOAA); Department of Defense (DOD); Environmental Protection Agency (EPA); Department of Health and Human Services—Public Health Service (PHS); Department of the Treasury—Customs Service (Customs); Department of Transportation—Coast Guard (USCG); Department of Energy (DOE); Department of Justice—Drug Enforcement Agency (DEA).

[b] Monitors animal diseases abroad.

[c] Monitors spread of human disease vectors within the United States.

[d] Regulates experimental releases of microbial pesticides.

[e] DOE lacks policies on NIS.

Table 3—Federal Coverage of Different Groups of Organisms [OTA Table 6-3]

	Movement into U.S. Restrict	Movement into U.S. Enhance	Interstate Movement within U.S. Restrict	Interstate Movement within U.S. Enhance	Regulate product content or labeling	Control or eradication programs	Fund or do introduction	Prevent eradication or control	Introduce or maintain	Prevention control eradication	Uses of species	Assist industry uses
Plants	APHIS, DOD, Customs, DEA	ARS[c], SCS[c]	APHIS, AMS	ARS, SCS, DOD[b]	APHIS, AMS	APHIS, FWS, BIA, BOR, NOAA, DOD	ARS[c], ASCS[c]	USFS, FWS, NPS, BLM, DOD	FWS, NPS, DOD	APHIS, ARS, SCS, CSRS, FWS, NPS, BLM, BOR, DOD	USFS[c], ARS[c], SCS[c]	ARS[c], SCS[c]
Terrestrial vertebrates	APHIS, FWS, DOD, PHS, Customs	DOD[b]	APHIS, FWS		FWS	APHIS, FWS	FWS	FWS, NPS	USFS, FWS, NPS, BLM, DOD	APHIS, FWS, NPS		
Insects (and arachnids)	APHIS, FAS, ARS, DOD, PHS, Customs	ARS[d], DOD[b]	APHIS	ARS[d], DOD[b]		APHIS, USFS	ARS[d], USFS[d], DOD[d]	USFS, NPS, BLM	USFS[d], NPS[d], BLM[d]	APHIS, USFS, ARS, CSRS, NPS, PHS	APHIS[d], ARS[d], ARS, NPS[d], DOD[d]	ARS[d], CSRS[d]
Fish	FWS, Customs, USCG		FWS	DOD[d]	FWS	FWS, BOR	FWS, BOR[d]	NPS, BLM	USFS, FWS, NPS, BLM, DOD	FWS, NPS, NOAA, EPA, USCG	ARS[e], CSRS[e], FWS[e], NOAA[e]	ARS[e], CSRS[e], FWS[de], NOAA[e]
Invertebrate (non-insect)	APHIS, ARS, FWS, DOD, PHS, Customs, USCG		APHIS, FWS	DOD[b]	FWS	APHIS				FWS, NPS, NOAA, EPA, USCG	ARS[d], NOAA[e], CSRS[e]	ARS[e], CSRS[e], DOD[d]
Microbes	APHIS, FAS, ARS, FWS, NOAA, DOD, EPA, PHS, Customs, USCG	ARS[d], DOD[d]	APHIS		EPA	APHIS, USFS, FWS	ARS[d], USFS[d]	USFS, NPS	USFS[d], NPS[d]	APHIS, USFS, ARS, CSRS, FWS, NPS, NOAA, USCG	ARS[d], CSRS[d], NPS[d]	ARS[d]

[b] Pests move unintentionally with equipment or due to construction.
[c] Plants for agriculture, horticulture, or soil conservation.
[d] Biological control agents.
[e] Aquaculture.

Federal Agency Legal Powers

The 21 government agencies identified by the OTA fall under the cabinet-level direction of 10 different government departments.[90] The most important of these agencies for dealing with NIS, including the Animal and Plant Health Inspection Service (APHIS), the Agricultural Research Service (ARS), the U.S. Forest Service (USFS), the U.S. Fish and Wildlife Service (FWS), and the National Park Service (NPS), all fall under the authority of two departments—the U.S. Department of Agriculture (USDA) and the U.S. Department of the Interior (DOI).

Federal government agencies get their power from a number of sources. One source of authority is the original or so-called organic acts that generally create a government department or agency and provide it with particular responsibilities and authority. Another common source of authority is a statute, such as the Lacey Act or Plant Pest Act or the other statutes described in previous sections, that direct the agency, or the executive generally, to act in some way—whether to achieve a goal, or respond to a problem, or develop procedures, or whatever.[91] A third source of authority derives from appropriations acts, which can explicitly or implicitly (by appropriating funds for specific purposes) provide government agencies with additional substantive authority.[92]

For example, and of most relevance to control of harmful NIS, the USDA finds its general authority in legislation known as the Organic Act of 1944.[93] The general provisions are often expanded and modified by later legislation, including the various substantive acts such as the new Plant Protection Act. Thus, over time, general concepts recognized in organic and other general pieces of legislation can be expanded to include ideas such as whether a plant pest is native or non-indigenous. As early as 1957, Congress recognized that some plant pests are alien or "imported."[94]

Congress creates some agencies, while others are created by the cabinet-level officers under the general authority of the department as a whole. When Congress creates a new agency, then that agency is likely to have its own organic (originating) statute. For example, the NPS, while part of the DOI, has its own National Park Service Organic Act, first passed in 1916.[95] The organic statutes for particular agencies might provide indirect authority for dealing with harmful NIS. For example, the National Park Service Organic Act directs the NPS to

> promote and regulate the use of the Federal areas known as national parks, monuments, and reservations . . . to conserve the scenery and the natural and historic objects and the wild life [sic] therein and to provide for the enjoyment of the same in such manner and by such means as will leave them unimpaired for the enjoyment of future generations.[96]

When agencies are created within the executive branch, Congress will both appropriate funds directed toward particular offices, and otherwise grant specific additional authority to those particular agencies. For example, there is no general authorizing act for APHIS,[97] which is the most important federal agency for preventing harmful NIS introductions, but Congress has granted

APHIS authority to contract for services to be performed outside the United States.[98]

Government authority to respond to harmful NIS arises from at least one additional source, which is international law that is reflected in treaties signed by the United States. Perhaps the best example of such legal authority is the Convention on International Trade in Endangered Species of Wild Fauna and Flora (CITES),[99] which provides additional authority for border inspections and creates an independent basis (indeed, an independent obligation), even in the absence of listing a species under one of the "black list" acts, for exclusion. The OTA report lists seven treaties with direct effects on harmful NIS and seven treaties with indirect effects on harmful NIS, including CITES.[100]

Apparent government authority to deal with harmful NIS appears in two additional settings: regulations and rules issued by relevant government agencies, and the activities of interagency "working groups" or councils. On the one hand, the rules and regulations of government agencies can provide the most specific illustrations of government response to harmful NIS. For example, regulations issued by the National Oceanic and Atmosphere Administration (NOAA), which has a policy role regarding various coastal resources, forbid "any person" from "introducing or releasing an exotic species of plant, invertebrate, fish, amphibian, or mammals" into the Florida Keys National Marine Sanctuary.[101] But regulations can also encourage the introduction of NIS, and even harmful NIS. For example, USDA regulations for a conservation reserve program allows "practices specific in the conservation plan that meet all standards needed to cost-effectively establish permanent vegetative or water cover, including introduced or native species of grasses and legumes, forest trees, and permanent wildlife habitat . . . ."[102]

Similarly, interagency working groups, which may also be interjurisdictional, and which may (or may not) be authorized specifically by statute, such as the Aquatic Nuisance Species Task Force, and the Federal Interagency Committee for Management of Noxious and Exotic Weeds (FICMNEW), are often the groups with the most direct and substantial interest in harmful NIS.

I refer to both the authority implicit in regulations and the authority in working groups as "apparent" because such regulations and groups can exercise only existing sources of legal authority; they cannot create new legal authority. Where substantial possible sources of authority exist, this may be a distinction without a difference. Moreover, to the extent that interagency working groups do not conduct activities that anyone can challenge, the lack of explicit legal authority may have no practical effect. To the extent, however, that one central question is what legal authority exists to deal with harmful NIS, regulations and working groups are not a source of such authority; indeed, they are not even evidence that such authority exists. Often agencies recognizing the general problem of invasive species or particular problems that appear to be within the agency's jurisdiction will not recognize or will sidestep questions of legal authority.[103]

If this combination of substantive statutes, general agency organic acts, various appropriations provisions, and binding international agreements have allowed 21 federal agencies to respond to varying degrees and in varying ways to harmful NIS, again an observer might fairly say: "Sure, this is a legal mess, but the total is, at least, the sum of the parts, and perhaps the parts, all together, make a working machine." If this were so, the legal mess would be a lawyer's quibble, and in the United States at least, those concerned about harmful NIS could focus solely on increasing appropriations and encouraging the various agencies to do more and to do what they do better.

A complete answer to the question of whether total sufficient legal authority exists to deal with harmful NIS requires a closer analysis than the scope of this chapter or the available literature can provide. A partial answer, however, is easy to provide. If the question is changed from "what are these myriad agencies doing?" to "what would we want government agencies to do in response to harmful NIS?" then huge gaps are revealed. That there may not be adequate federal legal authority to respond to the full range of issues raised by harmful NIS is suggested by a close examination of one other very important, and very odd kind of legal animal: two presidential Executive Orders directly addressing the problems of harmful NIS.

Executive Orders Addressing Harmful NIS

> A judge, like an executive advisor, may be surprised at the poverty of ically use-ful and unambiguous authority applicable to concrete problems of executive power as they actually present themselves. Just what our forefathers did envision, or would have envisioned had they foreseen modern conditions, must be divined from materials almost as enigmatic as the dreams Joseph was called upon to interpret for Pharaoh.
> Justice Robert H. Jackson,
> Youngstown Sheet & Tube Co. v. Sawyer,
> 343 U.S. 579, 634 (1952) (concurring)

Two Executive Orders, one issued by President Carter in 1977 and the other issued by President Clinton in 1999, directly address the problem of harmful NIS.

Executive Orders are an odd species of law, issued on occasion by the president.[104] They direct one or more federal agencies to act in a particular policy direction specified by the president. Executive Orders do not themselves create new government powers, and they cannot: legislative power is vested in the legislative branch (the Congress). The president can, however, rely on powers already vested in the executive branch by Congress, and those limited powers constitutionally committed to the president.

Why assess the effect of Executive Orders if they cannot create new legal authority? First, as the mass of possible legal authority in the prior sections suggests, the limits of the current authority remain unclear, and simply asserting greater authority might become a basis for some court (if a government action were properly challenged) to find authority in fact. Second, both Executive Orders on invasive species draw on the full range of available legal authority; in other words, they assert the maximum available authority in support of federal NIS efforts. This assertion of maximum authority highlights the necessity of understanding the greatest possible reach of current laws, at least in the absence of possible new or additional authority that might clarify current law, expand it, or fill gaps. Third, and related to the prior point, often the issue with regard to a problem with harmful NIS is not one of authority but of action, and of budgetary allocations, and in a unitary executive branch Executive Orders are the policy command of the president (at least in theory).

Executive Order No. 11987 (1977) (Carter)—Dramatic, Ignored, Defunct

President Carter issued Executive Order No. 11987 on May 24, 1977.[105] Although Executive Order No. 11987 has been entirely supplanted by Executive Order No. 13112, issued by President Clinton in 1999, it is still quite useful to review the fortunes of 11987, as it provides several lessons that might allow Executive Order No. 13112 a different and better fate.

Executive Order No. 11987 is an astounding document, as striking and unexpected, though not nearly as profound, as Charles Elton's classic 1958 book *The Ecology of Invasions by Plants and Animals*.[106] Some aspects of harmful NIS were of course part of public policy and debate by 1977, but NIS as a general issue had yet to strike public and political consciousness. For example, according to Devine the first effort to control any invasive plant in the Florida Everglades did not occur until 1969.[107]

Executive Order No. 11987 is not only unexpected because of its topic, but also because of its brevity, its clarity, and its more local, political timing. Executive Order No. 11987 is one page long. Discussions about it began within the White House only weeks after Carter took office in January 1977, and the order itself was issued as part of the first public policy statement on the environment by the Carter Administration. The heart of the order provides the following policy directives:

> (a) Executive agencies shall, to the extent permitted by law, restrict the introduction of exotic species into natural ecosystems on lands and waters which they own, lease, or hold for purposes of administration; and, shall encourage the States, local governments, and private citizens to prevent the introduction of exotic species into natural ecosystems of the United States.
> (b) Executive agencies, to the extent they have been authorized by statute to restrict the importation of exotic species, shall restrict the introduction of exotic species into any natural ecosystem of the United States.[108]

The short Executive Order included at least one other visionary aspect: it directed executive agencies to prevent the export of native (U.S.) species "for the purpose of introducing such species into ecosystems outside the United States where they do not naturally occur."[109] President Carter was not just concerned with U.S. ecosystems; he was concerned with the threat of NIS to the naturalness of all ecosystems.

Where did President Carter get the good idea that NIS were a bad idea? The answer, which emerges from a careful study of the Carter Presidential Papers, is that the interest of a handful of political advisors on the NIS issue, as well as Carter's own sensitivity to the impact of alien species, having lived in a farming area. This individual interest on the part of advisors and Carter himself was bolstered by the need to find early environmental initiatives that did not have substantial budget implications, since the funding decisions for Carter's first year in office had largely been set by the previous Congress and administration. The background statement issued with the release of the Executive Order included language that in its directness continues to help focus attention on harmful NIS issues even today, 27 years later. President Carter issued the Executive Order as part of an environmental message. The press covered the message, but largely ignored the exotic species Executive Order.

Executive Order No. 11987 had several dramatic flaws that ultimately proved fatal to its virtues. The most significant flaw was that the Executive Order included no complete procedure for implementing its policy directive. The order did direct the Secretary of the Interior, in consultation with the Secretary of Agriculture and other agencies, to "develop and implement, by rule or regulation, a system to standardize and simplify the requirements, procedures, and other activities appropriate for implementing" the order. The lack of specificity in this procedural language—in contrast to the strong substantive principles of the order—made this provision more harmful than helpful.

Executive Order No. 11987 disappeared from federal policy as dramatically as it first appeared. A September 15, 1977, memorandum written by the Council on Environmental Quality (CEQ) summarized the response of all federal agencies to the various aspects of the May 23, 1977, environmental message. Tucked away in this memorandum were a few lines on the question of the DOI's response to the directive to "develop legislation to restrict the impact of exotic plants and animals into the [United States]." The memorandum stated that "legislation is being developed with Agriculture," that agency progress was "adequate," and in what appears to be the final White House file entry on the subject, the "CEQ Progress Evaluation," that there were "delays in interagency meetings and in focus on problems."

Another flaw was that Executive Order No. 11987 defined "exotic species" to mean plants and animals "not naturally occurring, either presently or historically, in any ecosystem of the United States," while "native species" were those that did occur "in any ecosystem of the United States." These are political, not ecological boundaries. Executive Order No. 11987 simply did not recognize that movement of organisms among states and within states could cause problems similar to the introduction of organisms from abroad.[110]

A third problem with Executive Order No. 11987 was that it focused only on introductions into "natural ecosystems." While such a limitation reduced, to some extent, possible conflicts with commercial interests in industries such as agriculture and horticulture, the line between introductions in disturbed or artificial ecosystems on one hand and "natural" systems on the other may not be wise as a matter of science or policy. To the extent harmful NIS occur on disturbed or artificial land, and then move to more natural systems, and to the extent that the economic, ecological, or aesthetic harm is to disturbed or artificial systems, Executive Order No. 11987 may have created a barrier to proper regulation and policy.

A fourth flaw in Executive Order No. 11987 was the extent to which it focused only on new NIS introductions—the "release, escape, or establishment"—and seemed to ignore the possibility of reducing harm from the many NIS already established. Executive Order No. 11987 was issued 15 years before the OTA report, and the White House files and public statements suggest concerns for "hundreds" rather than the many thousands of NIS already in the United States. Still, even the most aggressive rules on new introductions would do little to stop the continuing and expanding harm from prior introductions, or from the inevitable occasional introductions that will occur even in a strict regulatory framework. The absence of a direct policy statement on established NIS is surprising to the extent that the signing statement and supporting executive branch documentation highlighted the harms from established invaders.

A fifth point about Executive Order No. 11987 is not so much a flaw as a warning sign not to read the currently legal authority too optimistically. While federal statutory legal authority to respond to harmful NIS has expanded somewhat since 1977, much of the legal framework, including the various "black list" acts and NEPA, were in place in 1977. The Carter White House files include several memoranda written in response to drafts that were circulated to cabinet and environmental agencies expressing support for the exotic species policy but doubts about whether available legal authority could support even the import and export policies that were the focus of the order.

The recognition among scientists, politicians, lawyers, and the public of the problems posed by harmful NIS has increased enormously since 1977, as suggested by the newspaper citation analysis in this chapter. Sophistication about the pitfalls of various kinds of administrative process is also considerably greater among lawyers now than 20 years ago. It is wrong, I think, to judge Executive Order No. 11987 as anything other than a truly bold but ultimately ineffectual statement of wise policy unfortunately ahead of its time.

Executive Order No. 13112 (1999) (Clinton)—Hopeful, Bureaucratic

What difference has 20 years made on executive policy? For one thing, Executive Order No. 13112,[111] promulgated by President Clinton on February 3, 1999, is a longer and more complex document, substantively and procedurally, than Executive Order No. 11987, which it replaced. Executive Order No. 13112 states its goal as preventing "the introduction of invasive species and provide for their control and to minimize the economic, ecological, and human health impacts that invasive species cause."[112]

In some ways the policy goals are more sweeping than Executive Order No. 11987. Executive Order No. 13112 includes control of existing invasive species as one of its primary goals. "Alien species" is defined in ecological, not political terms, as "with respect to a particular ecosystem, any species, including its seeds, eggs, spores, or other biological material capable of propagating that species, that is not native to that ecosystem."[113] Furthermore, "introduction" is defined to include "intentional and unintentional escape, release, dissemination, or placement of a species into an ecosystem as a result of human activity."

148

So far, so good. But Executive Order No. 11987 fell at least in part on its lack of process. How does Executive Order No. 13112 pursue its policy goals? Section 2 of the new Executive Order directs

[e]ach federal agency . . . to the extent practicable and permitted by law to use its programs and authority, subject to available funds, to pursue the following objectives:

(i) to prevent the introduction of invasive species;
(ii) to detect and respond rapidly to and control populations of such species in a cost-effective and environmentally sound manner;
(iii) to monitor invasive species populations accurately and reliably;
(iv) to provide for restoration of native species and habitat conditions in ecosystems that have been invaded;
(v) to conduct research on invasive species and develop technologies to prevent introduction and provide for environmentally sound control of invasive species; and
(vi) to promote public education on invasive species and the means to address them.[114]

The policy directive to all federal agencies whose actions may affect NIS is sweeping. Unfortunately, saying "everyone" has responsibility is a little like saying no one has responsibility. If the order stopped here, it would be only a more sophisticated, complete and current version of the Carter effort 22 years earlier.

However, Executive Order No. 13112 also creates an Invasive Species Council, made up of all cabinet officers with significant responsibility for NIS.[115] The council was required to issue an Invasive Species Management Plan within 18 months. The council is advised by an Advisory Committee whose responsibility is to "recommend plans and actions at local, tribal, State, regional, and ecosystem-based levels to achieve the goals and objectives" of the management plan.[116]

Executive Order No. 13112 uses many of the hottest federal management tricks in the book. The interagency council made up of cabinet officers places responsibility as high as it can go. Involving a wide range of cabinet-level officers increases the likelihood of a full airing of views, revelation of conflicts, and perhaps consistency, efficiency, and success of enforcement. Requiring a plan provides a device for action and commentary. Creating an advisory committee increases the chance of expert input and invests a number of people and organizations outside the government in the details of the council's work.

The National Invasive Species Management Plan (January 18, 2001):
Fail to Plan, Plan to Fail

The National Invasive Species Council issued its first draft management plan on July 10, 2000.[117] This first draft management plan was long (63 pages) and completely incoherent. It called for more funding and staff, but did not delineate either the problems or the solutions with any clarity.[118] It was a model of bureaucracies run amok.

149

The second draft management plan, issued on October 2, 2000,[119] was completely rewritten, and the main body of the text was one-half the length of the first draft, but with far greater substantive content. That plan, issued shortly before the 2000 presidential election and in the sunset of the Clinton Administration, was formally adopted by the cabinet officers making up the National Invasive Species Council on January 18, 2001, two days before the inauguration of President George W. Bush.[120] (By the time the plan appeared in print in October 2001, it was the Bush cabinet members on the council that appeared to a quick reader to be the plan's author.)

The 80-page *National Invasive Species Management Plan*, bearing the formal title *Meeting the Invasive Species Challenge*, is replete with specific goals for the council and for specific federal agencies, often with target dates attached. It is highly ambitious in detail if modest (indeed unclear) in ultimate aim. The spirit of the plan—hopeful, bureaucratic, nonspecific—can be illustrated with just a few goals for the council itself:

1. By April 2001, the Council will establish a transparent oversight mechanism for use by Federal agencies in complying with the Order and reporting on implementation. The oversight mechanism will employ an interactive process that engages public involvement . . . .
3. By January 2002, the Council will conduct an evaluation of current legal authorities relevant to invasive species. The evaluation will include an analysis of whether and how existing authorities may be better utilized. If warranted, recommendations will be made for changes in legal authority.
4. Starting in October 2001, each member Department of the Council shall submit an annual written report summarizing their invasive species activities, including a description of their actions to comply with the Order, budget estimates, and steps in implementing the Plan. These reports will be used in preparing the invasive species cross-cut budget and will help the Council in drafting the biannual updates to the year Management Plan.
5. By January 2002, the Council will prepare an analysis of barriers to coordinated and joint actions among Federal agencies, including legal and policy barriers and barriers relating to the transfer and pooling of funds for invasive species projects. The analysis will include consideration of a standard Memorandum of Understanding that would allow interagency transfer of funding for invasive species actions identified in the Plan.
6. By July 2002, the Council will identify at least two major invasive species issues, regulations, or policies where coordination is inadequate and will take action that fixes the problem.
7. Beginning with Fiscal Year (FY) 2003, and each year thereafter, the Council will coordinate and provide to the Office of Management and Budget (OMB) a proposed cross-cut budget for Federal agency expenditures concerning invasive species, and in particular will address implementation of the actions recommended in this and future editions of the Plan. The cross-cut budget will take into account views of the Advisory Committee, States, and the full range of stakeholders. In addition, it will be used as a tool for planning and coordination, giving emphasis to funding priorities to implement action items.
8. By January 2003, and every 2 years thereafter, the Council will give a report on success in achieving the goals and objectives of the current Plan, and issue an updated Plan. These updates and reports will be prepared in consultation with the

Advisory Committee and through mechanisms securing comment from stakeholders and the general public . . . .[121]

Despite their generality, most and perhaps all of these goals have not been met. It would have been optimistic to think that even a majority of these goals could be met if the plan had appeared at the start or in the middle of a new administration. But the shift to an administration where the council included Secretary of the Interior Gail Norton as a co-chair and Secretary of Defense Donald Rumsfeld and Secretary of State Colin Powell, among other cabinet officers, as members, made any progress on this plan unlikely.

Two general problems with the Invasive Species Management Plan stand out beyond its hyperactive, overstructured, action-item nature. The first is the extent to which the plan continues to define the invasive species problem largely in terms of current federal agency jurisdiction and authority, rather than as a cross-cutting issue for the federal government (and of immense relevance to states, localities, and private actors). Second, the draft does not include or require any measures of current collective harm and therefore offers no basis other than expenditure of energy and money for determining whether the policies proposed are effective or as efficient as possible. In the words of the old schoolroom saying: "Fail to plan, plan to fail."

The U.S. General Accounting Office (GAO) issued a report in October 2002 that concurs with these concerns.[122]

> While the National Invasive Species Council's 2001 management plan, *Meeting the Invasive Species Challenge,* calls for actions that are likely to help control invasive species, it lacks a clear long-term outcome and quantifiable performance criteria against which to evaluate the overall success of the plan....
> [T]he only available performance measure that can be used to assess overall progress is the percentage of planned actions that have been completed by the due dates set in the plan. By this measure, implementation has been slow. Specifically, the council departments have completed less than 20[%] of the planned actions that were called for by September 2000.... [W]hile the national management plan calls for many actions that would likely contribute to preventing and controlling invasive species, even if the actions in the plan were more fully implemented their effect would be uncertain because they typically do not call for quantifiable improvements in invasive species management or control.
> The national management plan does not clearly define a long-term outcome or measures of success as are called for by sound management principles. The executive order states that the management plan shall "detail and recommend performance-oriented goals and objectives and specific measures of success for federal agency efforts concerning invasive species." Consistent with that requirement, the council and its advisory committee adopted as one of their guiding principles that efforts to manage invasive species are most effective when they have goals and objectives that are clearly defined and prioritized....
> However, the council did not articulate in the plan a long-term outcome or condition toward which the federal government should strive. For example, the plan does not contain overall performance-oriented goals and objectives, such as reducing the introduction of new species by a certain percentage or halting the spread of established species on public lands. Instead, the plan contains an extensive list of actions that, while likely to contribute to preventing and controlling invasive species, are not clearly part of a comprehensive strategy.[123]

151

In earlier reports to Congress and executive branch officials in August 2000 and July 2001, the GAO had reported about the delay in developing federal policy under Executive Order No. 13122 and about the need for better rapid response capabilities, authority and funding across federal agencies.[124]

But in fairness to the drafters, even if the plan had been much better written, with measures of success and more clearly prioritized goals, the likelihood of great progress would be relatively slight given the horrible political timing, the environmental sympathies of the Bush Administration, and the terrible cloud of September 11, 2001, and the several wars that have followed. It is more than a little difficult to imagine Rumsfeld asking for the invasive species report following the update on the invasion of Baghdad.

Much of the success of any federal U.S. invasive species policy, but especially a policy emerging from within the executive branch, will turn on the attitudes of executive branch officials and funding and other direction and encouragement from Congress. At the present time, it is only the increasing, widespread recognition of the threat from invasive species that prevents a prediction that the National Invasive Species Council and the Invasive Species Management Plan will follow the path of Carter's 1977 Executive Order into oblivion.

One intriguing congressional twist to federal policy appeared in 2003 in the form of bills introduced in both the U.S. House of Representatives and the Senate that would codify and in some important ways modify President Clinton's Executive Order No. 13112.[125] Rep. Vernon Ehlers (R-Mich.) introduced H. 266, the House version of the bill, on January 8, 2003. He explained the bill:

> [The] authority [of the National Invasive Species Council] to coordinate the actions of Federal agencies has been limited. The General Accounting Office (GAO) recently recognized this problem . . . . GAO recommended that the Council study whether or not a lack of legislative authority has hampered its mission . . . .
>
> [H.R. 266 gives] the Council a clear statutory mandate . . . . It also makes the Council an independent entity within the Executive Branch . . . .
>
> [T]he Council must submit an annual list of the top priorities in several different areas related to addressing the threat posed by invasive species . . . . The legislation also calls on the Office of Management and Budget to develop a crosscut budget of all invasive species efforts in the Federal government. This is a necessary tool for the Council to coordinate efforts among the various Federal agencies.[126]

Perhaps codifying the responsibilities of Executive Order No. 13112 would increase the chance of substantial policy action; certainly it would reduce or eliminate ambiguities with regard to whether existing legal authority supported all of the actions specified in the Executive Order. In addition, in codifying the order Congress would put itself on notice to expect annual requests for funding to support NIS policies. If Congress is serious about invasive species, however, it will set clearer standards and measures, place clearer responsibility on the president and specific cabinet agencies, require far more specific reports, and commit more substantial funds to the area.

Specific agencies have made some visible progress as well on NIS issues, though typically what is evident from *Federal Register* notices and information on department websites are developments on single topics or in response to identified species. At each agency, progress has been a fraction of the systematic and detailed agency-specific requirements listed in the management plan. For example, APHIS has been moving toward implementing solid wood packing material regulations.[127] Solid wood packing material has been the subject of public concern based largely on invasions of the Asian longhorned beetle in New York City; solid wood packing material has also been the subject of guidelines issues by the International Plant Protection Convention (IPPC),[128] a multilateral convention to which the United States is a signatory. Similarly, following public concern and the directives of the National Invasive Policy Act of 1996, the Coast Guard has continued its efforts to pursue effective regulations and voluntary compliance with ballast water treatment and releases.[129] There is little evidence that federal agencies are living up to §2 of Executive Order No. 13112 or the demands of the management plan.

STATE LEGAL AUTHORITY REGARDING HARMFUL NIS

For many states, the range of actual and possible legal authority with regard to harmful NIS presents a picture as complicated as the federal situation. Indeed, inherent in any assessment of state legal authority is the additional dimension of limitations (if any) posed by federal law, and the very interesting and complicated questions raised by multistate, regional, and state and federal compacts, working groups, and parallel or joint state and federal policy implementation.

To make matters even more complicated, some federal laws specifically provide authority to assist and work with particular states. For example, the Hawaii Tropical Forest Recovery Act of 1992[130] included provisions designed to help Hawaii both protect native species and control non-native species. Other federal laws, including the Lacey Act, provide for federal enforcement of policy decisions made under state law. Still other federal laws have provisions encouraging (but not necessarily mandating) various state policies with respect to NIS. In this overview, I seek only to present the framework for understanding state NIS law generally, and to highlight some of the substantial variations among states in their legal response to harmful NIS.

States retain general power to do whatever they want with state lands. One obvious limitation on this applies to federal lands within state boundaries, a situation especially relevant to states in the West. Another obvious limitation on state lands policies applies to private lands, where an independent set of constitutional and statutory limitations together make up recognized private property rights. Still, as both a theoretical and a practical matter, U.S. states have an enormous range of power to prohibit, ignore, or even encourage harmful NIS within their borders.

In fact, state legal authority addressing harmful NIS varies enormously. Several states have substantial legal structures in place; others have substantial but incomplete legal and administrative structures, while still others seem hardly to have noticed the issue of harmful NIS at all. The OTA report summarized the law in all 50 states as of the early 1990s:[131]

- States prohibit importation and/or release of a median of only eight potentially harmful fish and wildlife species or groups. In a survey of state fish and wildlife agency officials, about one-third responded that their lists are too short.

- About one-quarter of the states lack legal authority over importation and/or release of one or more of the five major vertebrate groups (mammals, birds, fish, reptiles, and amphibians). Also, about 40% of state agencies would like to receive additional regulatory authority from their state legislatures.

- Among those states that do not have decisionmaking standards for approval of importation and/or release of non-indigenous fish and wildlife, none legally requires adherence to a scientific protocol when considering a proposal. A few states mandate scientific studies for certain proposals. About one-half the states require a general determination of potential impacts, defined broadly enough to include all ecological impacts. The rest lack vigorous decisionmaking standards.

- Most state agencies rate their own implementation and enforcement resources (staff, funding, or others) as "less" or "much less" than adequate; on average, they would like increases of resources of about 50% to meet their responsibilities.

- Several states present exemplary approaches to managing non-indigenous fish and wildlife. On the other hand, many States are underregulating in several important respects. Overall, States are not adequately addressing non-indigenous fish and wildlife concerns.[132]

Which states have "exemplary" approaches to managing NIS? A few states employ a "clean list" approach to new NIS introductions. The OTA report identifies Hawaii as the only state with a complete presumption against importation or release, and several other states—Florida, Georgia, Idaho, Kentucky, and Vermont—as states with partial "clean list" approaches. Most states have a "dirty" or "black" list approach, following the federal lead. The OTA provides a surprisingly long list of states that, it says, have no prohibitions whatsoever on importation or release, including Arizona, California, Massachusetts, and New Mexico; states with few restrictions include Nevada, New Jersey, Texas, and Virginia, though it is likely that most or all of these states have modified their policies on invasive species since the early 1990s, when the OTA did its research.

The accounting of state laws is incomplete without a full examination of state funding and actual agency behavior. The best illustration of state legislation appears in the 2002 volume from the Environmental Law Institute titled *Halting the Invasion: State Tools for Invasive Species Management*.[133]

States have been changing their laws relating to NIS over the past decade, as awareness of NIS issues has increased, and in light of the emergence of state-level plant pest councils and federal and state policy groups such as the Aquatic Nuisance Species Task Force and FICMNEW.[134] For example, Minnesota was listed in the OTA report as a state whose basic legal approach to NIS was a "black list" approach, and which listed more than five identified species or groups, i.e., it was among the states that appeared on this measure to be more aware of harmful NIS.[135] But in 1996, Minnesota passed a statute making it one of the most aggressive states in excluding harmful NIS. The new Minnesota laws create a strong white list approach. The Commissioner of Agriculture is directed to classify all exotic species as prohibited, unlisted, or unregulated.[136] Listing is to be based on the following criteria:

> Subd. 2. Criteria. The commissioner shall consider the following criteria in classifying an exotic species under this chapter:
>
> > (1) the likelihood of introduction of the species if it is allowed to enter or exist in the state;
> > (2) the likelihood that the species would naturalize in the state were it introduced;
> > (3) the magnitude of potential adverse impacts of the species on native species and on outdoor recreation, commercial fishing, and other uses of natural resources in the state;
> > (4) the ability to eradicate or control the spread of the species once it is introduced in the state; and
> > (5) other criteria the commissioner deems appropriate.[137]

Unlisted exotic species may not be introduced until the Commissioner of Agriculture has determined that the species is appropriate.[138] Regulated exotic species can only be introduced after obtaining a permit from the commissioner.[139] A person that allows introduction of an exotic species must notify the commissioner within 48 hours of learning of the introduction, and make every reasonable attempt to recapture or destroy it.[140] The person who allows release is liable for costs incurred by the state in capture or control of the animal "and its progeny."[141] A person who allows introduction and does not provide notice or make an attempt to recapture is subject to minor criminal sanctions.[142]

The new Minnesota law concerning NIS looks to be as strong as any state. These provisions focus on introductions and therefore do not describe a complete law regarding harmful NIS. The success of these provisions will depend on the administrative decisions made under the law, the willingness of citizens to follow the law, and the funding and support provided by the state legislature for the NIS review process.

Another dimension of state legal authority with respect to harmful NIS is that states will often have multiple agencies, offices, committees, and councils with authority over various aspects of the NIS problem. Because of the severity of NIS issues in Hawaii, for example, there is somewhat more literature on law and policy in the state, typified by an excellent 1992 report by the Nature Conservancy of Hawaii and the NRDC. This report includes a chart, reprinted here as Table 4, that illustrates the number of state agencies involved with harmful NIS in Hawaii. The chart also suggests the extent to which these state agencies interact or at least overlap with the many federal agencies involved in NIS issues.

Table 4: Hawaii's Control System

Discovery	Identification And Prescription	Treatment And Monitoring
INSPECTIONS AND MONITORING	**AGRICULTURAL PESTS**	**AGRICULTURAL PESTS**
HDOA/PQ	HDOA/PPC	HDOA/PPC
DOH/VCB	HSPA	HSPA
UHCES	BPBM	UHCES
	UHCES	USDA/ADC
AREA SURVEYS	Private Growers	USDA/ARS
HDOA/PPC		Private Growers
DLNR/DOFAW	**NATURAL**	
USFWS	**AREA PESTS**	**NATURAL**
NPS		**AREA PESTS**
BPBM	DLNR/DAR	
TNCH	USFWS	HDOA/PQ
HSPA	NPS	HDOA/PPC
	USFS	DLNR/DOFAW
INCIDENTAL DETECTIONS	BPBM	DLNR/DAR
	TNCH	USDA/ADC
HDOA/PC	FCC	USFWS
HDOA/PPC	Private Land Owners	NPS
DLNR/DOFAW		TNCH
DLNR/DAR	**HUMAN HEALTH**	FCC
UHCES	**PESTS**	Private Land Managers
USFWS		
NPS	DOH	**HUMAN HEALTH**
TNCH		**PESTS**
BPBM		
HSPA		DOH
Private Growers		
Private Biologists		
Private Land Owners		
Untrained Public		

Hawaiian law regarding harmful NIS law is among the strongest in the United States, no doubt due to the enormous impact NIS have had in Hawaii, as on many other islands. For example, Hawaiian law includes a general prohibition on the introduction of animals until they are evaluated and placed on a list of conditionally approved, restricted, or prohibited animals by the Hawaii Board of Agriculture.[143]

In addition to a strong policy and administrative structure supporting exclusion of NIS, Hawaiian law is striking for its aggressive recognition of the need to survey its lands for areas that are relatively pristine, as well as for those that have been harmed by NIS, and then to follow up by protecting the pristine lands and responding to invasions. The additional dimensions of a complete NIS law, including the identification of invasions and the mechanisms for responding to new invasions, as well as those already in place in Hawaii, seem to be absent from the law of many other states. The spirit, and perhaps the actual text of Hawaii Revised Statutes §152-6 (with NIS substituted for "noxious weed"), might serve as a model for other states and the federal system:

§152-6 Duties of the department; noxious weed control and eradication.

(a) The department shall maintain a constant vigilance for incipient infestations of specific noxious weeds on islands declared reasonably free from those weeds, and shall use those procedures and methods to control or eradicate the infestations of noxious weeds as are determined to be feasible and practicable.

(b) When the department determines that an infestation of a certain noxious weed exists on an island declared reasonably free from the weed, the department shall immediately conduct investigations and surveys as are necessary to determine the feasibility and practicability of controlling or eradicating the infestation. The department may also conduct investigations and surveys to determine the feasibility and practicability of controlling widespread noxious weed infestations. The methods of control or eradication adopted by the department for any noxious weed infestation shall cause as little damage to crops and property as possible.

(c) Upon determining that control or eradication of an infestation is practicable and feasible, the department shall immediately serve notice, either oral or written, on both the landowner of the property and the occupant of the property on which the infestations exist.... The notice shall set forth all pertinent information with respect to the infestation and notify the landowner and the land occupant of the procedure and methods of control or eradication.

(d) Upon the department's notification pursuant to subsection (c) above, the department may enter into a cooperative agreement with the landowner and land occupier for the control or eradication of the noxious weed infestation.

(e) Upon the department's notification pursuant to subsection (c) above, the department may entirely undertake the eradication or control project when it has been determined that the owner, occupier, or lessee of the land on which the noxious weed infestation is located will not benefit materially or financially by the control or eradication of the noxious weed; or when the noxious weed infestation is on state-owned land not leased or under control of private interest.[144]

Islands are special engines of endemism; they also tend to be especially vulnerable to invasion. It is not surprising, therefore, that Hawaii's laws regarding alien species are more developed than in most states, and that there is a steady stream of proposed legislation in the Hawaiian legislature responding, typically, to particular invasions.[145] Indeed, the Hawaiian legislature has enacted more than 20 new laws dealing with invasive species since 2001.

A complete analysis of state NIS laws is beyond the scope of this chapter. A complete analysis would require a state-by-state assessment not only of current laws, but also of current policies and budget allocations. This short survey, the available literature, and a sampling of state statutory and regulatory provisions provides sufficient information to conclude that states vary considerably in their response to invasive species, with most trailing behind the federal government in terms of their legal awareness of harmful NIS issues. This short review confirms that, the intriguing provisions in Hawaii and Minnesota notwithstanding, a complete legal response does not exist in even the most progressive states.[146]

Table 5: State Invasive Species Laws[147]

	General Non-Specific NIS Laws	Agriculture Farming, Nurseries, Ranching, Commerce	Forestry	Fisheries	Other Industries	Sporting and Pet	Environmental Protection	Total Laws Listed
Alabama	X	X						2
Alaska		X		X	X		X	2
Arizona		X						1
Arkansas		X						2
California	X	X		X	X	X	X	24
Colorado		X						2
Connecticut								0
Delaware		X						5
Florida	X	X		X	X		X	3
Georgia		X						1
Hawaii	X	X		X	X	X	X	9
Idaho	X	X						5
Illinois		X		X	X		X	7
Indiana		X					X	2
Iowa		X						4
Kansas		X						19
Kentucky		X						1
Louisiana		X						1
Maine		X	X	X	X		X	4
Maryland		X			X		X	3
Massachusetts		X					X	3
Michigan	X	X		X	X		X	10
Minnesota		X		X	X		X	7
Mississippi		X						1
Missouri	X	X						3

Table 5: State Invasive Species Laws (cont.)

	General Non-Specific NIS Laws	Agriculture Farming, Nurseries, Ranching, Commerce	Forestry	Fisheries	Other Industries	Sporting and Pet	Environmental Protection	Total Laws Listed
Montana		X						1
Nebraska	X	X				X		6
Nevada		X				X		6
New Hampshire		X		X	X		X	4
New Jersey		X				X		4
New Mexico	X	X						4
New York		X		X	X		X	5
North Carolina	X	X						4
North Dakota		X						3
Ohio	X	X						4
Oklahoma		X						1
Oregon	X	X			X		X	6
Pennsylvania		X						1
Rhode Island		X			X		X	2
South Carolina		X						3
South Dakota		X						4
Tennessee		X						3
Texas		X						2
Utah	X	X		X	X		X	5
Vermont		X			X	X	X	7
Virginia		X			X		X	4
Washington	X	X		X	X		X	6
West Virginia		X						1
Wisconsin		X			X		X	4
Wyoming		X						2

GAPS IN U.S. NIS LAWS

What *should* the law say about non-indigenous species? What role should government play in regulating NIS? What should the goals of NIS law be? What is the best way to achieve these goals?

This chapter began by asking whether there is any way to resolve the apparent paradox of a legal world with a huge amount of potentially relevant law and very little law that attacks the invasive species issue head-on or comprehensively. One resolution of this apparent paradox was to suggest that it is not a paradox at all when the question is expanded from "what laws exist?" to "what can (or cannot) be done under the laws that exist?" To make a similar point, there is no "much law"/"little law" paradox if the issue of invasive species has yet to be conceived in a unified or coherent fashion, though parts of the issue have been recognized. Indeed, if the issue of harmful invasive species has emerged clearly in U.S. public discourse only in the past decade, the odd incident of the Carter Executive Order in 1977 notwithstanding, then it would be even more surprising—perhaps more of a paradox—for comprehensive legislation to exist. Laws are rarely ahead of their time; it is hard enough to draft laws that adequately match the needs of their time.

While the present legal situation regarding harmful invasive species may well be common as a matter of the evolution of legal regimes for other issues and areas, that recognition does not obviate the need to consider the continued wisdom of the current framework. In other words, the increasing recognition of a large and coherent problem with harmful invasive species (coherence here does not mean simple, just "connected," or "understood as a whole") poses two fair challenges to the many piecemeal laws on the books: first, do the present array of laws address all essential aspects of policy and administration with respect to harmful invasive species, and second, whether or not the current laws address all (or most) essential issues, should the legal regime nonetheless be reworked into a simpler, more coherent, and more unified framework?

This final part identifies some of the important gaps in the collective set of current NIS laws and suggests critical issues that a good NIS law would address. It identifies three major problems with current U.S. NIS law: lack of vision, lack of completeness, and lack of coherence. It concludes with some initial reflections on the virtues of simpler and more coherent laws.

The Vision Gap: NIS and Natural Ecosystems

It is good when legal systems recognize that some NIS are harmful, as most if not all U.S. legal systems now do. But perhaps it is equally important that legal systems recognize that indigenous organisms and complete, functional, natural ecosystems populated by indigenous species have a special place and a special priority in policymaking. The important insight that NIS can cause enormous economic, ecological, and aesthetic harms may lead policymakers to focus on exclusion and control—to deal with the threats and negative consequences. A complete NIS law, though, would include a positive conception of ecological place. Especially for areas that are more natural and more wild, laws should express a general preference for indigenous over non-indigenous species, and treat even familiar non-indigenous species as exceptions to a favored norm.

The issues with respect to less wild and less natural areas, and especially with respect to agricultural land, are quite different. It would be awkward, to say the least, to apply a presumption against alien species to such systems which are almost entirely defined by introduced species, themselves highly modified through selective breeding and, now, through direct genetic modification. For agricultural areas, and perhaps in many other artificial or highly disturbed settings (homes, cities, and perhaps urban parks), a different set of presumptions with regards to alien species might apply. In such settings, the primary question might be the risk of alien species in those artificial contexts escaping into more natural or wild areas, or otherwise causing identifiable economic, ecological, or aesthetic harms.

Current federal law reveals multiple visions, some antagonistic to harmful NIS, some neutral, and some actually supportive of alien species introductions and protective of even harmful NIS now in place, even in more natural and more wild areas. In the new Executive Order No. 13112 there appears to be a general policy preference for indigenous over non-indigenous species where the order directs federal agencies to "provide for restoration of native species and habitat conditions in ecosystems that have been invaded." But Executive Order No. 13112 also limits its concerns to harmful NIS, and states no general policy against alien species even in more natural and more wild areas.

There are many different ways to state positive conceptions of the role of indigenous species and natural ecosystems. It would help in the design and implementation of wise NIS law and policies if there were some stated goal. Of course there are enormous philosophical and practical problems in almost any definition based on what is "natural" and what is "wild," given the pervasive effects of human presence and activities for long periods in much of the United States.[148] Perhaps invasive species laws need a principle of direction as much as one of destination. Perhaps an invasive species law would be a place to include, in a statement of principles, and at least with regards to more natural and more wild areas, Aldo Leopold's land ethic: "A thing is right when it tends to preserve the integrity, stability, and beauty of the biotic community. It is wrong when it tends otherwise."[149]

To point to a "vision gap" in current NIS laws may seem fairly abstract, and might suggest that the NIS problem—or at least its legal dimensions—is not so important after all. However, in the absence of some general statements of principle and identification of the goals to be achieved, it is hard to state coherent and complete legal or policy provisions, or to implement complex and wide-ranging laws, over time and place.

The Knowledge Gap

There may be no environmental issue of similar importance that is as little recognized to be a problem by the general public. This is true even as public awareness, reflected by an increase in news coverage, increases. The news stories are, for the most part, related to specific invasive species; they are not about, and often do not reflect, a more general concern with invasive species as a class.

The reasons for the relatively low standing of NIS issues are many and subtle. First, NIS problems are hard to see: it requires knowledge to differentiate between a native and invasive species, and to differentiate between harmful and benign alien species. When people look at their pets and their houseplants and their gardens, they do not usually think of these organisms as non-indigenous. The problem of NIS, therefore, is a problem in part of psychology (what is "seen") and in part of culture (what practices are considered proper).[150]

But many kinds of pollution other than biological pollution are nonobvious. The harms from other kinds of pollution may be easier, however, to perceive, especially when those harms are directly to human health. In addition, there are more accessible measures for other kinds of pollution, both in technical literature (assessing the risks from different pollutants) and in public and policy discourse (focusing on "smog days" or "superfund sites").

A complete NIS law would include both authority and process for expanding knowledge about NIS. NIS laws should mandate the development of ready measures for assessing the costs and benefits of NIS and of the activities (such as trade, travel, and horticulture) that may indirectly introduce harmful NIS.

The lack of knowledge extends beyond public awareness to basic science and wise conservation policy. Basic scientific questions that have been answered only in rough and preliminary terms include: how many NIS are there in the United States, and in each of the states? what are the pathways and rates of new introductions?[151] which NIS impose the greatest harm, and which NIS pose the greatest risk of harm over time? what are the most effective mechanisms for responding to different NIS? what are the most effective methods for reducing the rate of introductions? what standards should be applied to intentional introductions, including introductions in agricultural settings, of biological controls,[152] and of genetically engineered organisms?

Among the most important knowledge gaps address policy issues—applied biological and social science—that might establish a list of priorities with respect to NIS for each available policy dollar, as well as a sound basis for determining a proper total level of resources for NIS issues. It is easy to come up with long lists of invasive species and the various kinds of harm they cause. It is harder to determine a "top 10" list, because that requires an understanding of facts and a choice about values, neither of which exists in most U.S. contexts. It is harder still to determine whether the first priority is to respond to the most costly current invaders, or the most threatening future invaders, or the potential of new introductions, each of which requires a substantial knowledge base, and each of which may require very different administrative processes.

Therefore, a top priority for sound policy development is expanding the knowledge base about these multiple dimensions of the NIS problem, and developing management tools such as measures to assess the priorities across a huge number of needs and demands. Like hurricanes and earthquakes, it would serve sound policy purposes if we knew that a particular NIS (widespread or not yet an invader) was a "class 5" (or whatever scale was selected) and therefore deserved a particular priority response. Like many other aspects of environmental oversight, it would help to have regular reports, and a basis for establishing changes in the NIS problem over time.

The Crisis Response Gap

Current U.S. NIS laws are strongest, in general, at providing government agencies with power to exclude particular identified species, and to conduct various kinds of searches at points and through mechanisms of entry and transport. If a war metaphor is justified with respect to NIS—and the familiar and well-established language of invasions and invasiveness suggests the metaphor may be more useful here than in some contexts—then the law and policy should match the metaphor. Current law focuses on the front lines, but pays too little attention to the enemies that have already arrived, and are spreading within.

Among the gaps in most current U.S. laws are substantive and structural provisions aimed at identifying NIS that have been introduced, and responding to those invasions.[153] Like crime reports and the myriad other reports provided by the government to mark and measure important social and physical facts, the authority, tools, and procedures should exist to produce steady information and reports on the NIS problem. The authority should also exist to respond quickly, especially in circumstances where a quick response to a limited invasion might succeed at total suppression, while a delayed response might leave far more restricted options. In other words, a good law would authorize and fund an alien species strike force.

Information about NIS introductions and invasions is critical for assessing the proper response. While federal and state government agencies have found the authority to respond to particular invasions, only Hawaii appears to have a statute in place that creates an obligation to identify new invasions and respond to them. Explicit statutory authority should support both rapid and long-term strategic responses, depending on the scope of the invasion, the risk of harm from and nature of the invasive species, and the availability of control mechanisms.

Another surprising gap in U.S. NIS law involves intentional NIS introductions. Intentional NIS introductions arise in a wide variety of settings. Some of those settings may have notably higher risks for harm than others. In terms of current gaps, some harmful NIS continue to be sold even after their harmful properties are widely recognized, and even after regulatory efforts to control their spread are already in place. Purple loosestrife (*Lythrum salicaria*) is just one common example of such continued commercial distribution in the face of enormous evidence of harmful impacts.

A legal framework should exist for the regularized assessment of all proposed introductions, including the introduction of biological controls and genetically engineered organisms. Decisions about intentional introductions should be made based on explicit, public standards, and public processes.

Enlisting the Citizenry: The Role of Public Education

Again, the war metaphor may come to the aid of good law making. A culture and community that does not distinguish between indigenous species and NIS is one less likely to recognize or care about *harmful* NIS. When institutions and individuals who should know better—such as zoos and botanical gardens and fishing enthusiasts and nurseries—promote NIS, they illustrate the importance of encouraging a much broader understanding of the threats posed by harmful NIS.[154]

NIS laws can create extensive regulatory structures for assessing intentional introductions; they can also create formal civil or criminal liability for intentional and unintentional introductions. Such liability may be especially important with respect to the complex issues associated with intentional introductions for agricultural, pest control, horticulture, and sporting interests. But over time, better education about the threat of harmful NIS, including the training of citizens to help identify invasive species, may do more to lower the rate of introductions than formal regulatory or liability provisions for the individuals whose harmful behavior can be traced. (The point is not that regulatory and liability provisions are inappropriate, but that public awareness and education may be just as important.)

Coherence in Law

What determines whether an aspect of social policy is addressed by one law, 10 laws, or no law at all? What is the proper scope of law in any particular area? There are no absolute answers to these questions. Indeed, as a scholarly field, theories of legislation and law making are fairly impoverished. However, when the history of an area and the habits of law making have led to the promulgation of many related laws, it is probably a good time to consider whether there are logical or policy advantages to having fewer and more coherent laws in the area.

It is hard to imagine an area of law or policy more convoluted than the laws regarding harmful NIS, yet with great legal and knowledge gaps on key issues. This divergence framed the paradox noted at the beginning of this chapter. Pressures have already been brought to bear recently on the array of plant pest and noxious weed acts—one important piece of the much larger harmful invasive species puzzle—which led to the enactment of a new Plant Protection Act and the supplanting of one set of prior statutes. But continued divergence across the broader, coherent range of issues that describe the harmful invasive species problem provides a strong argument in favor of adopting a "uniform" or "organic" or "model" act.

The alternative to conceptualizing a uniform NIS statute is to assess the amenability of current laws in force to particular problems. The difficulty of this exercise is proportional to the number of relevant laws, to their uncertain scope, and to the absence of some clear statement of goals or measures against which to test the current legal provisions. This chapter has identified some of the typical gaps in current U.S. NIS laws. The OTA report and other publications have pointed to a variety of other gaps in federal and state law. This chapter has also noted the possibility that the limits of current federal legal authority may be more likely to be tested given the promulgation of the new Executive Order No. 13112 that relies on all available legal authority to support its policy directives.

During the past decade, Congress and executive branch agencies have appeared willing to respond to particular NIS issues, most notably in Executive Order No. 13112, and in statutes such as the Plant Pest Act. States, to varying degrees, also seem to be directing increasing political attention to harmful NIS. Both the federal and state governments could continue along this path, adding specific legal authority when needs arise, and encouraging appropriate funding within program, agency, and budget lines that are already established.

One argument in favor of working only with the idea of modifying current legal authorities is that there are many programs in place and established understandings, under the existing laws. However, a new organic NIS law would not necessarily need to replace current authorities, but could address general goals and priorities, set presumptions, and fill the kind of large gaps noted in this chapter, including various survey and reporting requirements that would help to increase the political and public awareness of NIS issues.[155] Such a core NIS law, for which there is no model currently in the United States, could dramatically help to increase awareness of NIS issues. A core law could also assist in explaining to Congress and state legislatures the funding priorities and demands for a wise response to harmful NIS.

A core NIS law could link pieces of the harmful NIS puzzle now left separate or unaddressed. It could link issues of intentional and accidental introduction on new NIS, assessment of NIS already released, and various control programs. A core NIS law could also assist in structuring NIS policies around ecological rather than political borders. In the area of intentional introductions, a core NIS law could provide a framework for considering and comparing the benefits and costs of introducing non-indigenous but naturally evolving species and those that are the product of genetic engineering.

An additional argument in favor of a new core NIS law is the growing evidence that the National Invasive Species Council has failed to demonstrate any substantial capacity to develop, implement, review and report on new policies that can make a difference. Indeed, it does not seem that the council has a sensible measure of "difference" it is trying to make. A locus of knowledge and policy on NIS is probably a good idea, but the political assumptions, authorities and hopes behind the creation of the council have not delivered sufficient progress. Don Schmitz and Daniel Simberloff have suggested the creation of a Center for Biological Invasions, an additional independent agency, modeled after the Centers for Disease Control, to address the massive knowledge and coordination problems raised by invasive species.[156]

A new core NIS law would demand the attention of all the political branches, the many interested private industries and individuals, and the public, and would increase the chance that the threat from invasive species will be contained. Every senator and representative with a concern about some particular invasive species should now see that the problem is unlikely to be addressed well, and new problems avoided, without the larger context, structure, and knowledge that better laws and institutions could provide.

CONCLUSION

Harmful NIS, and NIS generally, may present the single most important environmental issue overlooked, relative to its importance, in current law and policy. It may seem odd that an area of law that takes 50 pages to sketch and for which there is a "national plan" is an area strongly in need of new and better law. But that seems to be the case.

Even if lawyers might find the building blocks they need in current law to defend current or proposed government actions, no ecologist or policymaker would think a set of laws so fractured and designed for other purposes provides a wise foundation for NIS law and policy. Nor should any lawyer be satisfied with a legal framework that is so difficult to describe, understand, and apply. And no one, legislator, lawyer, scientist, or citizen, should be satisfied with the federal government's record thus far in preventing, identifying, or responding to invasive species.

APPENDIX: PRESIDENTIAL EXECUTIVE ORDERS ON NIS

a. Executive Order 11987 (May 24, 1977) (Jimmy Carter)
     42 Fed. Reg. 26969
     (E.O. 11987 was replaced by E.O. 13112).
Exotic Organisms
By virtue of the authority vested in me by the Constitution and the statutes of the United States of America, and as President of the United States of America, in furtherance of the purposes and policies of the Lacey Act and the National Environmental Policy Act of 1969, it is hereby ordered as follows:
     Section 1. As used in this Order:
     (a) "United States" means all of the several States, the District of Columbia, the Commonwealth of Puerto Rico, American Samoa, the Virgin Islands, Guam, and the Trust Territory of the Pacific Islands.
     (b) "Introduction" means the release, escape, or establishment of an exotic species into a natural ecosystem.
     (c) "Exotic species" means all species of plants and animals not naturally occurring, either presently or historically, in any ecosystem of the United States.
     (d) "Native species" means all species of plants and animals naturally occurring, either presently or historically, in any ecosystem of the United States. Section 2.
     (a) Executive agencies shall, to the extent permitted by law, restrict the introduction of exotic species into natural ecosystems on lands and waters which

they own, lease, or hold for purposes of administration; and, shall encourage the States, local governments, and private citizens to prevent the introduction of exotic species into natural ecosystems of the United States.

(b) Executive agencies, to the extent they have been authorized by statute to restrict the importation of exotic species, shall restrict the introduction of exotic species into any natural ecosystem of the United States.

(c) Executive agencies shall, to the extent permitted by law, restrict the use of Federal funds, programs, or authorities used to export native species for the purpose of introducing such species into ecosystems outside the United States where they do not naturally occur.

(d) This Order does not apply to the introduction of any exotic species, or the export of any native species, if the Secretary of Agriculture or the Secretary of the Interior finds that such introduction or exportation will not have an adverse effect on natural ecosystems.

Section 3. The Secretary of the Interior, in consultation with the Secretary of Agriculture and the heads of other appropriate agencies, shall develop and implement, by rule or regulation, a system to standardize and simplify the requirements, procedures and other activities appropriate for implementing the provisions of this Order. The Secretary of the Interior shall ensure that such rules or regulations are in accord with the performance by other agencies of those functions vested by law, including this Order, in such agencies.

b. Executive Order 13112 (February 3, 1999)
       (William J. Clinton)
       64 Fed. Reg. 6183

Invasive Species

By the authority vested in me as President by the Constitution and the laws of the United States of America, including the National Environmental Policy Act of 1969, Nonindigenous Aquatic Nuisance Prevention and Control Act of 1990, Lacey Act, Federal Plant Pest Act, Federal Noxious Weed Act of 1974, Endangered Species Act of 1973, and other pertinent statutes, to prevent the introduction of invasive species and provide for their control and to minimize the economic, ecological, and human health impacts that invasive species cause, it is ordered as follows:

Section 1. Definitions.

(a) "Alien species" means, with respect to a particular ecosystem, any species, including its seeds, eggs, spores, or other biological material capable of propagating that species, that is not native to that ecosystem.

(b) "Control" means, as appropriate, eradicating, suppressing, reducing, or managing invasive species populations, preventing spread of invasive species from areas where they are present, and taking steps such as restoration of native species and habitats to reduce the effects of invasive species and to prevent further invasions.

(c) "Ecosystem" means the complex of a community of organisms and its environment.

(d) "Federal agency" means an executive department or agency, but does not include independent establishments as defined by 5 U.S.C. §104.

(e) "Introduction" means the intentional or unintentional escape, release, dissemination, or placement of a species into an ecosystem as a result of human activity.

(f) "Invasive species" means an alien species whose introduction does or is likely to cause economic or environmental harm or harm to human health.

(g) "Native species" means, with respect to a particular ecosystem, a species that, other than as a result of an introduction, historically occurred or currently occurs in that ecosystem.

(h) "Species" means a group of organisms all of which have a high degree of physical and genetic similarity, generally interbreed only among themselves, and show persistent differences from members of allied groups of organisms.

(i) "Stakeholders" means, but is not limited to, State, tribal, and local government agencies, academic institutions, the scientific community, nongovernmental entities including environmental, agricultural, and conservation organizations, trade groups, commercial interests, and private landowners.

(j) "United States" means the 50 States, the District of Columbia, Puerto Rico, Guam, and all possessions, territories, and the territorial sea of the United States.

Sec. 2. Federal Agency Duties.

(a) Each Federal agency whose actions may affect the status of invasive species shall, to the extent practicable and permitted by law,

(1) identify such actions;

(2) subject to the availability of appropriations, and within Administration budgetary limits, use relevant programs and authorities to:

(i) prevent the introduction of invasive species;

(ii) detect and respond rapidly to and control populations of such species in a cost-effective and environmentally sound manner;

(iii) monitor invasive species populations accurately and reliably;

(iv) provide for restoration of native species and habitat conditions in ecosystems that have been invaded;

(v) conduct research on invasive species and develop technologies to prevent introduction and provide for environmentally sound control of invasive species; and

(vi) promote public education on invasive species and the means to address them; and

(3) not authorize, fund, or carry out actions that it believes are likely to cause or promote the introduction or spread of invasive species in the United States or elsewhere unless, pursuant to guidelines that it has prescribed, the agency has determined and made public its determination that the benefits of such actions clearly outweigh the potential harm caused by invasive species; and that all feasible and prudent measures to minimize risk of harm will be taken in conjunction with the actions.

(b) Federal agencies shall pursue the duties set forth in this section in consultation with the Invasive Species Council, consistent with the Invasive Species

Management Plan and in cooperation with stakeholders, as appropriate, and, as approved by the Department of State, when Federal agencies are working with international organizations and foreign nations.

Sec. 3. Invasive Species Council.

(a) An Invasive Species Council (Council) is hereby established whose members shall include the Secretary of State, the Secretary of the Treasury, the Secretary of Defense, the Secretary of the Interior, the Secretary of Agriculture, the Secretary of Commerce, the Secretary of Transportation, and the Administrator of the Environmental Protection Agency. The Council shall be co-chaired by the Secretary of the Interior, the Secretary of Agriculture, and the Secretary of Commerce. The Council may invite additional Federal agency representatives to be members, including representatives from subcabinet bureaus or offices with significant responsibilities concerning invasive species, and may prescribe special procedures for their participation. The Secretary of the Interior shall, with concurrence of the co-chairs, appoint an Executive Director of the Council and shall provide the staff and administrative support for the Council.

(b) The Secretary of the Interior shall establish an advisory committee under the Federal Advisory Committee Act to provide information and advice for consideration by the Council, and shall, after consultation with other members of the Council, appoint members of the advisory committee representing stakeholders. Among other things, the advisory committee shall recommend plans and actions at local, tribal, State, regional, and ecosystem-based levels to achieve the goals and objectives of the Management Plan in section 5 of this order. The advisory committee shall act in cooperation with stakeholders and existing organizations addressing invasive species. The Department of the Interior shall provide the administrative and financial support for the advisory committee.

Sec. 4. Duties of the Invasive Species Council.

The Invasive Species Council shall provide national leadership regarding invasive species, and shall:

(a) oversee the implementation of this order and see that the Federal agency activities concerning invasive species are coordinated, complementary, cost-efficient, and effective, relying to the extent feasible and appropriate on existing organizations addressing invasive species, such as the Aquatic Nuisance Species Task Force, the Federal Interagency Committee for the Management of Noxious and Exotic Weeds, and the Committee on Environment and Natural Resources;

(b) encourage planning and action at local, tribal, State, regional, and ecosystem-based levels to achieve the goals and objectives of the Management Plan in section 5 of this order, in cooperation with stakeholders and existing organizations addressing invasive species;

(c) develop recommendations for international cooperation in addressing invasive species;

(d) develop, in consultation with the Council on Environmental Quality, guidance to Federal agencies pursuant to the National Environmental Policy

Act on prevention and control of invasive species, including the procurement, use, and maintenance of native species as they affect invasive species;

(e) facilitate development of a coordinated network among Federal agencies to document, evaluate, and monitor impacts from invasive species on the economy, the environment, and human health;

(f) facilitate establishment of a coordinated, up-to-date information-sharing system that utilizes, to the greatest extent practicable, the Internet; this system shall facilitate access to and exchange of information concerning invasive species, including, but not limited to, information on distribution and abundance of invasive species; life histories of such species and invasive characteristics; economic, environmental, and human health impacts; management techniques, and laws and programs for management, research, and public education; and

(g) prepare and issue a national Invasive Species Management Plan as set forth in section 5 of this order.

Sec. 5. Invasive Species Management Plan.

(a) Within 18 months after issuance of this order, the Council shall prepare and issue the first edition of a National Invasive Species Management Plan (Management Plan), which shall detail and recommend performance-oriented goals and objectives and specific measures of success for Federal agency efforts concerning invasive species. The Management Plan shall recommend specific objectives and measures for carrying out each of the Federal agency duties established in section 2(a) of this order and shall set forth steps to be taken by the Council to carry out the duties assigned to it under section 4 of this order. The Management Plan shall be developed through a public process and in consultation with Federal agencies and stakeholders.

(b) The first edition of the Management Plan shall include a review of existing and prospective approaches and authorities for preventing the introduction and spread of invasive species, including those for identifying pathways by which invasive species are introduced and for minimizing the risk of introductions via those pathways, and shall identify research needs and recommend measures to minimize the risk that introductions will occur. Such recommended measures shall provide for a science-based process to evaluate risks associated with introduction and spread of invasive species and a coordinated and systematic risk-based process to identify, monitor, and interdict pathways that may be involved in the introduction of invasive species. If recommended measures are not authorized by current law, the Council shall develop and recommend to the President through its co-chairs legislative proposals for necessary changes in authority.

(c) The Council shall update the Management Plan biennially and shall concurrently evaluate and report on success in achieving the goals and objectives set forth in the Management Plan. The Management Plan shall identify the personnel, other resources, and additional levels of coordination needed to achieve the Management Plan's identified goals and objectives, and the Council shall provide each edition of the Management Plan and each report on it to the Office of Management and Budget. Within 18 months after measures have been recommended by the Council in any edition of the Management Plan, each Federal agency whose action is required to implement such measures shall either take the action recommended or shall provide the Council with an explanation of why the Action is not feasible. The Council shall assess the effectiveness of this order no less than once each 5 years after the order is issued and shall report to the Office of Management and Budget on whether the order should be revised.

Sec. 6. Judicial Review and Administration.

(a) This order is intended only to improve the internal management of the executive branch and is not intended to create any right, benefit, or trust responsibility, substantive or procedural, enforceable at law or equity by a party against the United States, its agencies, its officers, or any other person.

(b) Executive Order 11987 of May 24, 1977, is hereby revoked.

(c) The requirements of this order do not affect the obligations of Federal agencies under 16 U.S.C. §4713 with respect to ballast water programs.

(d) The requirements of section 2(a)(3) of this order shall not apply to any action of the Department of State or Department of Defense if the Secretary of State or the Secretary of Defense finds that exemption from such requirements is necessary for foreign policy or national security reasons.

Chapter 6 Endnotes

1. The author is Associate Dean for Faculty and Scholarship and Professor of Law, Emory University School of Law. E-mail: mmiller@law.emory.edu. He would like to thank Greg Aplet, Anita Bernstein, Bill Buzbee, Nick Fabian, Peter McAvoy, Richard Orr, Keith Pitts, Sarah Reichard, Robert Schapiro, and Ron Wright, each of whom offered insights on earlier drafts, and Stephanie Allen, Terry Gordon, Jason Herman, and Wendy Phillips for research support. The author wishes to express his appreciation for the insights into invasive species policy and politics provided by the National Invasive Species Council Policy and Regulation Working Group, which he served as nonfederal co-chair. *See* INTERIM REPORT: POLICY AND REGULATION WORKING GROUP OF THE INVASIVE SPECIES ADVISORY COUNCIL (2000), *available at* http://www. invasivespecies.gov/council/PR%20interim%20final2%20703.doc (last visited June 10, 2003).

2. OFFICE OF TECHNOLOGY ASSESSMENT (OTA), HARMFUL NON-INDIGENOUS SPECIES IN THE UNITED STATES (1993), *available at* http://www.wws.princeton.edu/~ota/ disk1/1993/9325_n.html (last visited Aug. 1, 2003) [hereinafter OTA REPORT].

3. *See* Wendy Wagner, *Congress, Science, and Environmental Policy*, 1999 U. ILL. L. REV. 181, 213 n.121; Colleen Krueger, *Congress' Own "Think Tank" Falls Victim to Cuts by GOP*, L.A. TIMES, Oct. 25, 1995, at A5.

4. OTA REPORT, *supra* note 2, at 3.

5. More recent reports have suggested that there are as many as 50,000 NIS in the United States. *See* David Pimental et al., *Environmental and Economic Costs Associated With Non-Indigenous Species in the United States*, Presentation at American Association for the Advancement of Science, Anaheim, Cal., January 1999, *available at* http://www.news.cornell.edu/releases/Jan99/species_costs.html (last visited Aug. 1, 2003).

6. The range of estimates of total NIS since the promulgation of the 1977 Executive Order by President Jimmy Carter has ranged across two orders of magnitude (1977 Executive Order—several hundred; 1993, OTA REPORT, *supra* note 2—5,000; 1999, Pimental et al., *supra* note 5,—50,000). The problems in assessing the total number of NIS, are in part definitional—including whether only harmful NIS are counted, and whether the range of established agricultural and other familiar species, e.g., dogs and cats, are counted. But the problems with accurate numbers also reflect a basic lack of knowledge. OTA REPORT, *supra* note 2, at 5.

7. *Id.* at 66 (citing U.S. DEP'T OF AGRICULTURE, U.S. FOREST SERVICE, PEST RISK ASSESSMENT OF THE IMPORTATION OF LARCH FROM SIBERIA AND THE SOVIET FAR EAST, Miscellaneous Publication No. 1495 (1991)).

8. OTA REPORT, *supra* note 2, at 66.

9. *Id.* tbl. 1-1.

10. M. LYNNE CORN ET AL., CONGRESSIONAL RESEARCH SERVICE, HARMFUL NON-NATIVE SPECIES: ISSUES FOR CONGRESS (1999) [hereinafter CRS REPORT] (citing Pimental et al., *supra* note 5).

11. David Wilcove et al., *Quantifying Threats to Imperiled Species in the United States*, 48 BIOSCIENCE 607 (1998). The January 2001 federal National Invasive Species Management Plan synthesizes and quotes these prior reports but does not provide additional estimates or analysis of the scope of the NIS problem in the United States. NATIONAL INVASIVE SPECIES COUNCIL, NATIONAL INVASIVE SPECIES MANAGEMENT PLAN (2001), *at* http://www.invasivespecies.gov/council/nmp.shtml (last visited June 4, 2003).

12. THE NATURE CONSERVANCY OF HAWAII & SUSAN MILLER & ALAN HOLT, NATURAL RESOURCES DEFENSE COUNCIL (NRDC), THE ALIEN PEST SPECIES INVASION IN HAWAII: BACKGROUND STUDY AND RECOMMENDATIONS FOR INTERAGENCY PLANNING (1992).

13. *Id* at 4.

14. ERIC REEVES, ANALYSIS OF LAWS AND POLICIES CONCERNING EXOTIC INVASIONS OF THE GREAT LAKES 1 (1999), *available*, along with other documents related to NIS issues in the Great Lakes, *at* http://www.michigan.gov/deq/0,1607,7-135-3313_3677_8314—,00.html (last visited June 3, 2003).

15. *See, e.g.,* UNION OF CONCERNED SCIENTISTS, THE SCIENCE OF INVASIVE SPECIES (2001), *available at* http://www.ucsusa.org/publication.cfm?publicationID=451 (last visited June 5, 2003); NATIONAL WILDLIFE REFUGE ASS'N, SILENT INVASION: A CALL TO ACTION (2002), *available at* http://www.refugenet.org/new-pdf-files/Silent%20Invasion%20pdf.pdf (last visited June 4, 2003).

16. Bob Dylan, *The Times They Are A-Changin'*, *on* THE TIMES THEY ARE A-CHANGING (1964). Bob Dylan surely did not have invasive species in mind when he penned these lyrics, but the lyrics make it seem like he did. A portion of the lyrics to that song follow, applicable then to social change and now to ecological change.

> Come gather 'round people
> Wherever you roam
> And admit that the waters
> Around you have grown
> And accept it that soon
> You'll be drenched to the bone.
> If your time to you
> Is worth savin'
> Then you better start swimmin'
> Or you'll sink like a stone
> For the times they are a-changin' . . .
> Come senators, congressmen
> Please heed the call
> Don't stand in the doorway
> Don't block up the hall
> For he that gets hurt
> Will be he who has stalled
> There's a battle outside
> And it is ragin'.
> It'll soon shake your windows
> And rattle your walls
> For the times they are a-changin' . . . .

17. There are some data problems with using the Lexis and Westlaw newspaper databases for general topic prevalence and incidence since the database has expanded somewhat over the years as new newspapers were added. The more recent information data is more accurate than the older data. Thus, the numbers before 1990 should be taken as only a loose indication of the prevalence of the terms. A rough calculation suggests that the database essentially doubled in size between the beginning of 1995 and the end of 1999. Since the frequency of references to alien species roughly quadrupled in the same period, the basic point still holds—that NIS have invaded popular media and that the scope of that media invasion is increasing. For a discussion and a more precise calculation of the change in the size of the Westlaw and Lexis news databases, see Ronald Wright, *The Abruptness of Action*, 36 CRIM. L. BULL. 401, 424-26 (2000).

18. Invasivespecies.gov, *Newsmedia on Invasive Species*, *at* http://www.invasivespecies. gov/new/newsmedia.shtml (last visited June 5, 2003) (chronological list, with links where available); Invasivespecies.gov, *Invasive Species News Sources*, *at* http://www. invasivespecies.gov/new/isnews.shtml (last visited June 5, 2003) (organized by topic)

19. ROBERT DEVINE, ALIEN INVASION: AMERICA'S BATTLE WITH NON-NATIVE PLANTS AND ANIMALS (1998).

20. CHRISTOPHER BRIGHT, LIFE OUT OF BOUNDS: BIOINVASION IN A BORDERLESS WORLD (1998). A more technical though still accessible overview of alien species in Florida appears in DANIEL SIMBERLOFF ET AL., EDS., STRANGERS IN PARADISE: IMPACT AND MANAGEMENT OF NON-INDIGENOUS SPECIES IN FLORIDA (1997).

21. *See* World Conservation Union, *New Journal Biological Invasions*, *at* http://www. issg.org/bioinvasions.html (last visited July 3, 2003).

22. OTA REPORT, *supra* note 2, at 11.

23. CRS REPORT, *supra* note 10, pt. IV.

24. *Id.* Introduction.

25. *See, e.g.*, The National Park Service Organic Act, Act of Aug. 25, 1916, 39 Stat. 535, codified at 16 U.S.C. §§1-4.

26. Lacey Act, as amended, 16 U.S.C. §§3371-3379; 18 U.S.C. §42.

27. *See* Robert Anderson, *The Lacey Act: America's Premier Weapon in the Fight Against Unlawful Wildlife Trafficking*, 16 PUB. LAND L. REV. 27, 36-53 (1995) (discussing history of Lacey Act):

> Although its coverage extended to animals, the Lacey Act was essentially a bird preservation and restoration measure designed to enhance and protect agriculture. Its language reflected Rep. Lacey's personal passion for the preservation of agriculturally beneficial birds and the eradication of harmful exotic species . . . . Lacey listed the primary threats to bird populations as excessive hunting of game birds by market hunters, the introduction of harmful exotic species that displaced native populations, and the millinery industry, which at that time consumed millions of birds each year for the production of ladies' hats.

> *See also* Davina Kari Kaile, *Evolution of Wildlife Legislation in the United States: An Analysis of the Legal Efforts to Protect Endangered Species and the Prospects for the Future*, 5 GEO. INT'L ENVTL. L. REV. 441, 446-48 (1993); STUART MCIVER, TRUE TALES OF THE EVERGLADES 5 (1989) (attributing passage of the Lacey Act to harvesting of birds from the Everglades).

28. 16 U.S.C. §3372.

29. *Id.* §3373(a)-(c).

30. *Id.* §3373(d).

31. *Id.* §3375(a).

32. *Id.* §3378(a). The nonpreemption of state law would have been clear enough from the general provisions of the Lacey Act since federal agencies are given enforcement power—the power to ban species—made illegal under the law of any state.

33. 18 U.S.C. §42.

34. An additional minor concern is that the listing powers may not include general ecological concerns, such as protection of ecosystem services, ecosystem function, or appearance. However, the list of concerns that are relevant to exclusion is sufficiently broad

that the Secretary of Agriculture can probably find a listed reason to exclude a particular animal species of concern.

35. The original Lacey Act did not include fish, a gap that was filled by the Black Bass Act of 1926, 16 U.S.C. §§851-856, repealed Pub. L. No. 97-79, 9b1, 95 Stat. 1079 (1981), and later amendments to both the Lacey and Black Bass acts, including a substantial set of amendments in 1969. *See* Anderson, *supra* note 27, at 44-48 (amendments expanded coverage of Lacey Act to include amphibians, reptiles, mollusks, and crustaceans).

36. 7 U.S.C. §§150aa-150jj.

37. Plant Quarantine Act of 1912, 7 U.S.C. §§151-157.

38. 7 U.S.C. §§2801-2814.

39. Federal Seed Act, 7 U.S.C. §§1551-1611.

40. *See* Pub. L. No. 106-224, 114 Stat. 358 (June 20, 2000), codified at 7 U.S.C. §§7701-7772.

41. One possible reading of the Lacey Act is that it leaves a technical gap in that there may be no authority for the federal government to limit introduction of species that threaten only wild lands. However, it is difficult to imagine a species that would impact wild lands but not wildlife or "wildlife resources." There does not appear to be any instance of the federal government failing to list a species because it believed it lacked the authority to do so.

42.

> Any importation or transportation of live wildlife or eggs thereof, or dead fish or eggs or salmonids of the fish family Salmonidae into the United States or its territories or possessions is deemed to be injurious or potentially injurious to the health and welfare of human beings, to the interest of forestry, agriculture, and horticulture, and to the welfare and survival of the wildlife or wildlife resources of the United States; and any such importation into or the transportation of live wildlife or eggs thereof between the continental United States, the District of Columbia, Hawaii, the Commonwealth of Puerto Rico, or any territory or possession of the United States by any means whatsoever, is prohibited except for certain purposes and under certain conditions as hereinafter provided . . . .

50 C.F.R. §16.3.

43. Pub. L. No. 106-224, §402(1), codified at 7 U.S.C. §7701.

44. *Id.* §403(10), codified at 7 U.S.C. §7702.

45. The agricultural and commercial focus of the Plant Protection Act is readily apparent from the comments of its sponsors. Speaking about the final version of the bill after consideration in conference, Rep. Charles Canady (R-Fla.) explained that the Plant Protection Act

> is designed to address a very real problem facing American agriculture. The United States loses thousands of acres and billions of dollars in farm production each year due to invasive species. Exacerbating this serious problem are the outdated and fragmented quarantine statutes that govern interdiction of prohibited plants and plant pests. Our agricultural sector needs a modern, effective statutory authority that will protect our crops from these destructive invasive species.
>
> [I]t was for this reason that I introduced the Plant Protection Act. This legislation, crafted in consultation with the USDA, will help to prevent the introduction and dissemination of invasive plants and pests by giving the Animal and Plant Health Inspection Service greatly enhanced investigatory

and enforcement tools. The Plant Protection Act will streamline and consolidate existing statutes into one comprehensive law and eliminate outdated and ambiguous provisions. It will also boost deterrents against trafficking of prohibited species by increasing monetary penalties for smuggling, and it will provide USDA with a comprehensive set of investigatory tools and ensure transparency for our trading partners.

Conference Report on H.R. 2559, 146 CONG. REC. H3816-01, 3820 (May 25, 2000).

46. In setting ranges for civil penalties, Congress included several unusual factors, including "ability to pay" and the "effect on ability to continue to do business." *See* 7 U.S.C. §7734(b).

47. The references to the use of science have a dual-edged quality. For example, §412(b) provides that "[t]he Secretary [of Agriculture] shall ensure that the processes used in developing regulations . . . governing consideration of import requests are based on sound science and are transparent and accessible." 7 U.S.C. §7712(b). The reference to "sound" science may be largely rhetorical; it may also place a burden of scientific proof whereby uncertainty and risk favor continued commerce or the status quo rather than action (or regulation). Other examples of "braking" actions by Congress in the Plant Protection Act include the requirement of "least drastic action" by the government with respect to threats from new plant pests and noxious weeds. 7 U.S.C. §7714(c)(2).

48. *See, e.g.*, 7 U.S.C. §7701(2) & (5). Further mischief may be caused by defining a "biological control organism" as "any enemy, antagonist, or competitor used to control a plant pest or noxious weed" since this definition does not distinguish between "classical" biological controls, where the control agent has evolved with the target in its home range, and the use of biological agents against unrelated targets. 7 U.S.C. §7702(2). *Compare* Marc Miller & Gregory Aplet, *Biological Control: A Little Knowledge Is a Dangerous Thing*, 45 RUTGERS L. REV. 285 (1993) (criticizing the increasing proposals for nonclassical biological controls).

49. Miller & Aplet, *supra* note 48, at 285.

50. *Id.*

51. Pub. L. No. 106-224, §436, codified at 7 U.S.C. §7756.

52. 7 U.S.C. §7756(a).

53. *Id.* §7756(b)(1).

54. *Id.* §7756(b)(2)(A)&(B). A special waiver for a state or political subdivision requires support by "sound scientific data or a thorough risk assessment." These are high and costly standards in the face of immediate and short-term threats, and may require substantial assistance by the federal government if the waiver will be in fact a way to take account of quite varied local needs and threats.

55. Wild Free-Roaming Horses and Burros Act of 1971, 16 U.S.C. §1334.

56. A large number of more focused federal laws dealing with specific invasive species problems might be used to defend particular federal government activities regarding harmful invasive species. Examples include the Virus-Serum-Toxin Act, 21 U.S.C. §§151-158, and various forestry acts, both national and region-specific.

57. 16 U.S.C. §§4701-4715.

58. 39 U.S.C. §3015.

59. Pub. L. No. 106-646, 104 Stat. 4762 (1990), codified in 16 U.S.C. §§4701-4715, reauthorized by Pub. L. No. 104-332, 110 Stat. 4073 (1996).

60. *Id.*

61. 16 U.S.C. §4712(a)(2).

62. National Invasive Species Act of 1996, Pub. L. No. 104-332, 110 Stat. 4073, 4091, codified at 16 U.S.C. §§4701 et seq.

63. *Id.* at §2(c), amending 16 U.S.C. §4712.

64. S. 525, 108th Cong. (2003).

65. 149 CONG. REC. S3179 (daily ed. Mar. 5, 2003). Sen. Carl Levin (D-Mich.), one of the principal sponsors, explained ballast water treatment requirements in the bill as follows:

> I understand that ballast water technologies are being researched and are ready to be tested onboard ships. These technologies include ultraviolet lights, filters, chemicals, deoxygenation, and several others. Each of these technologies has a different pricetag attached to it. It is not my intention to overburden the maritime industry with an expensive requirement to install technology. In fact, the legislation states that the final ballast water technology standard must be based on "best available technology economically achievable." That means that the EPA must consider what technology is available, and if there is not economically achievable technology available to a class of vessels, then the standard will not require ballast technology for that class of vessels, subject to review every 3 years. I do not believe this will be the case, however, because the approach creates a clear incentive for treatment vendors to develop affordable equipment for the market. Since ballast technology will be always evolving, it is important that the EPA review and revise the standard so that it reflects what is the best technology currently available and whether it is economically achievable. Shipowners cannot be expected to upgrade their equipment upon every few years as technology develops, however, so the law provides an approval period of at least 10 years.

> *Id.* at S3179.

66. *Id.* at S3179-80.

67. *See* UNION OF CONCERNED SCIENTISTS, THE NATIONAL INVASIVE SPECIES ACT (2002), *available at* http://www.ucsusa.org/publication.cfm?publicationID=383 (last visited June 5, 2003) (supporting reauthorization efforts to strengthen NISA).

68. 39 U.S.C. §3015 note.

69. Pub. L. No. 108-16 (signed into law on Mar. 23, 2003).

70. H.R. 695, 108th Cong. (2003).

71. S. 1051, 108th Cong. (2003).

72. S. 144, 108th Cong. (2003).

73. 42 U.S.C. §§4321-4370d, ELR STAT. NEPA §§2-209.

74. *Id.* §4332(c) provides:

> (C) include in every recommendation or report on proposals for legislation and other major Federal actions significantly affecting the quality of the human environment, a detailed statement by the responsible official on—
> > (i) the environmental impact of the proposed action,
> > (ii) any adverse environmental effects which cannot be avoided should the proposal be implemented,
> > (iii) alternatives to the proposed action,
> > (iv) the relationship between local short-term uses of man's environment and the maintenance and enhancement of long-term productivity, and

(v) any irreversible and irretrievable commitments of resources which would be involved in the proposed action should it be implemented.

Id. The regulations promulgated under the authority of NEPA chose to emphasize the requirements of "major" actions "significantly" affecting the environment. However, the current regulations suggest that intentional applications of biological control agents do trigger EIS requirements. *See* 7 C.F.R. §520.7:

§520.7 Preparation of an Environmental Impact Statement (EIS).
(a) Actions requiring EIS. An EIS will normally be prepared for:

(1) Proposals for legislation which are determined to be a major Federal action significantly affecting the quality of the human environment; or,

(2) Other major Federal actions significantly affecting the quality of the human environment. In the experience of ARS, an environmental impact statement shall normally be required in situations when a research project has advanced beyond the laboratory and small plot testing to full scale field testing over a very large area and involving the introduction of control agents . . . .

Regulations also provide a definition of what constitutes a "major" federal action. *See* 40 C.F.R. §1508.18:

"Major Federal action" includes actions with effects that may be major and which are potentially subject to Federal control and responsibility. Major reinforces but does not have a meaning independent of significantly (§1508.27). Actions include the circumstance where the responsible officials fail to act and that failure to act is reviewable by courts or administrative tribunals under the Administrative Procedure Act or other applicable law as agency action.

(a) Actions include new and continuing activities, including projects and programs entirely or partly financed, assisted, conducted, regulated, or approved by federal agencies; new or revised agency rules, regulations, plans, policies, or procedures; and legislative proposals (§§1506.8, 1508.17). Actions do not include funding assistance solely in the form of general revenue sharing funds, distributed under the State and Local Fiscal Assistance Act of 1972, 31 U.S.C. §§1221 et seq., with no Federal agency control over the subsequent use of such funds. Actions do not include bringing judicial or administrative civil or criminal enforcement actions. . . .

Id.

75. *See* San Francisco Baykeeper v. Corps of Eng'rs, 219 F. Supp. 2d 1001, 1016 (N.D. Cal. 2002) (U.S. Army Corps of Engineers (the Corps) not required to describe potential severe consequences of invasive species introduction through ballast water releases for two Port of Oakland construction projects because "because there was no 'credible scientific evidence' that such impacts would occur"); National Parks Conservation Ass'n v. Department of Transp., 222 F.3d 677, 30 ELR 20787 (9th Cir. 2000) (upholding sufficiency of "hard look" at alien species in EIS for expansion of Maui airport).

76. *See* Jonathan Cosco, *NEPA for the Gander: NEPA's Application to Critical Habitat Designations and Other "Benevolent" Federal Action*, 8 Duke Envtl. L. & Pol'y F. 345 (1998).

77. *See, e.g.,* Victor Flatt, *The Human Environment of the Mind: Correcting NEPA Implementation by Treating Environmental Philosophy and Environmental Risk Allocation as Environmental Values Under NEPA*, 46 Hastings L.J. 85 (1994); Bill Lockhart, *NEPA: All Form, No Substance?* 14 J. Energy Nat. Resources & Envtl. L. 415

(1994); Donald Zillman & Peggy Gentles, *NEPA's Evolution: The Decline of Substantive Review*, 20 ENVTL. L. 505 (1990); William Rodgers, *NEPA at Twenty: Mimicry and Recruitment in Environmental Law*, 20 ENVTL. L. 485 (1990); Nicholas Yost, *NEPA's Promise—Partially Fulfilled*, 20 ENVTL. L. 533 (1990).

78. 16 U.S.C. §§1531-1544, ELR STAT. ESA §§2-18.

79. *San Francisco Baykeeper*, 219 F. Supp. 2d at 1016 (upholding Corps' finding that Oakland port projects leading to additional release of ballast water not likely to jeopardize species listed under the ESA).

80. OTA REPORT, *supra* note 2, at 187.

81. 852 F.2d 1106, 18 ELR 21119 (9th Cir. 1998) (*Palila II*); 639 F.2d 495, 11 ELR 20446 (9th Cir. 1981) (*Palila I*). The power of the federal government to issue regulations under the ESA that include protection not just of endangered species but of the habitats that support them was upheld by the U.S. Supreme Court in Babbitt v. Sweet Home Chapter of Communities for a Great Or., 515 U.S. 687, 25 ELR 21194 (1995). *See* Ray Vaughan, *State of Extinction: The Case of the Alabama Sturgeon and Ways Opponents of the Endangered Species Act Thwart Protection for Rare Species*, 46 ALA. L. REV. 569 (1995). However, in *Sweet Home*, Justice Sandra Day O'Connor questioned whether the link between harm by the feral sheep to a plant that protects the palila bird was too tenuous to support the requirement of a "taking" under the ESA. 515 U.S. at 713-14 (O'Connor, J., concurring) (citing *Palila II*, 852 F.2d at 1106).

82. 16 U.S.C. §§528-531.

83. *Id.* §§1600-1687, ELR STAT. NFMA §§2-16.

84. 43 U.S.C. §§1701-1785, ELR STAT. FLPMA §§102-603.

85. 16 U.S.C. §668dd-668ee.

86. U.S. CONST. art. IV, §3. *See* Kleppe v. New Mexico, 426 U.S. 529, 6 ELR 20545 (1976) (upholding the constitutionality of the Wild Free-Roaming Horses and Burros Act, and its application on private lands that affect public lands).

87. 16 U.S.C. §§4901-4916.

88. *Id.*

89. Pub. L. No. 103-322, 108 Stat. 1796 (1994). The task force was charged with facilitating prosecution of federal and state laws relating to NIS, recommending ways to strengthen law enforcement regarding NIS "to prevent introduction of non-indigenous plant and animal species," *id.* §320108, codified at 42 U.S.C. §14221, and reporting to various congressional committees and federal agencies. What made Congress in 1994 think that criminal laws were avenue through which to deal with harmful NIS?

90. The cabinet-level departments that deal in some way with NIS issues include the U.S. Department of Agriculture, the U.S. Department of the Interior, the U.S. Department of Commerce, the U.S. Department of Defense, the U.S. Environmental Protection Agency (EPA), the U.S. Department of Health and Human Services, the U.S. Treasury, the U.S. Department of Transportation, and the U.S. Department of Justice.

91. In addition to the statutes described in the prior section—those with substantial and direct links to policy regarding harmful NIS—there are a large number of more or less obscure statutes that provide some authority that might be said to expand an agencies powers to deal with some aspect of the NIS problem. One example might be the Cooperative Forestry Assistance Act of 1978, which makes the U.S. Forest Service responsible for identifying and controlling forest pests. *See* 16 U.S.C. §§2101-2114, and 16 U.S.C. §1606.

92. The federal budgetary process is extremely complex. There are actually two required bills before any actual expenditure of funds, first a bill that "authorizes" expenditures, which may be part of a substantive act, and then a later bill that actually appropriates funds.

93. 7 U.S.C. §§147a et seq.; 7 U.S.C. §§428a et seq.

94. 1957 Amendments. Subsec. (a). Pub. L. No. 85-36 added "insect pests, plant diseases, and nematodes, such as imported fire ant, soybean cyst nematode, witchweed, spotted alfalfa aphid" following "or to prevent or retard the spread of."

95. 16 U.S.C. §§1-4, 22, 43.

96. *Id.*

97. General authority for APHIS is specified in a regulation in which the Secretary of Agriculture delegates relevant authority from various plant protection and pest control statutes. *See* 7 C.F.R. §371.3.

98. 7 U.S.C. §2277 provides:

    Funds available to the Animal and Plant Health Inspection Service (APHIS) under this and subsequent appropriations shall be available for contracting with individuals for services to be performed outside of the United States, as determined by APHIS to be necessary or appropriate for carrying out programs and activities abroad . . . .

    This provision was enacted in 1991. *See* Pub. L. No. 102-142, tit. VII, S. 737, 105 Stat. 915 (1991). The provision echoed similar authority first grant in a 1990 appropriation act. *See* Pub. L. No. 101-506, tit. VI, S. 641, 104 Stat. 1350 (1990).

99. 27 U.S.T. 1987, T.I.A.S. No. 8249, 993 U.N.T.S. 243 (1973).

100. *See* OTA REPORT, *supra* note 2, at 295. International agreements may also be a source of limitation on a country's power to develop domestic environmental policy. For example, world trade agreements might restrict NIS policies, such as comprehensive import restrictions and review, that were deemed a discriminatory or excessive restraint on free trade. *See* Marc L. Miller, *NIS, WTO, SPS, WIR: Does the WTO Substantially Limit the Ability of Countries to Regulate Harmful Non-Indigenous Species?*, 17 EMORY INT'L L.J. (forthcoming 2003).

101. 15 C.F.R. §922.163.

102. 7 C.F.R. §1410.23.

103. *See, e.g.*, U.S. EPA, HENRY LEE & JOHN CHAPMAN, NON-INDIGENOUS SPECIES—AN EMERGING ISSUE FOR THE EPA: VOLUME 1—REGION/ORD NON-INDIGENOUS SPECIES WORKSHOP REPORTS; VOLUME 2—A LANDSCAPE IN TRANSITION: EFFECTS OF INVASIVE SPECIES ON ECOSYSTEMS, HUMAN HEALTH, AND EPA GOALS (2001), *available at* http://www.epa.gov/owow/invasive_species (last visited June 8, 2003).

104. Michael Stokes Paulsen, *The Most Dangerous Branch: Executive Power to Say What the Law Is*, 83 GEO. L.J. 217, 220 (1995); Ronald Turner, *Banning the Permanent Replacement of Strikers by Executive Order: The Conflict Between Executive Order No. 12954 and the NLRA*, 12 J.L. & POL. 1 n.29 (1995) (Executive Orders "were not numbered until 1907 when the State Department organized all executive orders (including old orders on file) and numbered them consecutively; the designation Executive Order No. 1 went to an order issued by President Abraham Lincoln"). Frank Cross, *Executive Orders 12291 and 12498: A Test Case in Presidential Control of Executive Agencies*, 4 J.L. & POL. 483, 484 n.5 (1988).

105. Exec. Order No. 11987, 3 C.F.R. §116, ELR ADMIN. MAT. 45015 (1977).

180

106. CHARLES ELTON, THE ECOLOGY OF INVASIONS BY ANIMALS AND PLANTS 31-32 (1958).

107. DEVINE, *supra* note 19, at 166.

108. *See supra* note 105.

109. *Id.*

110. The OTA report reads these definitions as being "sufficiently vague to allow a species presently in one U.S. ecosystem to be 'exotic' in other U.S. ecosystems." OTA RE-PORT, *supra* note 2, at 167. I find this argument highly implausible, both because the language does not seem very "vague" in referring to "any ecosystem in the United States" and because in the face of ambiguous language a court would be likely to inter-pret the key terms in light of the "legislative history" (here the "executive history") which focused, with illustrations, only on introductions from outside the United States.

111. Exec. Order No. 13112, 64 Fed. Reg. 25 (Feb. 8, 1999), ELR ADMIN. MAT. 45105.

112. *Id.*

113. *Id.*

114. *Id.*

115. A possible exception to the list of relevant cabinet-level officers is the U.S. Attorney General, who has responsibility for enforcing criminal laws regarding NIS.

116. 64 Fed. Reg. at 25.

117. NATIONAL INVASIVE SPECIES COUNCIL, UNITED STATES INVASIVE SPECIES DRAFT MANAGEMENT PLAN: PREPARING FOR THE FUTURE (2000), *available at* http://www.invasivespecies.gov/council/draft711.pdf (last visited June 10, 2003).

118. *See, e.g., id.* at 17.

It will likely take several years to develop specific programs to phase in [a more effective approach]. Substantial additional funding and staff will also be necessary. These costs must be considered in the context of the addi-tional costs required to implement the fully existing laws and the substan-tial costs of future invasions that will be avoided through implementation of a more effective approach.

119. NATIONAL INVASIVE SPECIES COUNCIL, MEETING THE INVASIVE SPECIES CHAL-LENGE (Draft Management Plan) (2000), *available at* http://www.invasivespecies. gov/council/draft1002.pdf (last visited June 10, 2003).

120. NATIONAL INVASIVE SPECIES COUNCIL, MEETING THE INVASIVE SPECIES CHAL-LENGE (2001), *available at* http://www.invasivespecies.gov/council/mpfinal.pdf (last visited June 10, 2003).

121. *Id.* at 27-28.

122. U.S. GENERAL ACCOUNTING OFFICE (GAO), REPORT TO EXECUTIVE AGENCY OF-FICIALS, INVASIVE SPECIES: CLEARER FOCUS AND GREATER COMMITMENT NEEDED TO EFFECTIVELY MANAGE THE PROBLEM (2002), *available at* http://www.gao.gov/ new.items/d031.pdf. I write that the GAO report "concurs" with the views in this paper since GAO staff both discussed these issues with me in several telephone conversa-tions and read an earlier substantial draft of this chapter.

123. *Id.*

124. The GAO has responded to a series of requests from legislators on invasive species is-sues. In August 2000, the GAO described current federal and state funding for dealing with invasive species, and noted that a year and a half after President Clinton signed

Executive Order No. 13112 "[t]he Invasive Species Council has been slow in getting off the ground," and had yet to name people to two of four permanent staff positions. U.S. GAO, REPORT TO CONGRESSIONAL COMMITTEES, INVASIVE SPECIES: FEDERAL AND SELECTED STATE FUNDING TO ADDRESS HARMFUL, NON-NATIVE SPECIES (2000) (GAO/RCED-00-219), *available at* http://www.gao.gov/new.items/rc00219. pdf (last visited June 10, 2003). In July 2001, the GAO focused on the need for a more coherent national rapid response strategy. U.S. GAO, REPORT TO CONGRESSIONAL REQUESTERS, INVASIVE SPECIES: OBSTACLES HINDER FEDERAL RAPID RESPONSE TO GROWING THREAT (2001) (GAO-01-724), *available at* http://www.gao.gov/new. items/d01724.pdf (last visited June 10, 2003).

125. S. 535; H.R. 266, 108th Cong. (2003). The bills, creatively titled the "National Invasive Species Council Act," have been referred to committees, and have only a few sponsors.

126. H.R. 266, 149 CONG. REC. E42 (daily ed. Jan. 8, 2003).

127. U.S. Department of Agriculture, APHIS, 68 Fed. Reg. 27480 (May 20, 2003) (proposed rule). Issues registering on the federal agenda often generate prior or contemporaneous action in the most severely effected states. States enacting ballast water legislations since 1999 include Alaska (1999), California (1999), Illinois (1999), Maryland (2002), Michigan (1999), Oregon (2001), Washington (2002), and Wisconsin (2001). *See* REEVES, *supra* note 14.

128. United Nations Food and Agriculture Organization (FAO), International Plant Protection Convention New Revised Text Art. II (1997) (Approved by FAO Conference at its 29th Session in Rome).

129. *See, e.g.*, U.S. Department of Transportation, Coast Guard, Implementation of the National Invasive Species Act of 1996, 64 Fed. Reg. 26672 (May 17, 1999) (interim rule).

130. Pub. L. No. 102-574, 106 Stat. 4593, codified at 16 U.S.C. §§4502-4503.

131. OTA REPORT, *supra* note 2, at 201-31. The report lists key state statutes and regulations state by state, though unfortunately not in citation forms that are easy to use. *Id.* at 222-23.

132. *Id.* at 208-09.

133. ENVIRONMENTAL LAW INST., HALTING THE INVASION: STATE TOOLS FOR INVASIVE SPECIES MANAGEMENT (2002). The most current and complete list of state invasive species laws can be found at the Northeast Midwest Institute. *See* Northeast Midwest Inst., *Invasive Species State Laws*, *at* http://www.nemw.org/ANSstatelaws.htm.

134. *See, e.g.*, National Conference of State Legislatures, Environment, Energy, and Transportation Program, *Invasive Species Internet Report* (2001), *at* http://www.ncsl.org/ programs/ESNR/invaspecies.htm (last visited June 10, 2003).

135. Focusing on whether a state has a "black list" or "white list" or no list to introductions looks at only one of several relevant dimensions in dealing with harmful NIS. Perhaps the assumption is that if a state does not try to keep out harmful NIS, it is unlikely to be a leader in responding to NIS already in place.

136. MINN. STAT. §84D.04.

137. *Id.* §84D.04, sub. 2.

138. *Id.* §84D.06.

139. *Id.* §84D.07.

140. *Id.* §84D.08.

141. *Id.* §84D.08.

142. *Id.* §84D.13.

143. HAW. REV. STAT. §150-A-6 ("Any animal that is not on the lists of conditionally approved, restricted, or prohibited animals shall be prohibited until the board's review and determination for placement on one of these lists; . . . ."). *See also id.* tit. 11, ch. §150A.

144. *Id.* §152-6.

145. *See, e.g.,* Haw. H.B. No. 1949, House Draft 2 (Mar. 3, 2000) (Rep. Brian Schatz, D-25th Dist.) (a bill addressing alien aquatic organisms); Haw. H.B. No. 2973, House Draft 2 (Haw. 2000) (Rep. Joseph Souki, D-8th Dist.) (a bill making appropriations for alien miconia eradication).

146. Perhaps a complete legal response to harmful NIS could be cobbled together from the most thoughtful provisions from among the states and federal system, but this exercise does not seem more useful or promising than addressing directly the most common gaps in federal and state law.

147. Northeast Midwest Inst., *supra* note 133.

148. *See* Gregory Aplet, *On the Nature of Wildness: Exploring What Wilderness Really Protects,* 76 DENV. U. L. REV. 347 (1999).

149. ALDO LEOPOLD, A SAND COUNTY ALMANAC 262 (1966). *See* Eric T. Freyfogle, *The Land Ethic and Pilgrim Leopold,* 61 U. COLO. L. REV. 217 (1990). *See also* Bradley Karkkainen, *Biodiversity and Land,* 83 CORNELL L. REV. 1 (1997); J.B. Ruhl, *Biodiversity Conservation and the Ever-Expanding Web of Federal Laws Regulating Nonfederal Lands: Time for Something Completely Different?,* 66 U. COLO. L. REV. 555 (1995); A. Dan Tarlock, *Local Government Protection of Biodiversity: What Is Its Niche?,* 60 U. CHI. L. REV. 555 (1993).

150. *See* JOHN HEINZ CENTER FOR SCIENCE, ECONOMICS, AND THE ENVIRONMENT, STATE OF THE NATION'S ECOSYSTEMS: MEASURING THE LANDS, WATERS, AND LIVING RESOURCES OF THE UNITED STATES 76, 145, 169-70, 204, 222, 251, 261-62 (2002) (wisely suggesting that the presence of non-native species are one measure of ecological health; asks the misguided question "whether there is a time (e.g., 50 or 100 years) after which an introduced species is considered to be native").

151. *See generally* NATIONAL RESEARCH COUNCIL, COMMITTEE ON THE SCIENTIFIC BASIS FOR PREDICTING THE INVASIVE POTENTIAL OF NON-INDIGENOUS PLANTS AND PLANT PESTS IN THE UNITED STATES, PREDICTING INVASIONS OF NON-INDIGENOUS PLANTS AND PLANT PESTS (2002), *available at* http://www.nap.edu/books/0309082641.html (last visited June 10, 2003).

152. With Greg Aplet I have previously expressed hesitation about treating biological controls as anything other than invasive species, even if the cost-benefit and risk calculations come out in their favor many times. *See* Miller & Aplet, *supra* note 48.

153. *See* U.S. GAO, REPORT TO CONGRESSIONAL REQUESTERS, *supra* note 124 ("A major obstacle to rapid response is the lack of a national system to address invasive species . . . . Without such a system, obstacles to rapid response are less likely to be addressed and invasive species will continue to fall through the cracks.").

154. Zoos often sell seeds for plants from faraway places in giftshops. At some zoos, signs point out alien plants, and encourage use of plants appropriate to climate (but not necessarily appropriate to the local ecosystem).

155. KEITH PITTS & MARC MILLER, INTERIM REPORT: POLICY AND REGULATION WORKING GROUP OF THE NATIONAL INVASIVE SPECIES COUNCIL (2000), *available at*

http://www.invasivespecies.gov/council/PR%20interim%20final2%20703.doc (last visited June 2003).

156. Don Schmitz & Daniel Simberloff, Issues in Science and Technology Online, *Needed: A National Center for Biological Invasions* (2001), *at* http://www.nap.edu/issues/17.4/schmitz.htm (last visited June 10, 2003).

CHAPTER 7:
THE INTERNATIONAL PLANT PROTECTION CONVENTION AND INVASIVE SPECIES

by John Hedley[1]

The International Plant Protection Convention (IPPC),[2] revised in 1997, provides guidelines for common and effective action to prevent the introduction and spread of pests of plants and plant products. While the IPPC covers pests of both commercial cropping and the natural environment, it also deals with plant protection within a country as well as the spread of pests between countries. The activities and the legal status of national phytosanitary agencies operating in accordance with the IPPC can provide appropriate systems to protect not only commercial agriculture and forestry, but also the natural environment from many harmful non-native organisms.

The Agreement on the Application of Sanitary and Phytosanitary Measures (SPS Agreement)[3] of the World Trade Organization (WTO) has identified the IPPC as the treaty under which phytosanitary standards should be established. The principles inherent in the IPPC and the SPS Agreement provide a basis to set standards for phytosanitary measures concerned with trade issues. These principles suggest that countries may take action when necessary to protect plant health by prevention of introduction, eradication, or containment; that action should be based on the appropriate level of protection for each particular country; that pest risk analysis (PRA) be used in the development of restrictive measures; that countries should follow international standards where available; and that emergency action is permissible when situations require urgent action or there is insufficient information on which to base action.

The major elements of a national phytosanitary system include the following: import regulations to prevent the entry of potential pests; compliance systems to ensure import requirements are met; the use of PRAs for the development of import regulations; the maintenance of surveillance systems to determine the presence or absence of pests; the use of eradication or control programs to remove or restrict the spread of pests; and the use of export certification systems to ensure that exports meet the requirements of trade partners. National agencies are required to make every effort to employ the internationally accepted phytosanitary vocabulary to facilitate communication.

Phytosanitary legislation should set clear objectives, designate associated authorities, and include the power to set measures that deal with pests outside the country and manage those already within it. A law or statute should also have the power to set secondary level regulations and, if necessary, tertiary

185

level ministerial orders or directives as well. Such legislation must take account of any treaties to which the country is signatory that affect phytosanitary issues.

The critical component in the construction of phytosanitary measures is the PRA. To date, the environmental protection aspects of the PRA have not been engaged adequately enough to create measures that protect a nation's overall plant health status. Specific guidelines for the deployment of PRAs are needed, along with recourse to more information about environmental pests. In the long term, the maintenance of plant health status will be better achieved, not by the application of the precautionary principle, but through the use of PRAs to obtain technical justification both for action and for the use of the principle of emergency action.

The operation and status of a phytosanitary agency—to prevent introduction and to provide surveillance, eradication, and containment of pests—should establish the measures necessary to protect the natural environment from harmful non-native organisms. This must be associated with efforts to increase the availability of appropriate technical data and to undertake basic research.

INTRODUCTION

Although phytosanitary systems—or, in older terminology, plant quarantine systems—have been used for many years, it is only recently that they have received careful and detailed international scrutiny to ensure that they are fair, effective, and well-documented, with appropriate internationally accepted standards. Originally developed to protect agriculture, protection systems now cover both commercial and environmental concerns.

The IPPC functions as a standard-setting mechanism, which is recognized by the SPS Agreement of the WTO. The IPPC establishes standards for addressing plant pests, including "any species, strain or biotype of plant, animal or pathogenic agent injurious to plants or plant products"[4] (this IPPC definition of pest is used throughout this chapter). It is significant that this definition includes plants themselves—any plant that may have a directly or indirectly harmful effect on a cropping system or a natural environment. Thus, the IPPC covers many organisms given the general title of "invasive alien species."

This chapter examines the development of current practices and applications of phytosanitary measures, including the legal systems backing their use and the broader applicability of these systems to the maintenance of the natural environment and the biodiversity of species.

DEVELOPMENT OF THE CURRENT INTERNATIONAL PHYTOSANITARY SYSTEM

Phytosanitary systems have been used for many years,[5] long before the development of the first version of the IPPC, but the most significant developments have taken place over the past 10 years. The IPPC was first ratified in 1952 as an international treaty, "with the purpose of securing common and effective action to prevent the spread and introduction of pests of plants and plant products and to promote measures for their control."[6] A 1979 revision, which came into force in 1991, is the current version, with some 111 governments as contracting Parties. However, the convention was further revised in 1997. This updated version of the IPPC[7] is in the process of ratification and will come into force after acceptance by two-thirds of the contracting parties.

The IPPC provides a framework for international cooperation in the control of all plant pests, while also providing discipline in the measures taken against pests for regulatory purposes. It outlines both the duties of a national plant protection organization and the international obligations of each Member government. These include the responsibility to establish a national organization for plant protection and to outline the main functions of such a body; the authority to establish phytosanitary measures and the rules attached to the use of those measures; and the obligation to follow set rules for the use of phytosanitary certificates, as well as guidelines for international cooperation, regional plant protection organizations, and dispute settlement.

The convention has provided a framework for national officials to implement plant health protection systems appropriate to the needs of their country. It has provided internationally accepted requirements for officials to convince their governments that protection systems are essential. It has supported those trying to deal with opposing forces within their own governments that demanded protection or that required trade facilitation. With the 1997 revision of the IPPC linked firmly to the SPS Agreement, there are those who consider the treaty imbalanced in favor of trade facilitation. The revision has, however, clarified the concepts of the IPPC that are complementary to the SPS Agreement and has formalized the new IPPC institution and activities (its Secretariat, Commission, and standard-setting processes).

While the links to trade have been made explicit in the latest revision of the convention, the treaty still deals with general plant protection issues, and these include environmental issues. Plant protection officials who have been involved with the formation of import regulations as part of a plant protection system, and who have used PRA for this purpose, are aware of the need to protect the environment along with agriculture, horticulture, and forestry. These officials are even more aware of the difficulties inherent in the use of PRA to address environmental issues. Guidelines to deal with the problems raised by PRAs and environmental pest risk should be developed as soon as possible. This would allow these risks to be treated in a scientifically acceptable manner, with technical justification and regulations that have the same weight and force as regulations concerning the protection of agriculture, horticulture, and forestry.

The IPPC is noteworthy for its emphasis on international cooperation to prevent the introduction and spread of pests. However, the more prescriptive aspects of the convention have sometimes taken center stage. The development and use of phytosanitary certificates (model phytosanitary and re-export phytosanitary certificates were annexed to the convention), for example, have received much attention. Most countries that export plants or plant products have adopted the model phytosanitary certificate. Many quarantine officials have seen the phytosanitary certificate as the main outcome of the IPPC of 1952 and 1979. In practice, this was probably so, because standards were not developed or manuals produced to elaborate more concretely the principles described in the convention. But this situation has changed dramatically over time as principles and technically justifiable procedures have been developed and documented.

The major factor that has led to the development of phytosanitary science and administration during the past 10 years is the SPS Agreement. The SPS Agreement—one of the agreements forming the Uruguay Round of the General Agreement on Tariffs and Trade (GATT) talks, which instituted the WTO—provides a series of rules for the development and application of sanitary and phytosanitary measures. Its provisions cover the basic rights and obligations of Member nations.[8]

The WTO has given three organizations—the Codex Alimentarius Commission (CAC), the Office International des Épizooties (OIE), and the IPPC—the responsibility to create international standards in the areas of food safety, animal health, and plant health, respectively. The SPS Agreement has provided both a framework for the operation of phytosanitary measures and an impetus for the development and adoption of standards supplied through the IPPC. At the same time, it has increased acceptance and raised the status of phytosanitary measures. This has resulted in major activity in the phytosanitary area, where, formerly, there was only a rather out-of-date convention with no facility for developing and adopting standards.[9]

The development and adoption of international standards for phytosanitary measures are now the main tasks of the Interim Commission on Phytosanitary Measures (ICPM). Contracting Parties to the ICPM are supposed to engage in activities like providing technical assistance, encouraging the sharing of information, monitoring dispute settlement, surveying the state of plant protection in the world, and establishing cooperation with other relevant international organizations. To date, the commission has concerned itself only with the development and adoption of standards. The areas of technical assistance and dispute settlement are under discussion for future action, but, generally speaking, the ICPM has yet to define its international profile. The organization needs to adopt a sufficiently broad area of operation to be effective. Without the full incorporation of developing countries as well as the means to resolve problems below the level of the WTO, progress and effectiveness may be extremely limited.

As part of the cooperative activity of the IPPC, regional plant protection organizations aim to strengthen links between countries within specific regions to deal with phytosanitary issues. There are now nine such organizations, but, with no common structural or organizational guidelines, they have developed into a group of disparate institutions with quite different operational capabilities. For example, Comité Regional de Sanidad Vegetal Para el Cono Sur (COSAVE), with its links to Mercosur and its production of standards for its five Member countries, is quite different from the Asia and Pacific Plant Protection Commission (APPPC). The APPPC includes many different Member countries, from Pakistan to Korea to New Zealand; its biennial meeting is virtually its only common feature. There is no constancy of support present in all the regional organizations to allow them to be effectively used for the collection and dissemination of information and as fora for the discussion of matters of mutual interest.

The links of the phytosanitary community with other such norm-setting bodies are weak, apart from some connections on a personal basis between the staff of the relevant Secretariats. The IPPC Secretariat does have observer status at the SPS Committee meetings of the WTO.

PRINCIPLES OF PHYTOSANITARY SYSTEMS

As formal documentation of concepts, principles, and processes under the IPPC gathered momentum in the 1990s, principles relating to international trade became the first of the convention's published international standards.[10] Most of these principles were later noted in the 1997 revised IPPC.[11] While the CAC and the OIE—the other organizations that set standards for sanitary matters—have touched on international trade, they have not described the basic principles they regard as important in the same manner as has the IPPC.

Briefly, these principles include the following implications: countries have a sovereign right to utilize phytosanitary measures to regulate the entry of material that may carry plant pests; measures should be used only when necessary and be the least restrictive measures consistent with the pest risk involved; measures should be based on international standards where possible; measures may be changed to meet new conditions when they arise; measures should be published; and countries should make available a rationale for the measures they deploy. Furthermore, countries should accept as equivalent measures that, although not identical, produce the same effect. When using PRA to determine the strength of measures, countries should also understand that some risk of pest introduction always exists and should, therefore, agree to a policy of risk management. Countries should recognize pest-free areas as well. They may take emergency action when required and must notify exporting countries of noncompliance with import requirements.

The SPS Agreement, as noted earlier, created a number of rules that were intended to allow WTO Members to establish their own appropriate level of protection, but to prevent sovereign rights from being used for protectionist purposes. The most important of these rules are the criterion of necessity in SPS Agreement Articles 2.1 and 2.2; the scientific justification of measures in SPS Agreement Articles 2.2 and 5.2; the criterion of nondiscrimination in SPS Agreement Article 5.5[12]; pest-free areas in SPS Agreement Article 6; and the use of international standards in SPS Agreement Article 5.8. This agreement allows countries to give priority to plant health at the expense of trade, provided the measures are based on scientific data and so can be justified.[13]

From this list of principles, it is expected that each country will develop its own particular principles that deal with or emphasize its particular concerns. For example, Australia noted the following in a 1979 study on the adequacy of quarantine:

The fundamental principles of Australian Plant Quarantine may be summarized as follows:

• quarantine decisions should not be imposed unless the pest or disease found on imported plant material threatens the productivity of a local industry that is a substantial contributor to the economy;

• quarantine restrictions should not be imposed to protect Australian industries or to further other economic aims;

• research and cooperation between federal and state plant authorities are fundamental to the administration of Australian plant quarantine;

• cooperation with and advice from overseas bodies that oversee and study plant quarantine are essential;

• certification of cleanliness and health of plant material by other countries must be treated with caution;

• assessment of the possible effect that exotic pests and diseases may have in the Australian environment must be made conservatively so as to ensure that pest or disease entering the Australian environment cannot become an endemic environmental or agricultural pest; and

• education of both commercial importers and the traveling public on the need for quarantine measures and the possible consequences of the entry of exotic pests and diseases is essential.[14]

The Australian study stresses the need to avoid the misuse of phytosanitary restrictions. Note also that the study emphasizes the importance of phytosanitary measures to the protection of the environment, as well as the need to educate importers and the traveling public. The enunciation of such national viewpoints keeps the important points before administrators and legislators and helps them to develop consistent policies and regulations. Such principles also offer guides to trading partners and are thus useful in facilitating bilateral relations.

In summary, the following are the main implications of these principles for plant health:

• countries may take action when necessary to protect plant health, by prevention of introduction, by eradication, or by containment;

• action taken by a country should be based on an appropriate level of protection which each country selects for itself;

• countries should use scientific PRA to decide on the strength of any and all measures;

• where standards are available, countries should adhere to them; and

• countries may take emergency or provisional measures when situations require urgent action or when little information is available to determine a course of action.

At this time, there are very few international standards available, and those that are tend to be conceptual in nature, rather than practical and applicable to specific pests. So phytosanitary officials are left to construct regulations with the justification gained from PRAs. The principle of an appropriate level of protection remains obscure. There is no satisfactory definition of this concept that can be applied by plant health scientists or administrators. Theoretically, measures should be imposed only when the level of desired protection is known. The situation is eased somewhat by the fact that officials have some knowledge of the rigor of their own protection system. Furthermore, there are not many levels of strength available to phytosanitary agencies. The sooner the concept of an appropriate level of protection is defined in such a way as to allow for its effective application, the better.

OPERATIONAL ELEMENTS OF PHYTOSANITARY SYSTEMS

Plant health—in other words, the lack of pests and diseases—is a poorly recognized and much undervalued resource. A national phytosanitary system aims to protect the plant health of its country by regulating the means and/or mechanisms of pest entry where feasible, while imposing the least possible number of restrictions on trade. The major elements in the framework of such a system should include import regulations, compliance systems, PRAs, surveillance systems, eradication and control systems, and export certification systems. Each of these is discussed briefly below.

Successful phytosanitary systems are not grounded in inspections at ports or in the issuance of phytosanitary certificates, but rather, in the establishment of specific import regulations. Regulations—in whatever form, from legislation to administrative directives—identify the pests that a country believes constitute a potential danger to its plant health. They also identify the possible ways that these pests can enter their country and where measures can affect this entry. Finally, they set a range of import measures, from visual inspections to long periods in quarantine premises for intensive testing, that the country requires to protect its plant health resource.

Regulations may vary in rigour depending on diverse and particular risks, but when trade is involved, the development of import regulations must be followed by the implementation of adequate compliance systems to ensure that regulations are followed. Compliance systems are applied whenever movement of passengers, mail, transport machinery (ships, containers, planes), etc., is regulated.

To support its import regulations, a nation needs to undertake PRA. This requirement arises from the SPS Agreement and is stated in the 1997 revised IPPC. A PRA provides the technical justification for restrictive measures, and often it becomes the basis for discussion between countries when disputes over import requirements arise. More importantly, the technical justification provided by a PRA demonstrates the need for restrictive measures not only to the importer, but also to the citizens of the country itself. Such justification is essential to obtain public support. PRAs can also be used to identify research needs and priorities and to evaluate the measures of other countries.

To determine which pests could cause problems within a country if they were to enter and establish, a country needs to know what pests are already endemic. This is not always as simple and obvious a matter as it might seem. Surveys to determine the pests present in a country, coupled with the demand of continued surveillance to keep this list up to date, are extremely expensive. Furthermore, surveillance may have to be extended to include special areas which are pest-free and for which assurance is needed. The same applies for areas where a pest has been eradicated. Theoretically, surveillance for pests should be a regular function of national plant protection organizations, but in fact, this is rarely so because of the prohibitive costs involved.

The ability to eradicate pests from an area and the ability to control pests and restrict their spread are essential components of a phytosanitary arsenal. Eradication and control systems should, as mentioned above, have a substantial amount of surveillance or monitoring as part of their activities.

Nations normally respect each other's import requirements, and thus participate in a mutually beneficial system that protects everyone's plant health resources. Trading nations develop export certification systems to ensure that their products comply with an importing country's requirements. However, when a country does not believe that a trade partner is justified in its requirements, negotiations/dispute settlement procedures may ensue.

To facilitate understanding and communication between trading nations, it is necessary to have a comprehensive glossary, which defines terms in a scientific and rational manner. An explicit, scientific, nonemotive vocabulary is an essential tool for effective communication.

In the past, governments weighted phytosanitary measures to concentrate on the protection of agriculture, horticulture, and forestry. But this emphasis is today waning, as environmental protection issues gain steadily in importance. PRAs to determine the strength of phytosanitary measures that deal with pests of agriculture and forestry are now just as likely to be used for pests of the environment as well. The principles of technical justification and transparency demand this.

LEGAL ELEMENTS OF PHYTOSANITARY SYSTEMS

Phytosanitary regulations are drawn up with the knowledge that the balance of organisms that make up the natural resources of a country, whether in the natural environment or in the production of commercial crops, can be changed by the introduction of a new organism. Therefore, as much as possible, unintentional introduction of new organisms needs to be prevented, and the intentional importation of new organisms should take place only after due consideration.

Legislation is aimed initially at the assessment of risks (usually associated with the movement of people or products), then at the management of those risks by rules describing a series of controls, and finally at the discouragement of noncompliance with the rules. The management of risks requires the use of a cordon through which all craft, vehicles, goods, and people must pass. In some instances, an internal cordon will also be necessary.

The assertion of control forms the basic component of most phytosanitary law: either all plant material and associated transport are prohibited, or they are subject to quarantine until entry or quarantine release is granted. Some countries, though, take the reverse position: all material is permitted entry unless otherwise specified. This may be followed by the power to prohibit or to specify entry conditions in certain situations, and/or by ministerial orders with respect to the management of certain specified pests.

To prepare regulations that deal adequately with such situations, all viewpoints should be considered, including those responsible for forestry, fisheries, livestock, the environment, biological diversity, endangered species, and national parks. Consultation may be difficult, but it is essential. It should be remembered that those who take the risks are seldom those affected by a harmful introduction.

While it may be difficult to assess perfectly the dangers posed by the introduction of many organisms, it is nevertheless possible to make reasonable scientific judgments based on knowledge and experience. These judgments make up a PRA, which provides the requisite technical justification for all regulations promulgated.

To facilitate the operation of phytosanitary systems, a number of points must be addressed and clarified in legislation.[15] The areas that are usually covered include the following:

- title and purpose of the law, statute, or act;
- terms used with appropriate definitions;
- identification of the authority or government agency responsible for the act and the description of regulatory powers (regulations, rules, orders, etc.): the links with other governments' departments, e.g., Customs, ports authorities, commodity boards, post offices, would be indicated;
- appointment of officials and inspectors;
- measures associated with protection from pests outside the country, i.e., to prevent entry: import systems (licenses, standards), ports of entry, border controls, phytosanitary certificates, post-entry quarantine sites;
- measures associated with pests already in the country: pest surveillance, eradication or pest management programs, emergency measures;
- issuance of phytosanitary certificates for export and re-export;
- provisions for compensation;
- offenses and penalties;
- legal and administrative procedures (limitation of liability).

Thus, a phytosanitary law, statute, or act should have clear objectives and associated authorities, powers, offenses, and penalties, and should be enabling rather than prescriptive. It should have the power to establish regulations, ministerial orders, codes of practice, approvals, prohibitions, exemptions, restrictions, and provisional import permits. Such secondary legislation would prescribe the supplementary, administrative, and technical rules for implementing the act, i.e., regulations for the import of plants and plant produce, export regulations, and plant pest control regulations.

Tertiary-level ministerial orders or directives of similar authority are used in some countries to provide the technical detail necessary for the full implementation of an act or regulation. At this level, flexibility is necessary to cope with frequent changes of situation. Such directives may involve controls for importation (listed prohibitions, listed exemptions, standards for specified routine imports), pest management (programs for dealing with specified pests, movement controls to prevent pest spread or to establish free areas, response to emergency situations, e.g., outbreaks, and exportation (requirements for specified produce to specified markets).

New organisms, including all plants, should be assessed for weed status—and this should include all environments. The IPPC also allows for the consideration of pest aspects of genetically modified organisms. For export controls, systems need to be available to deal with the implementation of a phytosanitary certification procedure, which is part of the mutual respect for a trading partner's laws.

Finally, any system should take note of its relationship with other laws in the country and with obligations and requirements of other treaties to which the country may subscribe, such as the IPPC and its associated standards.

The above brief consideration of the legal elements of phytosanitary systems shows that a plant protection system based on the IPPC would have the structure and procedures to provide measures to deal with most of the plants that may be considered as harmful non-native organisms.

TERMINOLOGY

International discussions on phytosanitary measures have been facilitated by the use of a common, standard vocabulary. The Interim Commission on Phytosanitary Measures adopted the latest edition of the *Glossary of Phytosanitary Terms*,[16] known as ISPM 5, in 1999. Every attempt is made to obtain clarity and scientific usage for terms.

In the specific context of environmental issues, there is a need to adopt consistent usage of terms such as "endemic," "indigenous," "native," and their antonyms, as well as the more emotive terms such as "alien" and "invasive." The use of these terms implies a degree of potential danger that might not always be the case. The application of these terms to an organism needs to be justified. Usage of the term "invasive" might be restricted to those organisms fulfilling particular requirements and be qualified by information on date and place. A standardized, scientific, internationally accepted terminology would be a most useful adjunct to all discussions on this subject.

The phytosanitary community recognizes that effective plant protection derives from international cooperation. Part of this cooperation is the reporting of the distribution of pests—particularly the outbreak of new pests within a country. But most countries are reluctant to make such reports, because trade partners often react to such reports by instituting requirements that restrict or prohibit the importation of materials and products that may carry the reported pest. In some cases, such action is clearly justified, but in others, the reaction may amount to overreaction and not take into account the fact that an incursion was transient or that an outbreak was subsequently eradicated. To begin to remedy this situation, the ICPM has produced the standard *Determination of Pest Status in an Area*,[17] which recommends the use of terms that fully describe a pest's status in a particular country, terms such as: "transient: nonactionable"; "transient: actionable, under eradication"; "absent, pest eradicated." Single-word descriptors may be easier to use, but they frequently fail to impart the accurate and detailed information that is included in the descriptive phrases suggested above.

From these recommendations and the code of practice outlined in this standard, the ICPM will develop further standards on pest listing and pest reporting. This gives some indication of the seriousness with which the phytosanitary community views term definition and usage and its importance in international relations.

THE ENVIRONMENT AND PHYTOSANITARY SYSTEMS

Phytosanitary systems were initially developed to respond to concerns about the introduction and spread of pests that could affect cultivated plants. However, recognition that the natural environment needs to be protected as well has been evident for some years.[18] Consideration of this point must be integrated into the procedures adopted by phytosanitary officials to create regulations, since the IPPC covers not only commercial production of plants and the natural environment, but also both the direct and indirect effects of plant pests.

The scope of concern for harmful, non-native pests includes those organisms (plant and animal, marine, freshwater, and terrestrial) within the country that could spread or that could enter the country again, and those outside the country that could enter and establish. Of these, the IPPC deals with plants and their pests (plants, microorganisms that are plant pests, and animals that are plant pests), specifically with plant pests not in the country and all plants, not in the country, that may be injurious to plants or plant products. It also covers those pests that are in a country but that are not widespread. This means that the IPPC covers a great many of the concerns relating to the environment.

Considering those pests in a country, the IPPC supports eradication and containment programs. With the import of those pests already in the country, the IPPC provides for the regulating of regulated non-quarantine pests that are defined as those pests "whose presence in plants for planting affects the intended use of those plants with an economically unacceptable impact and which is therefore regulated within the territory of the importing party."[19] This is unnecessarily narrow in scope and should contain reference to environmental programs in addition to the reference to plants for planting. The ICPM is preparing a concept standard on this subject to clarify its implementation, but not, at this stage, with a view to its amendment.

PEST RISK ANALYSES

The requirement to use PRA in the creation of regulations has been emphasized for some time, but the use of an established, formal procedure is a recent development. In the past, some form of PRA would usually be applied to a potential pest entry—arising, for example, when access for a plant product was requested, but this PRA was often a very rudimentary type of analysis. PRA skills have developed slowly, due, in part, to a lack of resources and time available to phytosanitary officials. In many countries, the operational capabilities to conduct PRAs have been limited, but this situation is changing.

There is currently much greater recognition of the role that PRAs play in the setting of regulations. The availability of PRA guidelines and the greater availability of information have had a great effect on the willingness of phytosanitary officials to conduct PRAs. Also, the WTO dispute settlement system has made all Parties more conscious of the fact that import regulations may be disputed. If one country believes an import regulation of a trade partner is not technically justified, the problem can be bilaterally discussed and, if not resolved, referred to the WTO dispute settlement system. In the future, member countries may choose alternative systems for dispute settlement of lower profile issues. These less confrontational settlement procedures may involve either the SPS Committee, ad hoc consultations under the offices of the chair, or other mechanisms currently under development by the ICPM.

The IPPC now pays particular attention to environmental issues.[20] Yet some countries are reluctant to accept this, which only reinforces the ongoing concern of many countries that PRA with regard to environmental issues remains an extremely difficult task. Despite advances in the conduct of PRAs, the current guidelines[21] do not address the need for special features that emphasize environmental issues.[22] Furthermore, there is the difficulty of "converting" environmental impacts into economic terms for the purpose of estimating the cost of those impacts. In fact, there has been little consideration of this subject by the phytosanitary community. There needs to be discussion of the problems involved with environmental issues and, if necessary, the planning of a continuing research program.[23]

PRECAUTIONARY APPROACH

When discussing phytosanitary systems in relation to protecting the natural environment from invasive species, one of the most important concepts to consider is that of the precautionary approach. The precautionary approach can be interpreted strictly, in which case imports are permitted only when they have been proven to be safe. Under this interpretation, it may be justified or even mandatory, to limit, restrain, or prevent certain potentially hazardous actions without waiting for scientific justification beyond doubt. Under a more loose interpretation, import risk is dealt with by a careful assessment and the application of appropriate measures; where there is uncertainty, provisional measures may be applied which are then modified as soon as additional information is available.

One of the first enunciations of the precautionary approach is stated in Principle 15 of the Rio Declaration on Environment and Development: "In order to protect the environment, the precautionary approach shall be widely applied by States according to their capabilities. Where there are threats of serious or irreversible damage, lack of full scientific certainty shall not be used as a reason for postponing cost-effective measures to prevent environmental degradation."[24] This would imply that measures could be applied when serious and irreversible damage is possible, but the likelihood cannot be estimated due to a lack of data.

The SPS Agreement comments on this subject in Article 5.7:

> In cases where scientific evidence is insufficient, a Member may provisionally adopt sanitary or phytosanitary measures on the basis of available pertinent information, including that from the relevant international organization as well as from sanitary or phytosanitary measures applied by other Members. In such circumstances, Members shall seek to obtain the additional information necessary for a more objective assessment of risk and review the sanitary and phytosanitary measure accordingly within a reasonable period of time.[25]

This rule allows for provisional measures to be adopted when information is lacking, but it also requires a process of continuing investigation of risk and timely review of the provisional measure.

The first standard issued by the IPPC, *Principles of Plant Quarantine as Related to International Trade*, states in relation to emergency action:

> Countries may, in the face of a new and/or unexpected phytosanitary situation, take immediate emergency measures on the basis of a preliminary pest risk analysis. Such emergency measures shall be temporary in their application, and their validity will be subjected to a detailed pest risk analysis as soon as possible.[26]

This statement, like the two preceding it, suggests that a preliminary risk assessment, made with insufficient data, may be used to apply temporary or provisional measures, but it confines the use of these measures to situations requiring urgent action.

Thus, these statements from the Rio Declaration, the SPS Agreement, and the IPPC, all seem to suggest that the burden of evidence falls on proving an object, organism, or product harmful before restricting its importation, rather than restricting importation until an object, organism, or product is proven safe or harmless. And it seems clear that provisional measures should be based on some form of risk analysis.

Risk analysis is a process to estimate probability, i.e., the magnitude of effects and uncertainty. The process caters to the unknown. The guidelines for conducting PRAs are comprehensive, taking into account biological and economic data, as well as uncertainties that also must be assessed. Risk analysis should be a fundamental component in any precautionary approach, as it will ensure sound provisional measures.

The strict interpretation of the precautionary approach, i.e., that imports should be permitted only when proved to be safe, would allow the establishment of major prohibitions with a minimum of evidence or support, or even, possibly, the total absence of any supporting information. Such a system has enormous potential to cause trade problems. Phytosanitary restrictions have to be technically justified to make them acceptable to governments, industry, and citizens. The correct use of risk analyses, the application of provisional measures in instances of inadequate information or urgent situations, provides a substantial safety net for dealing with cases where there is concern that possible adverse consequences might arise from an import.

Finally, a note on managed risk will put the precautionary approach and the potential introduction of harmful organisms into context. It is impossible to stop completely the introduction and spread of organisms. There is no zero risk. The movement of organisms will take place despite the best endeavors of plant health officials. However, when and where the modes of entry of organisms believed likely to be damaging to an environment or cropping system can be identified, then every effort should be made to prevent such introductions taking place. PRA manages risk effectively by identifying the high-risk areas and thus focusing resources.

ADDITIONAL ASPECTS IN RELATION TO PHYTOSANITARY AND ENVIRONMENTAL INTERESTS

As part of recent developments in the formulation of international standards and the provision of technical assistance and information under the IPPC, links between phytosanitary systems and environmental interests have become increasingly evident. In June 2000, Members attending an Exploratory Open-Ended Working Group meeting of the ICPM discussed biodiversity in relation to the IPPC and considered creating some formal links between the IPPC and the Convention of Biological Diversity. As noted earlier, there is a pressing need for guidelines to address the consideration of environmental issues when conducting PRAs. The ICPM may be able to help with this task, as it is already dealing with standards for quarantine pests and regulated non-quarantine pests. The provision of appropriate biological data, as proposed by Marc Miller and Greg Aplet[27] and others, such as lists of pests associated with damage to particular environmental habitats, would further assist in undertaking PRAs.

Pest eradication and containment programs for phytosanitary purposes are much the same as eradication and containment programs of any non-indigenous pest. The primary constraint on any such program is usually financial. Eradication programs can be expensive in the short term, while containment programs are a continuing financial drain.

Many of the phytosanitary operational systems can apply to harmful non-native plant pests of the environment, so the components of phytosanitary legislation can support legislative action for the same organisms. However, some countries prefer to have the introduction of new organisms considered by a special agency. This separation of closely linked activities has its drawbacks. (Even if phytosanitary systems were applied to cover the introduction of all harmful non-native plant organisms, the coverage for genetically modified organisms, animal pests, and marine and freshwater problems would need to be dealt with by other legislation.)

Overall, the use of phytosanitary agencies to support the consideration of environmental issues would allow not only the most efficient use of existing knowledge, systems, and procedures, but also the building of integrated services. The advantages of using a phytosanitary service as a foundation, with its existing technical databases, legislation, and operational systems, far outweighs any advantage gained by creating a separate service to deal with non-indigenous environmental threats. Certainly this would be so for those developing countries that already have difficulty affording the institutions, facilities, and financial and human resources necessary to provide even a basic phytosanitary system.

CONCLUSION

Ultimately, there is little difference between a phytosanitary system used for the protection of production systems and one used for the maintenance of the natural environment and the biodiversity of species. Any differences are likely to be a matter of emphasis, in terms of the application of the precautionary approach by those concerned with the maintenance of the natural environment and the diversity of species.

Given the resources, phytosanitary systems can deal with many of the concerns about harmful non-native species (including weeds). All programs involved in protecting the plant health status of a country—the establishment of import requirements involving high biosecurity, or extensive (and expensive) surveillance systems, eradication programs or containment programs—require sound technical support to be effective and to engage appropriate resources. The use of PRA to provide technical justification is an essential part of any protection system. Systems involving PRA may well gain more support and resource share in the long term than the promulgation of the precautionary approach.

Effective progress in environmental protection can be made only with access to libraries of biological, climatic, and pest distribution information. Funds for basic research are required. This is why resourcing for the long term is so important and why the technical justification of all recommended regulations using PRAs is essential.

Chapter 7 Endnotes

1. Dr. John Hedley is presently National Adviser, Biosecurity Coordination and International Adviser for the Biosecurity Authority of the New Zealand Ministry of Agriculture and Forestry. He was the first Coordinator of the International Plant Protection Convention (IPPC) (1993-1995) and the first Chair of the Interim Commission on Phytosanitary Measures (ICPM) (1998-2001) and Vice Chair of the Interim Commission (2001-2003). He wishes to gratefully acknowledge the helpfulness of G. King, A. Matheson, and S. Rejasekar of the New Zealand Ministry of Agriculture and Forestry and R.L. Griffin and G. Moore of the United Nations (U.N.) Food and Agriculture Organization (FAO) in Rome.

2. U.N. FAO, International Plant Protection Convention New Revised Text, art. II (1997) (approved by FAO Conference at its 29th Session in Rome).

3. World Trade Organization (WTO), *Agreement on the Application of Sanitary and Phytosanitary Measures, in* THE RESULTS OF THE URUGUAY ROUND OF MULTILATERAL TRADE NEGOTIATIONS. THE LEGAL TEXTS (1994).

4. *See supra* note 2.

5. GEORGE H. BERG, PLANT QUARANTINE, THEORY, AND PRACTICE (Oganismo Internacional Regional de Sanidad Agripecuaria (OIRSA) 1991).

6. U.N. FAO, International Plant Protection Convention (Rome 1951).

7. U.N. FAO, International Plant Protection Convention (Rome 1999).

8. These include harmonization, equivalence, assessment of risk, pest-free areas and areas of low prevalence, transparency, control, inspection and approval procedures, technical assistance, special and differential treatment and consultations, and dispute settlement.

9. In 1989, the FAO agreed to set up an IPPC Secretariat to support the activities of the convention and to produce international standards for phytosanitary measures. By 1993, the Secretariat was operational and the first standard was adopted at the 1993 Session of the FAO Conference. In 1997, the FAO Conference adopted a revised convention, which established a Commission on Phytosanitary Measures. Until the revised convention is accepted, standard-setting under the IPPC is currently the responsibility of a body known as the ICPM.

10. U.N. FAO, PRINCIPLES OF PLANT QUARANTINE AS RELATED TO INTERNATIONAL TRADE (1995) [hereinafter ISPM Pub. No. 1].

11. Most of the principles relating to international trade set forth in the ISPM Pub. No. 1 are now noted in the 1997 revised IPPC (as indicated below with article numbers). They include general principles on sovereignty (VII, 1.), necessity (VI, 1. b), minimal impact (VII, 2. g), modification (VII, 2. h), transparency (VII, 2. b), harmonization (X, 4.), equivalence and dispute settlement (XIII). Specific principles noted include those on cooperation (VIII), technical authority (IV, 1.), risk analysis (IV, 2. f), managed risk, pest-free areas (IV, 2. e), emergency action (VII, 6.), notification of noncompliance (VII, 2. f), and nondiscrimination (VI, 1. b).

12. GATT provides two major rules that affect phytosanitary issues and deal with this matter more fully. The first is the Most-Favoured-Nation Treatment as found in Article I, Paragraph 1: "Any advantage, favour, privilege or immunity granted by any contracting party to any product originating in or destined for any other country shall be accorded immediately and unconditionally to the like product originating in or destined for the territories of all other contracting parties." WTO, GUIDE TO GATT LAW AND PRACTICE (1995). This rule prohibits any discrimination of requirements between

countries where similar conditions exist. The second is the National Treatment rule of Article III, Paragraph 4.

13. S. DURAND & J.P. CHIARADIA-BOUSQUET, NEW PRINCIPLES OF PHYTOSANITARY LEGISLATION (1997) (FAO legislative study No. 62).

14. Report from the Australian Senate Standing Committee on National Resources, The Adequacy of Quarantine and Other Control Measures to Protect Australia's Pastoral Industries From the Introduction and Spread of Exotic Livestock and Plant Diseases (1979).

15. U.N. FAO, PLANT QUARANTINE SECTION, SUGGESTED GUIDELINES FOR PLANT QUARANTINE ACT OR LAW (1983). *See also* LUIS M. BOMBIN, PLANT PROTECTION LEGISLATION (1984).

16. U.N. FAO, GLOSSARY OF PHYTOSANITARY TERMS, (REVISED) (1999) (ISPM Pub. No. 5) (revised version in publication).

17. U.N. FAO, DETERMINATION OF PEST STATUS IN AN AREA (1999) (ISPM Pub. No. 8).

18. RUSSELL C. MCGREGOR, THE EMIGRANT PESTS (1973) (a report to Dr. Francis J. Mulhern, Administrator, Animal and Plant Health Inspection Service, United States).

19. *See supra* note 2.

20. *Id.* pmbl. & art. IV, 2.b.

21. U.N. FAO, GUIDELINES FOR PEST RISK ANALYSIS (1996) (ISPM Pub. No. 2).

22. A new PRA standard has been adopted, U.N. FAO, PEST RISK ANALYSIS FOR QUARANTINE PESTS (2002) (ISBM Pub. No. 11).

23. Since the original presentation of this paper, a new PRA standard for quarantine pests has been published with supplements referring to economic and environmental matters under consideration. *See id.*

24. Rio Declaration on Environment and Development, U.N. Conference on Environment and Development, princ. 15, U.N. Doc. A/CONF.151/5/ Rev. 1, 31 I.L.M. 874 (1992).

25. WTO, *Agreement on the Application of Sanitary and Phytosanitary Measures* Art. 5.7, *in* THE RESULTS OF THE URUGUAY ROUND OF MULTILATERAL TRADE NEGOTIATIONS. THE LEGAL TEXTS (1994).

26. ISPM Pub. No. 1, *supra* note 10, princ. 14.

27. MARC MILLER & GREG APLET, MODEL PREVENTION OF HARM BY NON-INDIGENOUS SPECIES ACT (1995) (draft), *available at* http://www.law.emory.edu/~mmiller/ nisa1195.html (last visited Dec. 7, 2002).

CHAPTER 8:
INVASIVE ALIEN SPECIESAND THE MULTILATERAL TRADING SYSTEM

by Jacob Werksman[1]

International trade is one of the most important pathways for both the intentional and the unintentional introduction of alien species. The intentional introduction of alien species takes place through the importation of exotic plants and animals as commercial products. But alien species may also enter unintentionally, as byproducts of trade, e.g., through cross-breeding of exotics with local populations, as parasites of products, e.g., as an infestation or infection on agricultural products, or as "stowaways" during trade, e.g., in the ships, planes, or vehicles that deliver products. Furthermore, the unintentional introduction of alien species occurs not only by way of trade in goods, but also by way of trade in services, e.g., as parasites or stowaways through tourism. Not surprisingly, governments have used their authority and responsibility to regulate commerce at their borders as a primary means of controlling the introduction of alien species. As the volume and geographical spread of trade grows, this regulatory challenge will increase, particularly for developing country governments.

This chapter examines the potential interaction between the policy objectives and rules associated with efforts to regulate the introduction of alien species, and those designed to promote and protect free trade. Free trade rules, as represented by the agreements of the World Trade Organization (WTO), generally recognize the right of governments to impose rules necessary to protect domestic animal and plant life and health. However, WTO rules may not take full account of the specific concerns of officials and nongovernmental organizations (NGOs) working to protect native biodiversity from the threat of invasive alien species.

For example, WTO rules abhor distinctions made on the basis of national origin. Discrimination against or between products or services on the basis of their "foreignness" runs contrary to the WTO's central principles that prohibit *imported* products or services from being treated less favorably than "like" *domestic* products or services. Such distinctions are considered inherently suspect and probably motivated by efforts to protect domestic industries from foreign competition. Thus, under free trade rules, regulators seeking to ban the import of a product must justify their request with something more substantial than the mere fact of the foreignness of the product. By contrast, as other chapters in this collection suggest, rules that seek to prevent the introduction of "alien" species are primarily concerned with excluding that which is foreign, i.e., "non-native." The somewhat arbitrary manner in which some governments and groups have chosen to define what is native and what is not, may pose particular difficulties with trade rules.

WTO rules increasingly rely on science as an "objective" arbiter to determine when governments can reasonably restrict trade in products and services as a means of protecting animal and plant life. Evolving interpretations of WTO rules suggest, for example, that defending a quarantine measure against a WTO challenge requires a scientific risk assessment. Such assessments can be both technically difficult and expensive. WTO rules could substantially limit the scope and ability of governments to take precautionary actions in the absence of supporting scientific evidence. While the impact or potential impact of a number of alien introductions has been well documented, concerns about other species and pathways remain hypothetical or unstudied. Aggressive, precautionary regulations against the introduction of alien species are thus potentially vulnerable to conflicts with free trade rules.

WTO rules and practices also look toward multilaterally negotiated, internationally agreed upon standards as a means of striking a reasonable balance between national concerns about environmental protection, and global concerns about trade protectionism. If an appropriate international institution has adopted an international standard on the regulation of alien species, the WTO rules may, in certain circumstances, defer to this standard. This deference is based on the rationale that a large, representative grouping of states is unlikely to agree to standards that are discriminatory, arbitrary, or protectionist. However, as other chapters in this book demonstrate, the international community is still struggling to agree on global standards to define, identify, and regulate alien species. Thus far, there are no concrete or definitive internationally agreed upon rules that might help defend a national measure against a WTO challenge. The WTO's broadly applicable trade rules and its powerful dispute settlement system will fill this regulatory vacuum unless or until other international institutions develop specific rules related to the trade in alien species.

This chapter reviews the landscape of WTO law and practice relevant to the regulation of alien species. After a brief review of the general rules governing trade in products and services, the analysis focuses on the Agreement on Sanitary and Phytosanitary Measures (SPS Agreement).[2] The discussion reviews specific challenges facing regulators of alien species as they struggle to comply with SPS disciplines, including conforming to international standards, carrying out scientific risk assessments, ensuring consistency in the application of levels of protection, and designing least trade-restrictive alternatives.

THE WTO

The agreement establishing the WTO entered into force January 1, 1995. The WTO agreements establish legally binding disciplines that govern the trade in goods and services, and the enforcement of intellectual property rules among 140 Members.[3] The agreements also established the WTO as a formal international organization authorized to monitor the implementation of these disciplines, to resolve disputes that arise between WTO Members, and to negotiate and implement new rules. WTO law draws upon 40 years of practice under the General Agreement on Tariffs and Trade (GATT),[4] a narrower and more loosely organized institution, which focused on trade in products.

One of the most innovative institutional aspects of the WTO is its dispute settlement system, which can issue binding judgments and authorize retaliation against WTO Members who fail to comply with their obligations.[5] WTO Members must answer complaints brought against them by other Members. The WTO's ad hoc arbitration panels and its Appellate Body (AB), both of which decide disputes, provide reasoned and authoritative clarifications of WTO rules on a case-by-case basis. Once a dispute is resolved, if a WTO Member fails to comply with a panel or AB report, the "losing" Member can be subject to trade sanctions by the complaining Member. As disputes arise and are then resolved, a dynamic and evolving set of new understandings emerges from these changing legal and factual contexts.

The WTO dispute settlement system is thus crucial to understanding and predicting the interaction between trade rules and other national and international rules. There have, however, only been two WTO disputes to date, both of which fall under the SPS Agreement, that deal directly with regulatory measures designed to deal with the introduction of alien species. While the analysis of the SPS Agreement is the focus of this chapter, other WTO agreements will be mentioned as well to provide a fuller context of the development and potential application of trade law to alien species regulation.

The WTO agreements most relevant to this analysis are the Multilateral Agreements on the Trade in Goods, in particular the GATT of 1994; and the WTO SPS Agreement; as well as the General Agreement on Trade in Services (GATS).[6] The WTO agreements that apply, either individually or in combination, to a particular measure designed to regulate alien species depend upon the nature of the threat being regulated, the nature of the measure designed to regulate that threat, and the way in which the measure impacts trade. The most common measures to regulate introductions through trade pathways are border controls designed either to bar unintentional introductions or to regulate intentional introductions. These measures can include mandatory advanced notification and other documentation, import licenses, quarantine, and fumigation.[7] An intentionally introduced species may be subject to further regulation after it has crossed the border, such as permits conditioned upon monitoring and containment procedures, and restrictions on breeding, sale, and resale.[8] Whether the alien species is the product itself, or "hitchhiking" on a product or service, measures that slow or hinder the flow of commerce fall under the WTO's jurisdiction.

GATT (1994)

The GATT as amended in 1994 (GATT 1994) consists of the general rules designed to govern the trade in products that were developed through 40 years of practice under the original GATT agreement, adopted in 1947. The 1994 WTO agreements that are now in force not only retain and clarify the original GATT rules, but have also brought into force more detailed agreements on specific kinds of products and measures. The GATT's general disciplines govern all products traded between WTO Members unless they are expressly overridden by the more specific and recent agreements. These GATT rules will be briefly reviewed here before moving on to an in-depth discussion of the SPS Agreement—the WTO agreement most likely to be invoked in the context of regulating alien species.

The GATT rules potentially relevant to the regulation of alien species include a prohibition against the use of trade bans,[9] rules aimed at eliminating discrimination on the basis of the national origin of products,[10] and general exceptions that allow Members to deviate from the rules in certain limited circumstances.[11]

GATT Article XI forbids WTO Members from instituting or maintaining prohibitions or quantitative restrictions on the importation of products from other WTO Members (through quotas, import licenses, or other measures). Such bans are the most obvious manner in which governments interfere with free trade, and the GATT rules are designed to ensure that they can only be maintained in the most limited circumstances. Trade bans that are aimed at alien species as products or that are designed to prevent their introduction as parasites or stowaways on other products would be a prima facie violation of Article XI and would have to be justified under an exception.

GATT Article III (National Treatment) and Article I (Most-Favored-Nation Treatment) prohibit measures that directly or indirectly discriminate between "like products" on the basis of their country of origin. These rules are based on the assumption that if two products are physically alike in all relevant characteristics, there can be no legitimate regulatory basis for discriminating between them. Articles III and I have been interpreted broadly to catch not only any regulation that discriminates "on its face," i.e., that expressly distinguishes on the basis of national origin, but also any regulation that is facially neutral, but discriminates in its effect. Restrictions on the sale, resale, or use of alien species, if these species are demonstrably "like" an unregulated species of domestic origin or are "like" another unregulated foreign species, might violate these GATT provisions. Determinations of "likeness" made by GATT and WTO panels have focused on a comparison of the physical characteristics of the products, and the regulatory risks associated with those physical characteristics.[12]

Measures that are found to violate Articles XI, I, or III:4 may, nevertheless, qualify for an exception under GATT Article XX. Such an exception requires a two-step process. First, the Member defending the measure bears the burden of provisionally justifying the measure under one of the policy objectives enumerated in subparagraphs of Article XX. A measure shown to be *necessary* to the protection of "human, animal or plant life or health"[13] or, under certain conditions, *related to* the conservation of natural resources[14] may qualify for an exception. Either of these exceptions could be applicable to alien species regulations. The more restrictive of the two, Article XX(b), requires the importer to defend the measure by showing it is the least trade-restrictive means reasonably available for achieving the measure's objective.[15] The second step of the process to qualify for an exemption under Article XX requires the Member to demonstrate that the measure is not being applied in an arbitrary or unjustifiable manner, or as a disguised restriction on trade.[16]

The absence of an internationally recognized definition of an "alien invasive" species could not only raise difficulties for the defense of a regulation designed to distinguish between otherwise "like" products under Article III, but also complicate efforts to demonstrate, in accordance with Article XX, that a regulation is, in fact, not "arbitrary."[17] No alien species-related disputes arose under the GATT prior to the entry into force of the WTO, despite the fact that use of quarantine and licensing provisions designed to regulate and prevent the introduction of invasive species have been quite common for some time.[18] With regard to the regulation of intentional introductions, the absence of disputes may reflect the very low volume of instances of introduction, as well as widespread acceptance of the need to control trade in exotics by potential exporters concerned about the loss of their native biodiversity. With regard to the regulation of unintentional introductions as parasites and stowaways, the absence of disputes may reflect a broad recognition that such measures are indeed necessary to protect domestic animal (sanitary) and plant (phytosanitary) health. Nevertheless, concern that governments were using such SPS measures for illegitimate purposes led to the negotiation, as part of the Uruguay Round, of the SPS Agreement, which greatly elaborates disciplines intended to implement, in particular, the GATT Article XX(b)'s health-based exceptions. As discussed below, several alien-species related disputes have subsequently arisen under the SPS Agreement.

THE GATS

While the GATT and SPS Agreement govern measures affecting trade in products, they do not apply to measures designed to prevent the introduction of alien species through the provision of a service, such as tourism by ship or plane. These regulations would most likely fall under the GATS. The GATS contains general rules on nondiscrimination, specific commitments on market access, and general exceptions similar to those in the GATT.

An analysis of the interaction between alien species regulation and the GATS is made more difficult by the unique structure of the agreement. The GATS allows a large degree of differentiation in obligations from Member to Member. Thus, the scope of each Member's obligations would need to be assessed separately. Members are entitled, when acceding to the GATS, to opt out of certain measures and sectors related to Most-Favored-Nation Treatment. Similarly, each Member binds itself to the GATS Market Access obligations on a sector-by-sector basis and may negotiate to retain noncompliant measures in specific areas of its trade in services.

If, for example, a Member were to make a broad commitment to liberalizing its tourism sector, but then put in place SPS measures that banned the entry into port of vessels suspected of carrying alien species, like cruise ships, then other Members might challenge these measures. The panel's analysis would likely follow the same pattern described above in the GATT context, testing whether or not the SPS measures were applied in a discriminatory manner. Are the service providers (the tourist ships) subject to the SPS measures "like" those service providers allowed into port? Thus far, there is no WTO jurisprudence to guide a determination of a "like" service provider. If the service providers were found to be "like," the measure would have to be defended on the basis of a GATS "exception." These exceptions, like those under the GATT, allow Members, in limited circumstances and for specific reasons, to put in place measures that might otherwise violate the GATS. The measures would have to be shown to be "necessary to protect human, animal[,] or plant life or health."[19] While this provision has yet to be applied or clarified through a WTO dispute, it would likely be interpreted in the same manner as the parallel provision in the GATT Article XX, which requires the importer to demonstrate that the measure is the "least trade-restrictive" measure reasonably available to achieve the particular safety objective. However, if the measure were applied in a manner that was neither directly nor indirectly discriminatory, and that had a sound scientific basis, it is difficult to see why it would not survive such a challenge.

AGREEMENT ON THE APPLICATION OF SPS MEASURES

The WTO SPS Agreement regulates, among other things, trade measures that governments put in place:

> 1. to protect human, animal[,] and plant life from risks arising from the entry, establishment or spread of pests, diseases, disease-carrying organisms, or disease-causing organisms; and
> 2. to prevent or limit other damage within the territory of the Member from the entry, establishment or spread of pests.[20]

Because alien species entering as parasites or stowaways are likely to be characterized as "pests," the SPS Agreement, rather than the GATT, is the trade agreement most relevant to their regulation. While the SPS Agreement recognizes the right of WTO Members to put SPS measures in place, they must do so only to the extent necessary to protect human, animal, or plant life or health. Furthermore, when identical or similar conditions prevail, the measures must be enacted in a manner that does not arbitrarily or unjustifiably discriminate between Members.

Unlike the GATT, which assesses whether a Member has unjustifiably discriminated between otherwise "like products," the SPS Agreement tests whether the measure at issue is a scientifically justified and proportionate response to the risk at hand. This approach avoids the complex and abstract challenge of interpreting the word "like." It focuses instead on the direct analysis of the risks associated with the product, the level of protection necessary to prevent the risk, and the relationship between the level of protection and the chosen measure.

Thus far, three WTO disputes have tested the SPS Agreement,[21] two of which could be characterized as dealing with alien species. In the first, known as Australia-Salmon, Canada challenged a series of SPS measures that Australia put in place to prevent the introduction of some 24 "disease causing agents" suspected to be present in fresh Canadian salmon. The Australian ban on the import of Canadian salmon was challenged by Canada as scientifically unjustified. The study upon which the Australian ban was based indicated that the exotic nature of the viruses and bacteria at issue provided an important motivation behind the measures.[22] But a WTO panel and the AB subsequently struck down the Australian measure for failing to meet the SPS Agreement's requirements for risk assessment. The criteria against which the Australian risk assessment was tested are discussed below.

The second relevant dispute, known as Japan-Varietals, between Japan and the United States, arose over the fumigation procedures that Japan required on imports of fruits and nuts to prevent the introduction of the coddling moth, a pest exotic to Japan. The Japanese regulation required each variety of a particular fruit or nut to be tested to demonstrate the effectiveness of the fumigation process in eradicating the moth. The United States objected to this "varietal" approach as being unnecessarily trade-restrictive and scientifically unjustified. The WTO AB agreed that the measure failed to meet the SPS Agreement's provisions requiring sufficient scientific evidence. Principles developed from this case on the sufficiency of scientific evidence are discussed below.

Together, these two cases demonstrate that a national SPS measure, to comply with the SPS Agreement, must observe the following key principles:

- Harmonization with agreed upon international standards as a basis for SPS measures;
- Application of risk assessment procedures based on scientific principles and evidence;
- Consistency in the application of appropriate levels of protection;
- Use of the least trade-restrictive alternatives; and
- Transparency through publication of trade measures.

Harmonization With International Standards

The SPS Agreement defines harmonization as the "establishment, recognition[,] and application of common [SPS] measures by different Members."[23] Where an international SPS standard exists, WTO Members are required to *base* their SPS measures on such a standard.[24] But *basing* an SPS measure on an international standard does not excuse a Member from fulfilling its other obligations under the SPS Agreement. However, if a Member's SPS measure *conforms to* an international standard, the measure will enjoy the benefit of a presumption (albeit one that can be rebutted) that the measure is consistent with the relevant provisions of the SPS Agreement and the GATT. The WTO AB has indicated that a measure in conformity with an international standard is one that "would embody the international standard completely and, for practical purposes, converts it into a municipal standard."[25]

Under the SPS Agreement, international standards, guidelines and recommendations are defined as those developed by international organizations specifically identified in the agreement. The three international standard-setting organizations recognized under the WTO operate under the umbrella of the United Nations (U.N.) Food and Agriculture Organization (FAO).[26] The Codex Alimentarius Commission was established in 1962 as a joint undertaking of the FAO and the World Health Organization. It sets standards on food safety and human health, concerning particularly food additives, veterinary drug and pesticide residues, contaminants, methods of analysis and sampling, and codes and guidelines of hygienic practice.

The International Office of Epizootics develops standards and guidelines on pests and diseases of animals (but not animals themselves as pests). It was created in 1924 to facilitate trade in animals and animal products, with a view both to protect the health of consumers and to prevent the spread of diseases. The International Plant Protection Convention, adopted in 1951,[27] provides a framework for international cooperation to secure common and effective action to prevent the introduction of pests of plants and plant products, and to promote appropriate measures for their control.

For matters not covered by these three organizations, the SPS Committee, which the WTO established to oversee the implementation of the SPS Agreement, may identify additional standards promulgated by international organizations that are open to membership by all WTO Members. More than 50 international and regional instruments, including the Convention on Biological Diversity (CBD)[28] and the Cartagena Protocol on Biosafety,[29] now deal one way or another with the introduction, control, and eradication of alien species.[30] Nevertheless, the SPS Committee has yet to identify additional organizations as official sources of international standards.

An international standard can, however, be used either as a shield or a sword against a national SPS measure, depending on the situation. If such a standard exists, a Member may rely upon it to defend a relevant national measure, but the Member may also be called upon to justify any trade restriction based upon a departure from that standard.

Promoting or requiring the use of international standards in the regulation of trade is one means by which the WTO agreements discourage disguised discrimination, encourage trade liberalization, and ease the burden of administering trade rules. In theory, if a standard has received the endorsement of an international body, it is widely recognized as a legitimate means of regulating a genuine threat. If all Members are aware of and seek to apply the same standard, importers and trade officials will enjoy a greater predictability and conformity of regulation. However, as with many environmental and health-based issues, not all governments share the same values or perceptions of risk regarding domestic biodiversity and alien species. This may mean that, as international standards on alien invasive species emerge, they will form around "least common denominator" solutions that place "high standard" countries outside the range of what has been endorsed internationally.

Sufficient Science and Risk Assessment

SPS measures must be based on "scientific principles." Unless they are in conformity with international standards, as discussed above, measures must be justified by a scientific risk assessment. This risk assessment provides the rationale both for the setting of an appropriate level of protection and for the design of an SPS measure adequate to achieve that level of protection. Decisions adopted by the WTO AB have begun to provide more specific guidance with regard to the elements of a proper risk assessment, as well as the relationship between the risk assessment, the process of establishing the appropriate level of protection, and the final design of the SPS measure. Indeed, the SPS disputes to date have turned in part on both the adequacy of the risk assessment upon which the importing government relied, and the relationship between the assessment and the SPS measures on which it was based.

Under the SPS Agreement, a risk assessment prepared by a Member must do three things:

> 1. Identify the invasive alien species whose entry, establishment, or spread a [M]ember wants to prevent within its territory, as well as the potential biological and economic consequences associated with the entry, establishment, or spread of these invasive alien species;
> 2. Evaluate the likelihood of entry, establishment, or spread of these invasives, as well as the associated potential biological and economic consequences; and
> 3. Evaluate the likelihood of entry, establishment[,] or spread of these invasive alien species according to the SPS measure that might be adopted.[31]

It is not sufficient that a risk assessment merely conclude there is a *possibility* of entry, establishment, or spread of an invasive alien species. A proper risk assessment must evaluate the *likelihood or probability* of entry, establishment, or spread. There should be a rational or objective relationship between the SPS measure at issue and the available scientific information. Demonstrating this relationship will depend on the particular circumstances of each case, including the characteristics of the measure and the quality and quantity of the scientific evidence.[32]

Differences in perception lie behind many SPS disputes, as importers and exporters often disagree about whether or not risks associated with particular products are based on "sufficient science." Many international environmental declarations and agreements include the "precautionary principle," which is intended to guide states when developing regulation in contexts where there are significant gaps in scientific knowledge, but where the risks of inaction are, nevertheless, potentially high.[33] The irreversibility or potential irreversibility of the threats posed by the introduction of alien species is likely to raise issues about the applicability of the "precautionary principle."

The application of the precautionary principle has proved particularly controversial in the context of trade. Exporting nations are promoting international trade in a product they have deemed "safe" for sale and consumption at home, and thus tend to resent any implication that their product might fail to meet importers' standards. They presume that the "precautiousness" of an importing government is more likely to be fueled by a desire to protect a domestic industry than to protect consumers, native plants, or wildlife.

When governments have sought to invoke the precautionary principle in an SPS dispute, the WTO AB has recognized that "responsible, representative governments commonly act from perspectives of prudence and precaution where risks are of irreversible nature."[34] The precautionary principle, however, cannot override the procedures for risk assessment required by the SPS Agreement.[35] Provisional measures may be applied where relevant scientific evidence is insufficient,[36] but these provisional measures may not be maintained indefinitely. Additional information for a more objective risk assessment must be actively sought, and the measure must be reviewed within a reasonable period of time.[37]

The SPS Agreement's insistence on "sufficient science" may raise particular challenges for importers seeking to regulate alien introductions. For example in the coddling moth dispute, Japan claimed that "for practical reasons, the importing country was at a disadvantage in respect of the gathering of sufficient information on exotic pests (which did not exist domestically), for varieties that often were not produced in Japan."[38] Japan argued unsuccessfully that because of this asymmetry of information, the exporting government should have the burden of proving that any alternative to the importer's measure would achieve the required level of protection.

Consistency of Application in Levels of Protection

The SPS Agreement states the following:

> With the objective of achieving consistency in the application of the concept of the particular SPS protection, each [M]ember shall avoid arbitrary or unjustified distinctions in the levels it considers to be appropriate in different situations, if this situation would result in discrimination or a disguised restriction on international trade.[39]

Members must ensure that SPS measures do not arbitrarily or unjustifiably discriminate between Members where identical or similar conditions prevail.[40] These provisions taken together require Members to be consistent when they deal with risk over a range of measures and products.

This provision is likely to prove controversial for the simple reason that governments rarely regulate with perfect consistency. Regulatory challenges tend to arise in an ad hoc manner, as scientific understanding of a risk and the public and political pressure necessary to respond to it emerge. Regulatory responses depend upon government priorities, the strength of vested interests and choices about the application of limited resources.

While it may be reasonable to assess consistency of regulation within a narrow range of regulatory activity, the broader the range of activity, the more likely that inconsistencies will arise. In Australia-Salmon, the AB assessed the consistency of import bans on fresh, chilled, or frozen salmon with regulations designed to regulate imports of herring, cod, haddock, eel, sole for human consumption; herring for use as bait; and live ornamental fin fish. It found that this broad scope of comparison was justified when situations "involve *either* a risk of entry, establishment[,] or spread of the same or a similar disease, *or* a risk of the same or similar 'associated potential biological and economic consequences.'"[41] This approach presents an opportunity to encourage a broad range of alien species regulation, on the basis that piecemeal approaches could provoke WTO challenges. However, if the requirement of consistency is interpreted too strictly, it could prevent the development of regulation in an incremental manner.

The Australia-Salmon dispute also highlighted the need for regulators to avoid depending too heavily on the mere "exoticness" of an SPS threat to justify onerous restrictions at the border. One of Canada's many allegations was that Australia had failed to put in place internal regulations consistent with those required at the border for those disease agents that were exotic to some parts of Australia, but endemic to others. The measure failed for other reasons, but the arguments raised suggest that once an alien species has been introduced, border controls should be combined with internal efforts to eradicate or control the spread of the threat.[42]

Alternative/Less Restrictive Trade Measures

Reflecting the jurisprudence developed under the GATT, a national SPS measure must not be more trade-restrictive than is necessary to achieve the appropriate level of protection.[43] A measure is deemed trade-restrictive if there is another, available SPS measure, which, taking into account technical and economic feasibility, would achieve the appropriate level of protection without restricting trade as much as the contested measure.[44]

In Australia-Salmon, the fact that the relevant measure, which would have required the heat-treatment of fresh salmon, destroyed the intended end use of the product helped support a conclusion that less trade-restrictive alternatives (such as testing and quarantine) could have achieved the same level of protection. If the measures were directed at banning the introduction of an alien species as the product itself, it is difficult to imagine a more trade-restrictive alternative to an outright ban on the trade.

Transparency

Members are required to notify other countries in advance, except in emergency situations, of any new or changed SPS measure that could affect trade, and to solicit comments from trade partners on the proposed measure. These notifications are publicly available documents, and each Member must establish an office to respond to requests for more information. Furthermore, to enhance transparency, WTO Members must promptly publish all SPS measures in a manner that enables interested Members to become acquainted with them.[45] This ensures protection against disguised barriers to trade.

CONCLUSION

The SPS Agreement constitutes an elaborate attempt to reconcile national interests to protect human, animal, and plant health with trade interests. It highlights the need for Members to harmonize their approaches through competent international organizations. At the same time, it recognizes the difficulties of this approach and the sovereign right of Members to establish their own priorities and adopt their own national SPS measures as long as these measures are based on adequate scientific information.

The two cases involving alien species that have come before the WTO thus far have resulted in protective regulations being struck down, primarily on the basis of insufficient scientific evidence and unacceptable risk assessments. While in both cases the importing government's cases were quite weak, there are nonetheless some grounds for concern that strict interpretations of WTO rules could work to limit or chill the development and application of progressive alien species regulation.

At present, the SPS Agreement is the only international legal instrument in force that governs trade-related aspects of alien species regulation, and that is backed by a compulsory dispute settlement system. Its science-based disciplines, and relatively narrow interpretation of the precautionary principle may well restrict the discretion of national governments to design aggressive regulation in this area. The SPS Agreement's deference to international standards does, however, provide an additional incentive for agreeing multilaterally to specific international rules to prevent the spread of alien species through trade.

The rules and guidelines concerning alien species developed in the context of the CBD may be particularly significant in the future. In 1998, the Conference of the Parties (COP) requested the CBD Subsidiary Body on Scientific, Technical, and Technological Advice (SBSTTA) to develop "guiding principles for the prevention, introduction, and mitigation of impacts of alien species."[46] As requested, the SBSTTA has developed the *Interim Guiding Principles for the Prevention, Introduction, and Mitigation of Impacts of Alien Species*. Governments particularly concerned about alien species regulation may wish to support and promote this process with a view to creating more latitude to regulate alien species in a precautionary manner when acting in the face of scientific uncertainty.

Chapter 8 Endnotes

1. Jacob Werksman is Environmental Institutions and Governance Adviser, Bureau for Development Policy, United Nations Development Programme. This chapter was written for the World Conservation Union (IUCN) while Mr. Werksman was a Senior Lawyer at the Foundation for International Environmental Law and Development (FIELD), London. Mr. Werksman would like to thank Nattley Williams, Legal Officer at the IUCN Environmental Law Centre, for her assistance in preparing an initial draft of this chapter. The views expressed are the author's.

2. WTO, *Agreement on the Application of Sanitary and Phytosanitary Measures, in* THE RESULTS OF THE URUGUAY ROUND OF MULTILATERAL TRADE NEGOTIATIONS. THE LEGAL TEXTS (1994) [hereinafter SPS Agreement].

3. On February 1, 2003, WTO membership stands at 145. *See* WTO, *Members and Observers, at* http://www.wto.org/english/thewto_e/whatis_e/tif_e/org6_e.htm (last visited Mar. 31, 2003).

4. GATT, *opened for signature* Oct. 30, 1947, General Agreement on Tariffs and Trade, Text of the General Agreement (July 1986) [hereinafter GATT].

5. When joining the WTO each Member agrees, under the WTO's Dispute Settlement Understanding, to answer all disputes brought against it and to abide by the resulting judgments. Any WTO Member who feels benefits it was expecting under the WTO have been "nullified or impaired" by another Member's failure to comply with WTO rules can request the establishment of a panel of arbitrators to hear the case. Each WTO panel is formed ad hoc, and is composed of three to five trade experts appointed either by agreement between the disputants, or, should they fail to agree, by the head of the WTO's administrative body. After both oral and written pleadings, the panel issues a report. The panel's report is generally considered binding upon the disputants, unless it is rejected by a consensus of the WTO membership, or it is appealed. Rejection by consensus is extremely unlikely, as it would require the support of the entire membership, including the Member who "won" the dispute. Appeal, however, is extremely common, as either disputant is entitled to appeal any mistake of law made by the panel. The WTO Appellate Body (AB), a standing body composed of seven internationally recognised legal experts appointed by the WTO Membership, hears the appeal. The AB hears each appeal in a division of three Members, and its reports are generally considered binding upon the disputants, unless rejected by a consensus of the entire membership. If a WTO Member fails to comply with an adopted panel or AB report, the complaining Member can request the authorization of a trade sanction at a level equivalent to the damages resulting from the continuing noncompliance. Such sanctions usually take the form of an increase in the tariffs that can be assessed by the complaining Member against products or services exported by the noncomplying Member.

6. General Agreement on Trade in Services, Apr. 15, 1994, 36 I.L.M. 354 (entered into force Jan. 1, 1995) [hereinafter GATS].

7. CLARE SHINE ET AL., A GUIDE TO DESIGNING LEGAL AND INSTITUTIONAL FRAMEWORKS ON ALIEN INVASIVE SPECIES 63 (2000) [hereinafter IUCN GUIDE].

8. *Id.* at 52, 59.

9. GATT, *supra* note 4, art. XI.

10. *Id.* arts. I, III.

11. *Id.* art. XX.

12. The test for a "like product" in the context of Article III:4, which applies to all "nonfiscal" measures, was articulated by the WTO AB, when testing the legitimacy of

a French ban on the import and internal sale of asbestos and asbestos-containing products. It calls for a case-by-case determination in which a panel should assess, among other things, the product's properties, nature, and quality; its end uses in a given market; its tariff classification; and consumers' tastes and habits. European Communities—Measures Affecting Asbestos and Asbestos-Containing Products, AB-2000-11, WT/DS135/AB/R, at 31–56 (Mar. 12, 2001).

13. GATT, *supra* note 4, art. XX(b).

14. *Id.* art. XX(g).

15. The reasonable availability of alternatives cannot be based solely on administrative ease, but can be based on, among other things, the importance of the value being pursued by the regulation, and whether an alternative regulation could achieve the same level of protection as the challenged measure. *Id.* at 60-63.

16. United States—Import Prohibitions of Certain Shrimp and Shrimp Products, WT/DS58/AB/R (Oct. 12, 1998).

17. See discussion on definitions of "alien invasive species" in IUCN GUIDE, *supra* note 7, at 1-5.

18. See review of existing domestic legislation on alien species in *id.* at 37-48.

19. GATS, *supra* note 6, art. XIV(b).

20. SPS Agreement, *supra* note 2, Annex A.

21. EC—Measures Concerning Meat and Meat Products, WT/DS26/AB/R, WT/DS48/AB/R (Jan. 16, 1998) [hereinafter EC-Hormones]; Australia—Measures Affecting Importation of Salmon, WT/DS18/AB/R (Oct. 20, 1998) [hereinafter Australia-Salmon]; and Japan—Measures Affecting Agricultural Products, WT/DS76/AB/R (Feb. 22, 1999) [hereinafter Japan-Varietals]. The WTO reports on these disputes are available on the WTO website: *World Trade Organization, at* http://www.wto.org (last visited Dec. 9, 2002).

22. As summarized by the WTO Panel, the Australian study concluded:

> There was a possibility that up to 20 disease agents exotic to Australia might be present in Pacific salmon products and although the probability of establishment would be low, there would be major economic impacts which could seriously threaten the viability of aquacultural operations and the recreational fishing industries, in addition to adverse environmental impacts on the built environment of Australia. The Report considered that should any of the 20 diseases become established, they would almost certainly be ineradicable.

Australia-Salmon, *supra* note 21, at Panel Report, ¶ 2.30.

23. SPS Agreement, *supra* note 2, Annex A, §2.

24. *Id.* arts. 3 and 12.4.

25. EC-Hormones, *supra* note 21.

26. SPS Agreement, *supra* note 2, art. 3.4.

27. U.N. FAO, International Plant Protection Convention, Rome 1951, revised in 1979 and 1997 (latest versions not yet in force).

28. U.N. Environmental Program (UNEP), Convention on Biological Diversity 31 I.L.M. 818 (1992).

29. UNEP, Cartagena Protocol on Biosafety, Montreal (Jan. 29, 2002).

30. IUCN GUIDE, *supra* note 7, at 13 and Annex I.

31. Australia-Salmon, *supra* note 21.

32. Japan-Varietals, *supra* note 21.

33. The precautionary principle, as stated in Rio Declaration, Principle 15, holds that "lack of full scientific certainty shall not be used as a reason for postponing cost effective measure to prevent environmental degradation." Rio Declaration on Environment and Development, U.N. Conference on Environment and Development, princ. 15, U.N. Doc. A/CONF.151/5 Rev. 1, 31 I.L.M. 874 (1992).

34. EC-Hormones, *supra* note 21.

35. *Id.*

36. SPS Agreement, *supra* note 2, art. 5.7.

37. Japan-Varietals, *supra* note 21.

38. *Id.* at AB Report, ¶ 4.29.

39. SPS Agreement, *supra* note 2, art. 5.5.

40. *Id.* art. 2.3.

41. Australia-Salmon, *supra* note 21 at 44, AB Report, ¶ 146.

42. *Id.* at 116, AB Report, ¶ 13.

43. SPS Agreement, *supra* note 2, art. 5.6.

44. Japan-Varietals *supra* note 21; Australia-Salmon, *supra* note 21.

45. SPS Agreement, *supra* note 2, art. 7 and Annex B.

46. Decision IV/1, 1998.

CHAPTER 9:
THE REGULATION OF GENETICALLY MODIFIED ORGANISMS AND ITS RELATIONSHIPS WITH INVASIVE SPECIES

by Julian Kinderlerer[1] and Paul Phifer[2]

Genetically modified organisms (GMOs) are not, by default, invasive species. Given the variety of novel traits modern biotechnology may be able to confer on a variety of organisms, some genetic modifications may result in an increase of a species' invasive ability, while some may serve to decrease that ability. The introduction of a novel organism into a new environment does not inherently make that species invasive. It is not until that species spreads, persists, and causes environmental, economic, or human health-related harm that it becomes an invader, and there is no evidence that the process of genetic modification inherently increases the likelihood that a particular species will invade.

Invasive species and GMOs do, however, present similar scientific and regulatory challenges. Both are novel organisms, and the introduction of any novel organism into an environment almost always entails scientific unknowns, making risk assessments important yet often difficult. Further, the questions policymakers and regulators ask the scientists who assess these risks are: which of these species have the potential to cause damage? what is the potential extent of this damage and is it manageable? how do the potential benefits stand in relation to the risks?

Both GMOs and invasive species also involve significant trade aspects, among both developed and developing countries. Agricultural products of biotechnology are becoming more common globally, and an increasing number of developing countries are turning a critical eye toward these crops and their potential benefits. Further, while the international and domestic regulation of certain novel organisms has been in existence for decades, e.g., plant protection and quarantine systems, the regulation of both invasive species and GMOs is currently a central issue for several international discussions, such as the International Plant Protection Convention[3] and the Convention on Biological Diversity.[4]

Another similarity between GMOs and invasive species is the potential for unauthorized releases. While the release of most GMOs stem from some formal authorization, pollen drift and unintentional introductions are believed to have occurred. Some invasive species stem from intentional introductions, e.g., Nile perch in Lake Victoria, but many others come unintentionally, e.g., zebra mussels in the Great Lakes of the United States. Unintentional introductions of invasive species may occur along predictable pathways, such as through ballast water exchange, yet not all pathways are known, and managing these avenues of invasion can be extremely difficult.

This chapter divides roughly into two sections. The first entails the who, why, and how of GMO regulations, both internationally and within Canada, the European Union (EU), and the United States. The chapter provides both an historical perspective on why GMOs are regulated as they are and a discussion of some of the federal and international bodies tasked with regulating these organisms. The second section concerns the similarities encountered when conducting risk assessments associated with the introduction of any novel organism into a new environment. We close with a discussion about some of the lessons learned from GMOs and how these might inform the regulation of invasive species.

THE REGULATION OF GMOs

The use of biotechnology to modify the behavior of organisms we use in our environment is not new. Much of agriculture involves the use of biological systems to provide a product substantially different from the starting material. Deliberate manipulation of organisms to produce a specific product has been practiced for millennia, and few of our modern crops bear a close resemblance to the ancestral plants from which they are derived. There are many products and varieties on the market that could not have been achieved "naturally," if that is defined as not requiring human intervention in the fertilization process.

Early Stages of Biotechnology

The invention of new techniques in biology during the late 1960s and early 1970s forced many scientists to start thinking about the implications of their research, as Susan Wright has discussed in her book *Molecular Politics*.[5] Sydney Brenner wrote to the Ashby Committee (1975)[6]:

> It cannot be argued that this is simply another, perhaps easier way to do what we have been doing for a long time with less direct methods. For the first time, there is now available a method which allows us to cross very large evolutionary barriers and to move genes between organisms which have never had genetic contact.[7]

Scientists' worries about the implications of this new technology led in July 1974 to the simultaneous publication of an open letter in the journals *Nature*, *Science*, and the *Proceedings of the National Academy of Science*. Scientists were asked not to manufacture organisms that might carry unknown or novel antibiotic resistance or where the manufactured bacteria could make toxins. They were also asked to refrain from experiments involving animal virus deoxyribonucleic acid (DNA). Though it was seen as calling for a moratorium on the use of the technology, the letter only asked for a partial delay on particular experiments. It also proposed a scientific conference to "review scientific progress in this area and to further discuss appropriate ways to deal with"[8] the putative hazards posed by the technology. The letter further suggested that a committee nominated by the National Institutes of Health (NIH) in the United States prepare guidelines for the safe use of the new technology.

In Britain, the Ashby Committee was set up in January 1975 to examine the potential hazards posed by the ability to alter the genetic composition of microorganisms apparently at will. The committee's report would serve as the foundation for almost all later legislation and guidelines introduced for the regulation of GMOs in containment. It recommended the use of disabled organisms to minimize the hazards should any modified organism escape from the confinement of the laboratory. It recommended genetic manipulation techniques be allowed to proceed but with rigorous safeguards, including containment and precautionary measures to protect those working in the laboratories. The committee believed the containment measures recommended in the report would be more than sufficient to protect the environment (including the general public).

The conference called for in the open letter of July 1974 was held in Asilomar, California, in February 1975. The meeting recommended the partial moratorium be lifted and guidelines for research replace it. The view, held on both sides of the Atlantic, was that the hazards of this new biotechnology ought to be confronted through research. Perhaps most importantly, the conference stressed primarily scientific issues should be addressed at this time rather than any social or economic concerns that might arise from the use of the technology in the future. In the discussions at the meeting, however, the participants identified a major concern, which remains at the heart of the debate today: whether there is sufficient information known to predict risk or hazard from the release of these organisms.

It was suggested during the conference that the public has a right to become involved in assessing new technology, and to make an erroneous assessment. It was argued the committee appointed by the NIH could make an initial assessment based on science, but that the policymaking process should extend beyond the narrow issue of safety to the broader questions of human impact.

The legacy of the structures put in place by scientists in these formative years of biotechnology are still with us. There continue to be arguments about a risk assessment having to be "science-based," and the extra difficulties that might arise if socioeconomic considerations were brought into the regulatory process. Within most regulatory circles across most countries, scientific advice has been paramount, as has been the general acceptance that scientists can predict the risk associated with the use of biotechnology.

In the United States, this approach led first to the introduction of the NIH guidelines, which provided the mechanisms by which risk to human health or to the environment posed by the confined use of modified organisms could be assessed and contained. In Britain, initially, guidelines were produced which enabled scientists to assess the likely problems that might be caused by a particular microorganism and hence assess the level of containment that ought to be used in order to ensure its safe use. By 1978, though, Britain had instituted a formal regulatory system.

In the United Kingdom, the Genetic Manipulation Advisory Group (GMAG) was set up under the scientific auspices of the Medical Research

Council and the Health and Safety Executive. The British Health and Safety (Genetic Manipulation) Regulations[9] were the first set of formal regulations anywhere in the world. In 1984, the GMAG were replaced by the Advisory Committee on Genetic Modification (ACGM) that still advises the Health and Safety Executive on the contained use of modified organisms. Its scope is clear, including the health and safety of those working in the contained environment and (later) the assessment of any damage to the environment that might occur in the event of escape or incidental release. Ethical and social issues are not within the remit of the committee. Scientists and industry in the United Kingdom consider this regulatory structure for the contained use and field trial of GMOs to work effectively without significantly restraining ongoing work.

REGULATION IN THE UNITED STATES

The majority of transgenic crops grown in the world have been in the United States. The decision not to introduce specific laws for the regulation of biotechnology may have helped in the rapid commercialization of the technology. It is therefore educative to examine the regime instituted by the federal authorities in the United States to ensure all organisms introduced into the environment are safe. The U.S. decision in 1986 not to introduce new regulatory structures for transgenic organisms rested on the argument that potential risk should be determined on the basis of the specific organism, rather than the method by which it is made.

In the United States there is no *specific, independent* regulatory system for ensuring the safe use of biotechnology in either the laboratory or the factory, where the release of an organism is restricted. Instead, existing laws have been reinterpreted to allow their application to many if not all of the modified products likely to be introduced in research facilities or onto the market in the United States. The policy document that establishes the U.S. strategy for regulating products of biotechnology is called the *Coordinated Framework for Regulation of Biotechnology.*[10] This framework outlines the role of each relevant agency in regulating the products of biotechnology. The NIH guidelines,[11] for example, are for laboratory or factory use and must be followed by recipients of government funding. Regulations the Occupational Safety and Health Administration has created for general factory safety also apply to biotechnology. And in most cases, the U.S. Food and Drug Administration (FDA) regulates new animal drugs, biologics, or human drugs; while the U.S. Department of Agriculture (USDA) is the lead regulatory agency for deliberate release of genetically modified plants into the environment.[12] USDA also requires a permit for interstate movement and importation of USDA-regulated articles from one contained facility to another. Finally, the U.S. Environmental Protection Agency (EPA) regulates the deliberate release and field testing of pesticide-producing organisms.

The USDA

The USDA, with its Animal and Plant Health Inspection Service (APHIS), is the primary regulatory authority for any deliberate release of GMOs into the U.S. environment. The prime function of APHIS is to protect U.S. agriculture against plant and animal pests. Oversight by APHIS begins when a "regulated article"[13] is introduced into the United States, a process monitored by a stringent permit system.[14] APHIS is responsible for the regulation of importation, interstate movement, and environmental release of transgenic plants that contain plant pest components.[15]

There are two formal permit procedures: one covers introduction into the United States (this does not include creation of the article by recombinant techniques in a laboratory) and interstate movement of "regulated articles," while the other covers releases into the environment of "regulated articles" for field tests.[16] An informal "courtesy" permit system is also available for persons handling articles that are not listed, a process that allows APHIS to confirm (or otherwise acknowledge) the nonregulated status of the article. Persons handling articles for which there is not a published exemption from oversight are actively encouraged to use the "courtesy" permit system so that APHIS can remain abreast of all introductions into the United States. It would appear that all novel introduced articles will be investigated as to their plant pest potential by APHIS, whatever their origin.

Although APHIS has authority to investigate all "regulated articles," using a sophisticated risk assessment process, it concentrates on those that may pose a threat to the agricultural crops of the United States. It does not emphasize diseases of nonagricultural species. Transferring genes among plants that are not important to agriculture is only relevant if there is some likelihood that the genes will cross back into the agricultural (managed) environment. APHIS' stated aim is the protection of American agriculture.[17] To this end, all plant "regulated articles" are handled by the Plant Protection and Quarantine section of APHIS. Animal "regulated articles" are be handled by the Animal Care section, or the Veterinary Services section.

APHIS has responsibilities for evaluating "Petitions for Determination of Nonregulated Status."[18] Such a petition must include information collected by an applicant to demonstrate the product poses no potential for plant pest risk, which is interpreted to mean the organism is as safe to grow as its nonengineered equivalent. The petitions are open to public comment. APHIS also asserts that its definition for plant pests is broad, as it includes direct or indirect injury, disease, or damage to plants, plant parts, or processed or manufactured products of plants.

If APHIS grants nonregulated status, the plant may then be grown, tested, or used in breeding programs without any further oversight by APHIS, although it would still be subject to review by other agencies. APHIS permits for release are not equivalent to permits for marketing of a product as other statutes may apply.

EPA

EPA also has regulatory authority for deliberate releases of some GMOs into the environment. EPA registers certain pesticides produced in transgenic plants prior to their distribution and sale and establishes tolerances for the pesticides in the plants. EPA also reviews and grants permits for field testing plants that produce such pesticides when the field tests are more than 10 acres. EPA administers both the Federal Insecticide, Fungicide, and Rodenticide Act (FIFRA)[19] and the Toxic Substances Control Act (TSCA).[20] Under FIFRA, EPA controls the production and use of pesticidal substances, which includes pesticidal substances expressed in plants as a result of genetic engineering. Under TSCA, EPA controls the use of microorganisms that are included in its definition of chemical substances: all new chemical substances are presumed toxic and are subject to regulatory control.

Under FIFRA, EPA controls certain plant GMOs if they produce a pesticide (in which case the Agency regulates the pesticide and not the plant, e.g., residues in food and impact upon nontarget species), or if they cause a new use of a registered pesticide. Linking herbicide-resistant plants to a specific commercially available herbicide may be considered a new use. Under TSCA, EPA controls all microbes that are not covered by other statutes (such as FIFRA or the Federal Food, Drug, and Cosmetic Act (FFDCA) administered by the FDA).[21] Although it has authority to control microbes in containment, it has chosen not to do so because of the existing NIH guidelines; it does not control subcellular constructs of animal or plant origin either. EPA has also restricted its actions to microbes that are substantially dissimilar to the "natural" strains and microbes that present pathogenic characteristics only.

The FDA

The FDA, an agency of the U.S. Department of Health and Human Services, is the primary agency responsible for food safety in the United States. However, it shares a number of its functions with other agencies.[22] The FDA implements the FFDCA which establishes the standard for safety, which states that food is safe if it is in an unadulterated condition.[23] With regulatory authority for food and feed use in the United States, FDA regulates modern biotechnology largely as food additives and if modification can be shown to have "adulterated" a food. So far, FDA has clarified its position concerning foods from new plant varieties only. It has not issued policies concerning foods from new animal varieties or concerning new drugs, or new animal drugs.[24] However, the policies FDA adopts concerning these other genetically modified products will, most likely, follow the same lines as those currently regulating products from genetically modified plants.

Companies developing GMO foods are encouraged to voluntarily notify FDA before marketing the new food. A report by the U.S. General Accounting Office states:

Notification leads to a two-part consultation process between the agency and the company that initially involves discussions of relevant safety issues and subsequently the company's submission of a safety assessment report containing test data on the food in question. At the end of the consultation, FDA evaluates the data and many send a letter to the company stating that the agency has no further questions, indicating in effect that it sees no reason to prevent the company from marketing the GMO food.[25]

FDA issued a proposed rule in January 2001 to make the premarket notification mandatory by companies.[26] As of this writing the proposed rule had not yet been finalized.

REGULATION IN CANADA

The Canadian Food Inspection Agency (CFIA) regulates the importation, environmental release, and feed use of plants with novel traits, which may include, but are not limited to, transgenic plants. Health Canada has jurisdiction over novel foods, including food products derived from transgenic plants.[27] Like the United States, Canada has chosen to regulate all novel organisms, rather than merely relying on genetic modification to trigger regulation. The federal framework that regulates biotechnology products defines "biotechnology" as "the application of science and engineering in the direct or indirect use of living organisms or parts or products of living organisms in their natural or modified forms."[28] This broad definition covers all organisms, their parts and products, whether traditionally developed or developed through newer molecular techniques like genetic engineering. Biotechnology is, therefore, a series of techniques, not a product, and these techniques are applied in many sectors to develop goods and services of value to the economy.

In 1992, the Canadian government introduced a framework to regulate biotechnology that attempted to maintain current standards for the protection of workers, the general public and the environment. The government chose to use existing legislation to set guidelines for products of modern biotechnology. Thus, all new biotechnology products "are assessed based solely on established procedures for identification of safety concerns."[29] The Canadian Department of the Environment explained in 1996 how these established procedures and institutional responsibilities would apply to biotechnology products:

> Another key principle of the federal framework is the use of existing legislation and institutions to clarify responsibilities and avoid duplication. This principle means that departments now regulating products developed using traditional techniques and processes will be responsible for regulating products developed using newer biotechnology techniques and processes. Regulatory departments such as Agriculture and Agri-Food Canada, the Department of Health and the Department of the Environment have developed considerable expertise over a period of many years in addressing safety questions related to a variety of products including conventional biotechnology products. As part of the framework, the Department of the Environment and the Department of Industry, in cooperation with other Departments involved in the regulation of biotechnology products, coordinated the establishment of appropriate standards and responsibilities for environmental assessments for the federal government.[30]

Under this framework, for example, Canada's Environmental Protection Act is meant to ensure no new substance is introduced into the marketplace without an assessment as to its toxicity and the risk it poses the environment.

REGULATION IN THE EU

An examination of the relevant EU legislation on GMOs may provide what some have called a picture of a "harmonized regulatory framework . . . (that) provide(s) for the protection of human health and the environment."[31] The Royal Society has described genetic modification and the release of GMOs as tightly regulated.[32] However, this picture of harmony and tight regulation has not been extensively tested for few agricultural products of biotechnology, for example, have been approved for marketing within Europe.

In 1990, the EU introduced three directives that have a direct bearing on the use of transgenic organisms. The Directive on Contained Use of Genetically Modified Microorganisms[33] (modified in 1998)[34] provides a basis for assessing the risk posed by research establishments or industrial and commercial premises where modified organisms are used in containment. The directive only applies to microorganisms (including animal and plant cells in tissue culture), but may be extended by member countries to cover all organisms used in containment. It provides a mechanism for the identification of the containment procedures needed to ensure the safe use of organisms. The Deliberate Release Directive (90/220)[35] requires a risk assessment and consequent risk management whenever deliberate experimental releases into the environment are contemplated or where there is an intention to market a GMO. The third directive (90/679)[36] applies to all "biological agents" used in the workplace, including GMOs. It requires risk be assessed and appropriate containment be used for every organism.

The Food Regulation (258/97)[37] supersedes the terms of the Deliberate Release Directive when products are to be sold as food, and requires the environmental risk assessment be at least as rigorous as that required under the previous directive.

The Preamble to the Deliberate Release Directive identifies the necessity for "harmonized procedures and criteria for the case-by-case evaluation of the potential risks arising from the deliberate release of GMOs into the environment."[38] It also states that the introduction of GMOs into the environment should be carried out according to the "step-by-step" principle, under which "the containment of GMOs is reduced and the scale of release increased gradually, step-by-step, but only if evaluation of the earlier steps in terms of protection of human health and the environment indicates that the next step can be taken."[39]

In principle, Directive 90/220 was to provide a predictable procedure that includes risk assessment and risk management precautions. Each individual country within the EU was expected to implement the directive through their own national laws. One of the primary objectives of the Deliberate Release Directive was the maintenance of the open market, to provide a level playing field on which trade may proceed. Unfortunately, the principles of risk assessment were not clear, and different Member states have interpreted the requirements differently, resulting in confusion and lack of certainty on the part of applicants.

Hence, on March 12, 2001, Directive 2001/18 was introduced to provide a more efficient and transparent regulatory system, thereby replacing Directive 90/220, and becoming the new Deliberative Release Directive. Further, on March 8, 2001, Decision 2001/204 was adopted to supplement Directive 90/219 regarding the criteria for establishing the safety, for human health and the environment, of certain types of genetically modified microorganisms. The European Commission also proposed a regulation to set up a European Community framework for the labeling and traceability of GMOs and products produced from GMOs.[40] Directive 2001/18 was adopted July 2, 2003.

Building on many of the elements in Directive 90/220, Directive 2001/18 has explicit requirements for environmental risk assessments that must be performed prior to release of a GMO or a product produced from a GMO into the environment or marketplace, including the importation of such goods. This directive also requires notification to the national competent authority prior to the release of a GMO or product of a GMO, and subsequent monitoring of potential cumulative long-term effects.

Two of the most controversial elements of Directive 2001/18 are its requirements that

- [i]n order to ensure that the presence of GMOs in products containing, or consisting of, [GMOs] is appropriately identified, the words[:] "This product contains genetically modified organisms" should appear clearly either on a label or in an accompanying document,[41] and
- It is necessary to ensure traceability at all stages of the placing on the market of GMOs as or in products.[42]

Traceability in this context means, "the ability to trace GMOs and products produced from GMOs at all stages of the placing on the market throughout the production and distribution chains . . . . Importantly, effective traceability provides a 'safety net' should any unforeseen adverse effects be established."[43]

These labeling and traceability requirements are controversial due to their potential impacts on international trade and existing trade agreements, e.g., are these requirements cost effective and do they erect an unnecessarily barrier to trade? Yet, these requirements are partially in response to a strong public demand within the EU for consumer information and public or environmental safety measures. Such tensions between trade and public and environmental safety concerns arise for both GMOs and invasive species given that invasive species are often associated with aspects of trade, e.g., ballast water exchange of cargo ships in ports or agricultural pests disseminated via trade in agricultural products.

SELECT INTERNATIONAL AGREEMENTS ON GMOs

There have been multiple attempts to produce a set of guidelines or a legally binding international treaty that might allow consistent treatment of GMOs (or living modified organisms) transported across international borders. In the early 1990s, the United Nations (U.N.) Industrial Development Organization produced a set of guidelines for the development of legislation. This "Voluntary Code of Conduct for the Release of Organisms Into the Environment" addressed some of the issues needed to ensure the harmonization of requirements for assessing the risks of modified organisms to the environment:

> The advent of new molecular and cellular techniques of genetic modification has led to the continuing emergence of products (including organisms) of biotechnology that promise substantial benefits and improvements to the quality of life. These techniques are available now, but to be safely and effectively used, they must be applied according to a number of principles.[44]

The code recommended that each country should have the following scientific and technical expertise:

- a national assessment and decisionmaking structure(s);
- specific scientific advisory bodies;
- mechanisms to gather information on local agronomic and environmental conditions; and
- systems for the provision of information to, and education of, the public.

The code noted that:

- virtually all countries have quarantine procedures or similar mechanisms for managing the import of new plants, animals, or microorganisms. An adaptation of these mechanisms through specific organism-related scientific advisory bodies could provide a means of handling new biotechnology products. In addition, such procedures could be extended to include review of new domestically produced GMOs.[45]

In the early 1990s when the Organization for Economic Cooperation and Development (OECD) examined the informational requirements for each European country that had regulatory or guideline control over the release of modified organisms, the OECD found that almost all countries required the same or similar information upon which to base a risk assessment. But the interpretation of the data differed by country because of the various national legal structures through which the technology was regulated.

The International Plant Protection Convention (IPPC)[46] improves international cooperation to control pests and plant disease partially by establishing recommended standards by which risk assessments should be conducted. The IPPC decided to draft standards related to invasive species and products of biotechnology. The IPPC is centrally concerned with pests that cause economic damage to crop plants, yet in 2000 they began to consider pests that cause damage to the environment.

Chapter 16 of Agenda 21, adopted at the United Nations Conference on Environment and Development in Rio de Janeiro in 1992,[47] requires governments to consider international cooperation on the "Environmentally Sound Management of Biotechnology." It also requires governments to take appropriate measures to ensure developing countries have both effective participation in biotechnological research activities and priority access to the results and benefits of biotechnology on a fair and equitable basis.

The United Nations Environment Program (UNEP) produced a set of Guidelines on Biosafety[48] in an attempt to achieve such technological equity and provide a uniform baseline for the regulation of biotechnology throughout the world. These guidelines "seek to ensure safety in biotechnology development, application, exchange[,] and transfer through international agreement on principles to be applied on risk assessment and management."[49] The UNEP Technical Guidelines mark a significant attempt to rationalize the structure of national regulation that would, if implemented, lead to similar processes in a number of countries.

However, the central international agreement concerning the environmental aspects of the transport of GMOs (more specifically, living modified organisms (LMOs) has now become the Cartagena Protocol on Biosafety (commonly referred to as the Biosafety Protocol (BSP)).[50] The BSP is a treaty under the Convention on Biological Diversity (CBD),[51] and its objective is to "contribute to ensuring an adequate level of protection in the field of the safe transfer, handling[,] and use of [LMOs] resulting from modern biotechnology that may have adverse effects on the conservation and sustainable use of biological diversity."[52] On January 29, 2000, the BSP was completed and it came into force September 11, 2003.[53]

Essentially, the BSP establishes the process and architecture for an information-sharing system that provides the importers of LMOs with the information they need to make informed import decisions, and the exporters the relatively predictable export process they desire. Some of the key provisions to this process are the advance informed agreement (AIA), the risk assessment criteria, the Biosafety Clearing House (BCH), and the handling, transporting, packaging, and identification requirements.

Article 7 of the BSP requires that prior to the first intentional transboundary movement of an LMO, the country of import must be provided the risk assessment information they need to make import decisions. The content of this information, at the minimum, must be in accordance with the risk assessment criteria outlined in Article 15 of the BSP. To facilitate the exchange of this and other required information under the BSP, the BCH has been established. The BCH is a World Wide Web and, if needed, paper database that is the central repository of information on:

- risk assessments of LMOs,
- each BSP Party's existing laws, regulations, and guidelines for the implementation of the BSP,
- any relevant bilateral, regional, and multilateral agreements and arrangements; and
- "final decisions regarding the importation or release of [LMOs]."[54]

In addition, the BSP requires that any LMO intended for direct use as food, feed, or processing, be clearly identified that it "may contain" an LMO and that it is not intended for intentional introduction into the environment. Those LMOs intended for introduction into the environment of the importer must be identified, according to the BSP, as an LMO, as must be their identity and relevant traits or characteristics. The actual details of how these identification requirements will be implemented are as of this writing still undefined. The first Meeting of the Parties to the BSP is to take place in Malaysia, February 2004. To facilitate implementation of the multiple requirements of the BSP, UNEP and the Global Environmental Facility (GEF) are conducting a nearly $40 million, three-year capacity-building project (2001-2004) to assist countries in their creation of a domestic regulatory structure to address GMOs.[55]

RISK ASSESSMENT OF NOVEL ORGANISMS WITHIN THE ENVIRONMENT

Risk analysis developed from experience in the chemical industry, where significant information could be known about a particular chemical and the likely hazards that would be encountered when it was released into an environment. This information often allows for a quantitative analysis, with the probabilities of multiple outcomes calculable. In these analyses, it is sometimes even possible to evaluate the cost of remediation, and therefore approach a formal cost-benefit analysis and identify the most practicable manner of minimizing risk. Yet, introducing novel organisms into a new environment potentially presents many variables and often an associated lack of information, making it difficult to conduct such a formalized quantitative risk assessment. Further, not all introductions of novel organisms, whether they be potential invasive species or GMOs or both, are intentional. Therefore, some risk assessments are solely to calculate the risks of novel organisms unintentionally being introduced, establishing and spreading and causing biological or ecological harm.

The most direct way of proceeding in these complex circumstances is to depend on experience of the transference of genes in similar, wild-type organisms and the multiple modern pathways of invasive species, and use analogy as a method of predicting behavior. That is, look at how novel organisms have established and spread previously in the wild or agricultural settings and use the lessons learned to predict future invasions.

Almost all of the environmental risk assessments that are performed rely on the collection of data about donor and host organisms and the physical pathways, such as cargo ships and vectors used in the transfer of genes. A typical approach to risk assessments for the introduction of novel organisms, therefore, uses the experience of a collection of scientists from dissimilar backgrounds to assess or audit potential risk, and thereby combine their collective experience to provide a qualitative result.

The initial prediction of hazards that might be expected from the release of novel organisms, including GMOs, is based on the properties of the organisms themselves. These risk assessments become more complex when they attempt to consider indirect or delayed effects on the environment. A basic example here is predicting invasiveness: it is extremely difficult to identify whether a novel organism will become invasive (even given the examples of similar or identical species in other environments), and any estimate of the risks of introducing a novel organism will vary with the organism and the environment to which it is being introduced. We should expect potential ecological and environmental changes from the introduction of novel organisms, and the important questions are: How extensive might this change be? Can it be mitigated? How do the risks fare in comparison to the potential benefits of introducing that organism?

GMOs may present risks that differ in quality from invasive species, given the breadth of potential characteristic traits that might be conferred through modern biotechnology. For example, GMOs may also have altered allergenic or toxic properties. Their toxicity to animals or insects that feed on them may change, with implications for the environment into which they are released. The risk of harming nontarget species, or making plants less or more attractive to insects, while difficult to estimate, is nevertheless an important aspect of a risk assessment for novel organisms.

In the face of the complexity of conducting quantitative risk assessments that incorporate multiple environmental variables, two general approaches can be described for conducting risk assessments on the release of novel organisms into a new environment. These options are not exclusive and can operate in a complementary fashion.

A detailed testing procedure prior to release of a novel organism can be implemented. This option might describe an ideal approach, yet it is difficult to identify all of the tests that need to be performed before an organism may be considered safe. For example, it is not always possible to identify potential delayed or indirect impacts that have a low probability of occurrence, but carry a high cost if they do occur.

Another approach would be to rely on some form of "substantial equivalence." Here one assumes that if most of the characteristics of the comparable and previously safe organism are unchanged, and only those novel traits are observed, then the novel organism is as safe as the comparable organism. This approach assumes one can identify all the significant, even unintentional, differences of the novel organisms, and can understand how these differences might interact with the new environment.

CONCLUSION

There are direct similarities between how individual countries and international trading partners should assess the risks of releasing any novel organism into a new environment, whether that organism is a GMO or a potentially invasive species, or both. Risk assessments will assist with the discovery of organisms that may threaten human health or the environment. Many countries and multiple international agreements are already implementing such systems. The value of an impact analysis that considers the risks (to the environment and to human health) of introducing a novel organism, the benefits that might accrue from the organism's release, as well as the risks associated with not introducing the organism is clear. However, implementing effective and accurate analysis for the potential release of all novel organisms is nearly impossible, especially for the organisms that are released unintentionally. So, what is to be done?

The first step in any improvement of the risk assessment process would be an increase in the acquisition of data. Data need to be collected for ordinary organisms within a variety of environments so that risk analysis using comparable species and ecosystems can be conducted. Further, systems need to be devised that will facilitate the efficient exchange of biological, ecological, and risk assessment information within and between countries. These systems can also share insights into emerging or existing invasive species and their prevention or control. Such systems are taking shape, e.g., the BSP BCH. A similar information-exchange system for invasive species is being created through the broader Clearing House Mechanism of the CBD, in conjunction with the Global Invasive Species Program.

Once information is exchanged, countries need the capacity to turn this information into effective management decisions. This is where projects like the UNEP/GEF capacity-building project are needed, though there is much more work to be done.

Ours desire for international trade, the creation of new products, whether through biotechnology or other means, and the protection of human and environmental health creates problems that are not easily solved, yet deserve our attempt to find a resolution.

Chapter 9 Endnotes

1. Paul Phifer currently works on forest and endangered species policy for the U.S. Fish and Wildlife Service (FWS). Previously, he was a lead negotiator for the U.S. Department of State on the issue of the transboundary movement of genetically modified organisms (GMOs). He worked extensively on the Cartagena Protocol on Biosafety (commonly referred to as the Biosafety Protocol (BSP)) under the Convention on Biological Diversity (CBD). Part of his time at the Department of State, he served as a Diplomacy Fellow with the American Association for the Advancement of Science (AAAS). Dr. Phifer received his Ph.D. in conservation biology from the University of Minnesota, in 1998.

2. Prof. Julian Kinderlerer is the Assistant Director of the Sheffield Institute of Biotechnological Law and Ethics based in the University of Sheffield. He is a biochemist who has moved from research interests in theoretical aspects of enzymology and enzyme kinetics to looking at law, ethics, risk assessment, and risk analysis in biotechnology. He is now in the Faculty of Law at the University of Sheffield. The views expressed here are solely those of the authors and do not represent the views of the FWS or the U.S. government.

3. United Nations (U.N.) Food and Agricultural Organization (FAO), International Plant Protection Convention (Rome 1951) (revised in 1997 and 1999).

4. 31 I.L.M. 818 (1992).

5. SUSAN WRIGHT, MOLECULAR POLITICS DEVELOPING AMERICAN AND BRITISH REGULATORY POLICY FOR GENETIC ENGINEERING, 1972-1982 (1994).

6. Ashby Committee (1975) Report of the Working Party on the Experimental Manipulation of the Genetic Composition of Micro-Organisms, January 1975, United Kingdom CMND 5880.

7. Wright, *supra* note 4 at 75. *See also id.* at 142.

8. Letter from Paul Berg et al. to the editor, *reprinted in* 185 SCIENCE 303 (1974).

9. Enacted in 1978.

10. This policy was published as Coordinated Framework for Regulation of Biotechnology: Announcement of Policy and Notice for Public Comment, 51 Fed. Reg. 23302 (June 26, 1986).

11. The latest amended version of the current NIH guidelines became effective April 29, 1999, and can be found in the *Federal Register* at 64 Fed. Reg. 25361 (May 11, 1999). The original NIH guidelines can be found at 59 Fed. Reg. 34496 (July 5, 1994).

12. An organism may be regulated if it has been genetically engineered from a donor organism, recipient organism, vector, or vector agent that is a plant pest or contains plant pest components. Other modified organisms may be regulated articles if they have been engineered using unclassified organisms or if the Animal and Plant Health Inspection Service (APHIS) determines that the genetically engineered organism is a regulated article.

13. "Regulated articles" are listed by APHIS regulations; unlisted organisms may also be treated as a "regulated article" by APHIS if there is any reason to believe that the organism is, or will be, a plant pest. To this end, oversight by APHIS covers all forms of, and all components of, plant or animal pests. Therefore, GMOs that have been engineered from a donor, recipient, vector, or vector agent that is a plant pest or contains plant pest components are treated as "regulated articles."

14. The proposed rule was published in the *Federal Register* at 51 Fed. Reg. 23352-66 (June 26, 1986); and the final rule was published in the *Federal Register* at 52 Fed. Reg.

22892-915 (June 16, 1987); the final version of simplifications to the regulations were published in the *Federal Register* at 62 Fed. Reg. 23945-58 (May 2, 1997). The regulations are set out at 7 C.F.R. §340: "Introduction of Organisms and Products Altered or Produced Through Genetic Engineering Which Are Plant Pests or Which There Is Reason to Believe Are Plant Pests."

15. Summary Report, Canada—U.S. Bilateral Discussions on Agricultural Biotechnology, July 15-16, 1998, Ottawa, Ontario, Canada.

16. *See* Introduction of Organisms and Products Altered or Produced Through Genetic Engineering Which Are Plant Pests or Which There Is Reason to Believe Are Plant Pests, 7 C.F.R. §340, *at* http://www.aphis.usda.gov/ppq/biotech/7cfr340.html (last visited July 7, 2003).

17. APHIS states its mission at: USDA, APHIS, *About Aphis, at* http://www.aphis.usda. gov/lpa/about/welcome.html. APHIS also has a Wildlife Services section; this is not concerned with the impact of agriculture on the environment, but with the prevention of wildlife damage to crops and the protection of rare and endangered species.

18. *See supra* note 15.

19. 7 U.S.C. §§136-136y, ELR STAT. FIFRA §§2-34.

20. 15 U.S.C. §§2601-2692, ELR STAT. TSCA §§2-412.

21. Statement of Policy: Microbial Products Subject to the Federal Insecticide, Fungicide, and Rodenticide Act and Toxic Substances Control Act, 51 Fed. Reg. 23302 (June 26, 1986); Microbial Products of Biotechnology; Proposed Regulation Under the Toxic Substances Control Act, 59 Fed. Reg. 45526 (Sept. 1, 1994); Plant-Pesticides Subject to the Federal Insecticide, Fungicide, and Rodenticide Act (FIFRA) and the Federal Food, Drug, and Cosmetic Act (FFDCA); Proposed Policy; Notice, 59 Fed. Reg. 60496 (Nov. 23, 1994); Plant-Pesticides Subject to the Federal Insecticide, Fungicide, and Rodenticide Act; Proposed Rule, 59 Fed. Reg. 60519 (Nov. 23, 1994); Plant-Pesticides; Proposed Exemption From the Requirement of a Tolerance Under the Federal Food, Drug, and Cosmetic Act, 59 Fed. Reg. 60535 (Nov. 23, 1994); Plant-Pesticides; Proposed Exemption From the Requirement of a Tolerance Under the Federal Food, Drug, and Cosmetic Act for Nucleic Acids Produced in Plants, 59 Fed. Reg. 60542 (Nov. 23, 1994); Plant-Pesticides; Proposed Exemption From the Requirement of a Tolerance Under the Federal Food, Drug, and Cosmetic Act for Viral Coat Proteins Produced in Plants, 59 Fed. Reg. 60545 (Nov. 23, 1994).

22. The USDA is responsible for enforcing standards of wholesomeness and quality of primary agricultural produce in the United States through its inspection and grading functions. It is solely responsible for meat, poultry, and eggs, which it inspects via its Food and Safety Inspection Service. The USDA enforces standards set by the FDA in food sanitation and hygiene and cooperates with the FDA for the detection and prevention of food contamination. The Centers for Disease Control are also responsible for preventing food-borne diseases and vector-borne diseases. The FDA enforces tolerance limits for pesticides in food and standards for bottled water quality set by EPA. The FDA is not responsible for the oversight of alcoholic beverages (except of certain wines): this is the responsibility of the Bureau of Alcohol, Tobacco, and Firearms of the U.S. Department of the Treasury. Nor is it responsible for the oversight of seafood or aquaculture, which the National Marine Fisheries Service, a part of the U.S. Department of Commerce, covers.

23. 21 U.S.C. §342. A food is deemed adulterated if, among other things, it contains an added poisonous or deleterious substance that may render the food injurious to health or if it contains an unapproved food additive.

24. Statement of Policy: Food Derived From New Plant Varieties, 57 Fed. Reg. 22984-23005 (May 29, 1992).

25. U.S. GENERAL ACCOUNTING OFFICE, GENETICALLY MODIFIED FOODS: EXPERTS VIEW REGIMEN OF SAFETY TESTS AS ADEQUATE, BUT FDA'S EVALUATION PROCESS COULD BE ENHANCED (2002) (GAO-02-566).

26. The FDA's Center for Food Safety and Applied Nutrition (CSFAN) is responsible for this proposed rule. *See* U.S. FDA, *CSFAN, at* http://www.cfsan.fda.gov (last visited July 7, 2003). The proposed rule can be found at Premarket Notice Concerning Bioengineered Foods: Proposed Rule, 66 Fed. Reg. 4706 (Jan. 18, 2001).

27. *See supra* note 14.

28. New Substances Notification Regulations Amendment: Canadian Environmental Protection Act, Department of the Environment, August 1996.

29. *Id.*

30. *Id.*

31. House of Lords Select Committee on the European Communities (1999) EC Regulation of Genetic Modification in Agriculture Second Report Volume 1 Report HL 11-I ¶ 39.

32. Royal Society, Genetically Modified Plants for Food Use (Sept. 1998), The Royal Society, 6, Carlton House Terrace, London, SW1Y 5AG, UK.

33. EC Directive 90/219/EEC (1990), The Contained Use of Genetically Modified Micro-Organisms, O.J. L117 (May 8, 1990) 1-14.

34. EC Directive 98/81/EEC (1998) amending EC Directive 90/219/EEC, The Contained Use of Genetically Modified Micro-Organisms, O.J. L330 (Dec. 5, 1998) 13-31.

35. EC Directive 90/220/EEC (1990), The Deliberate Release Into the Environment of Genetically Modified Organisms, O.J. L117 (May 8, 1990) 15-27.

36. Council Directive 90/679/EEC of November 26, 1990, The Protection of Workers From Risks Related to Exposure to Biological Agents at Work (seventh individual directive within the meaning of Article 16(1) of Directive 89/391/EEC), O.J. L374 (Dec. 31, 1990) 1-12.

37. EC Regulation 258/97 (1997), Novel Foods and Novel Food Ingredients, O.J. L43 (Feb. 14, 1997) 1-7.

38. EC Directive 2001/18/EC of the European Parliament and of the Council on the Deliberate Release Into the Environment of Genetically Modified Organisms and Repealing Council Directive 90/220/EEC, pmbl. ¶ 18 (Mar. 12, 2001), *available at* http://europa.eu.int/eur-lex/pri/en/oj/dat/2001/l_106/l_10620010417en00010038.pdf (last visited July 7, 2003).

39. *Id.* pmbl. ¶ 24.

40. *See* Proposal for EC Directive 2001/0180, Regulation of the European Parliament and of the Council, Concerning Traceability and Labelling of Genetically Modified Organisms and Traceability of Food and Feed Products Produced From Genetically Modified Organisms and Amending EC Directive 2001/18/EC (July 25, 2001), *available at* http://europa.eu.int/eur-lex/en/com/pdf/2001/en_501PC0182.pdf (last visited July 7, 2003).

41. *See supra* note 37, pmbl. ¶ 40.

42. *Id.* pmbl. ¶ 42.

43. *See supra* note 39.

44. UNITED NATIONS INDUSTRIAL DEVELOPMENT ORGANIZATION (UNIDO), BIOSAFETY INFORMATION NETWORK AND ADVISORY SERVICE (BINAS), VOLUNTARY CODE OF CONDUCT FOR THE RELEASE OF ORGANISMS INTO THE ENVIRONMENT (1991), *available at* http://binas.unido.org/binas/regulations/unido_codes.pdf (last visited July 7, 2003).

45. *Id.*

46. U.N. FAO, International Plant Protection Convention New Revised Text, art. II (1997) (approved by FAO Conference at its 29th Session in Rome).

47. U.N. Conference on Environment and Development, Agenda 21, U.N. Doc. A/CONF.151.26 ch. 16 (1992).

48. *See* UNEP INTERNATIONAL TECHNICAL GUIDELINES FOR SAFETY IN BIOTECHNOLOGY (1995), *available at* http://www.unep.org/unep/program/natres/biodiv/irb/unepgds.htm (last visited July 7, 2003).

49. *Id.* art. 1.2.

50. CBD, *Cartegena Protocol on Biosafety, at* http://www.biodiv.org/biosafety (last visited Sept. 23, 2003).

51. 31 I.L.M. 818 (1992). The CBD is a legally binding agreement (Rio de Janeiro, 1992), which has been signed by over 150 countries. It came into force on December 29, 1993. The CBD has three key objectives: (1) the conservation of biological diversity; (2) the sustainable use of this diversity; and (3) the fair and equitable sharing of the benefits arising out of the utilization of the genetic resources.

52. *See also supra* note 49, art. 1.

53. *Id.*

54. *Id.* art. 20.3.

55. UNEP, *UNEP—GEP Biosafety Projects, at* http://www.unep.ch/biosafety/ (last visited Sept. 23, 2003).